THE SCREAMING CITADEL

It is a time of turmoil for the galaxy. While the evil Galactic Empire remains strong, the forces of the Rebel Alliance continue to struggle for freedom from their oppressive grasp, establishing a secret outpost on Horox III, deep in the Outer Rim.

Young rebel pilot Luke Skywalker, struggling to forge his destiny, is at a loss. He can feel the Force, but without the proper training, he cannot become the Jedi Knight he is certain he must become.

Meanwhile, the rogue archaeologist and sometime scoundrel Doctor Aphra has come into possession of a very valuable – and very dangerous – artifact... one containing the recorded consciousness of an ancient Force user. If only she could reactivate it....

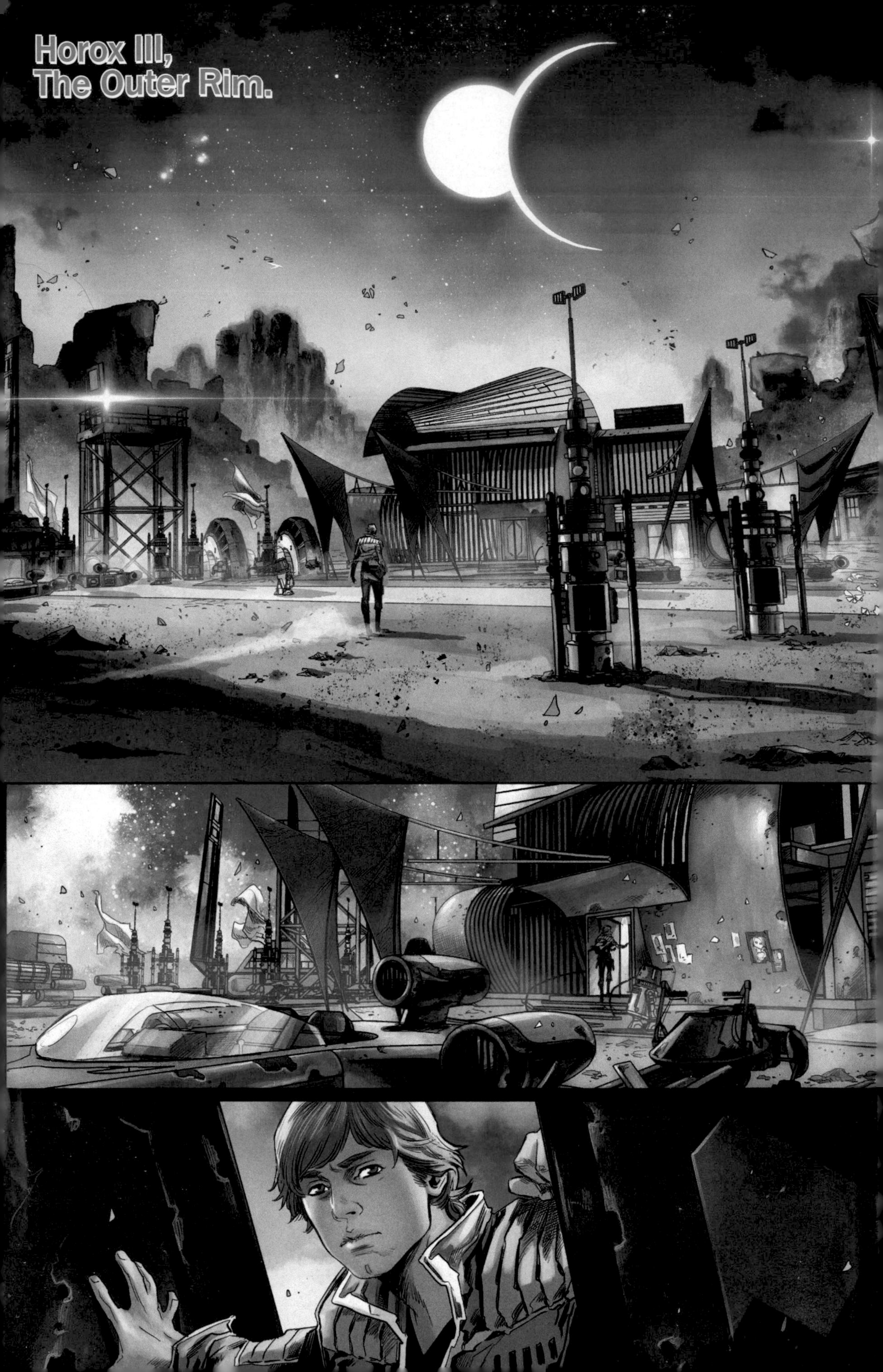
Horox III,
The Outer Rim.

SCREAMING CITADEL

Story   **KIERON GILLEN & JASON AARON**

STAR WARS: THE SCREAMING CITADEL #1

Writer   **KIERON GILLEN**
Artist   **MARCO CHECCHETTO**
Color Artist   **ANDRES MOSSA**
Letterer   **VC's JOE CARAMAGNA**

STAR WARS #31-32

Writer   **JASON AARON**
Artist   **SALVADOR LARROCA**
Color Artist   **EDGAR DELGADO**
Letterer   **VC's CLAYTON COWLES**

STAR WARS: DOCTOR APHRA #7-8

Writer   **KIERON GILLEN**
Artist   **ANDREA BROCCARDO**
Color Artist   **ANTONIO FABELA**
Letterer   **VC's JOE CARAMAGNA**

Cover Art   **MARCO CHECCHETTO**
Assistant Editor   **HEATHER ANTOS**
Editor   **JORDAN D. WHITE**
Executive Editor   **C.B. CEBULSKI**

Editor in Chief   **AXEL ALONSO**
Chief Creative Officer   **JOE QUESADA**
President   **DAN BUCKLEY**

For Lucasfilm:
Senior Editor   **FRANK PARISI**
Creative Director   **MICHAEL SIGLAIN**
Lucasfilm Story Group   **JAMES WAUGH, LELAND CHEE, MATT MARTIN**

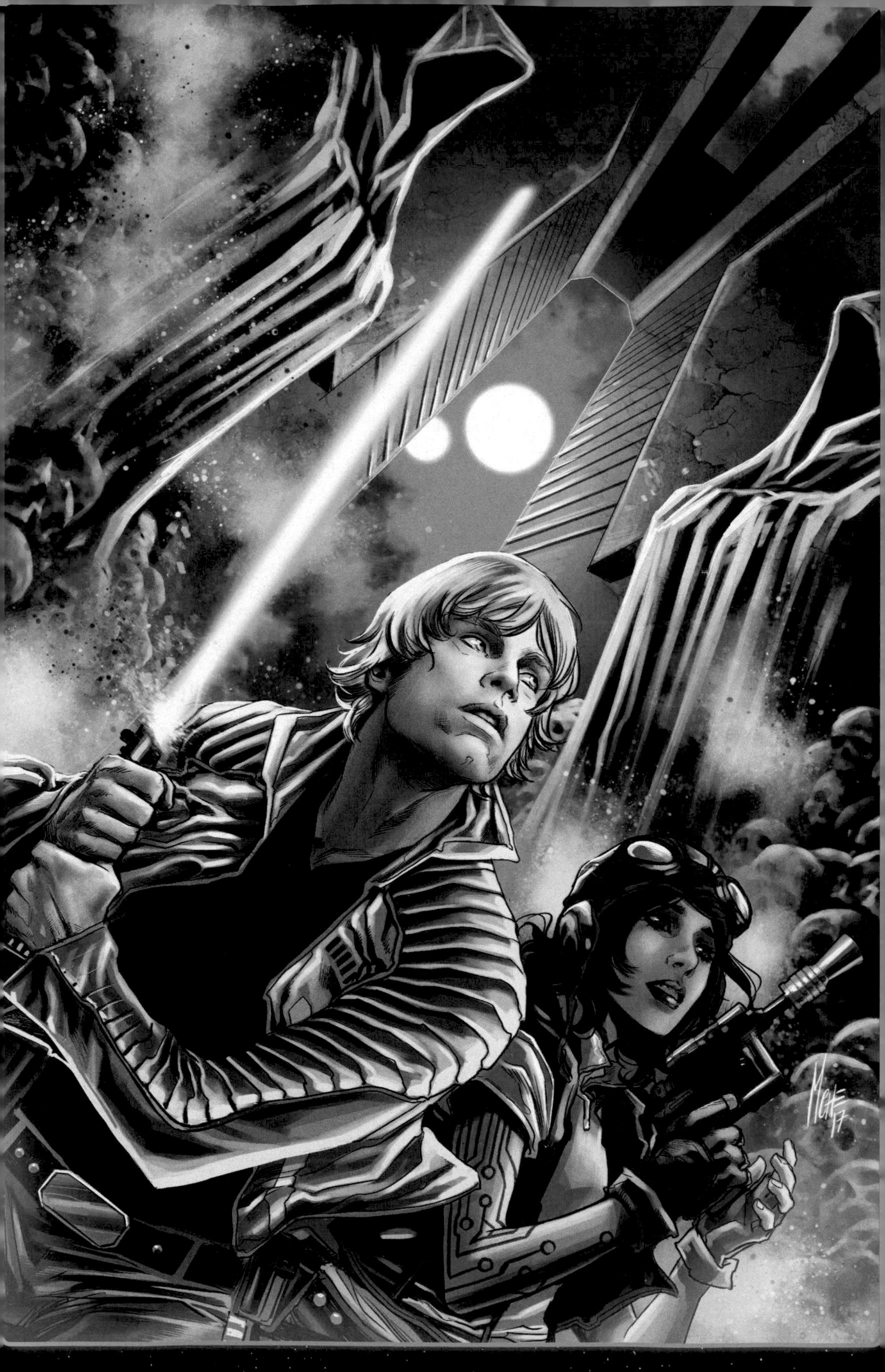

STAR WARS: THE SCREAMING CITADEL 1

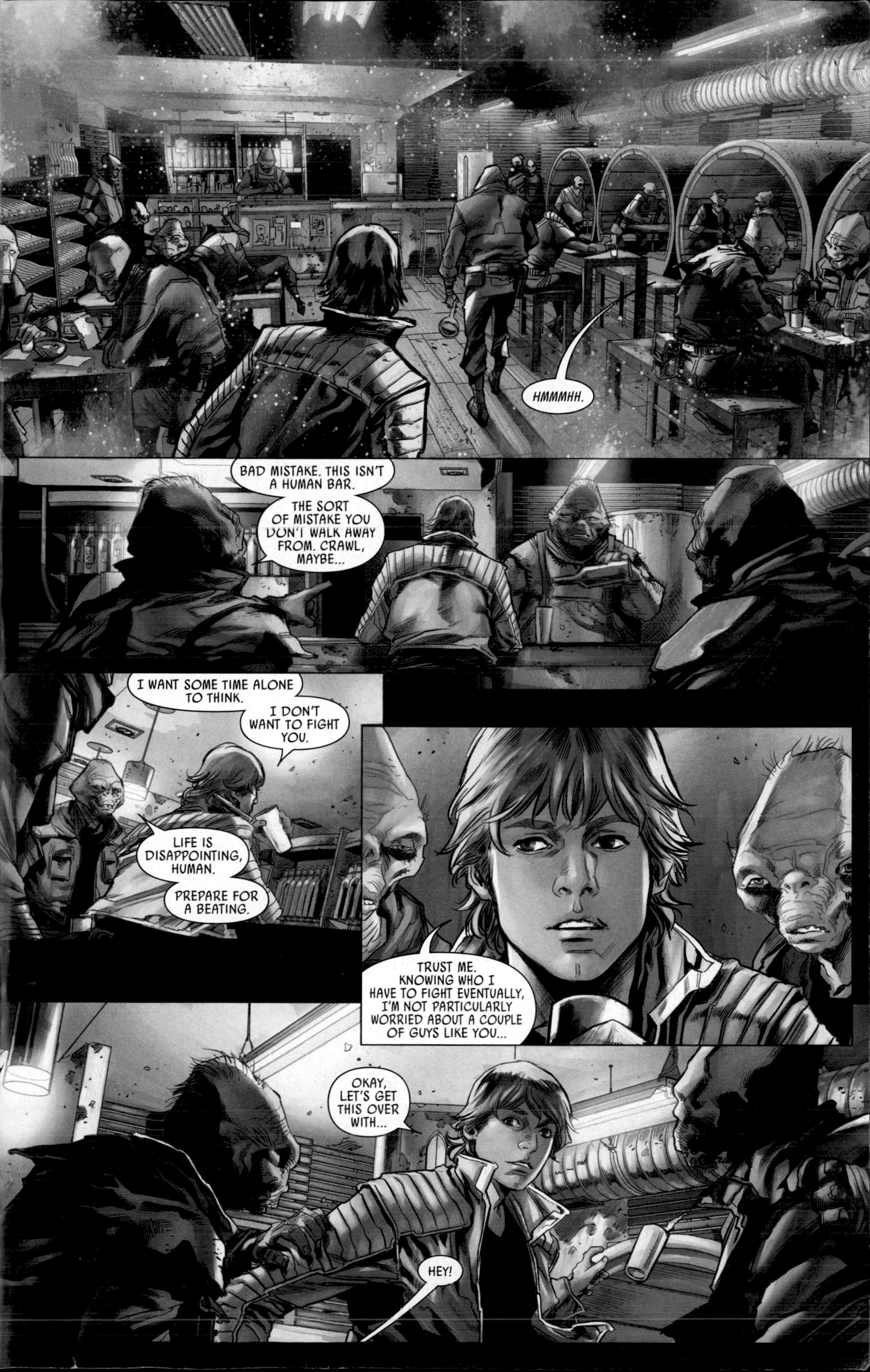
HMMMHH.
BAD MISTAKE. THIS ISN'T A HUMAN BAR.
THE SORT OF MISTAKE YOU DON'T WALK AWAY FROM. CRAWL, MAYBE...
I WANT SOME TIME ALONE TO THINK.
I DON'T WANT TO FIGHT YOU.
LIFE IS DISAPPOINTING, HUMAN.
PREPARE FOR A BEATING.
TRUST ME. KNOWING WHO I HAVE TO FIGHT EVENTUALLY, I'M NOT PARTICULARLY WORRIED ABOUT A COUPLE OF GUYS LIKE YOU...
OKAY, LET'S GET THIS OVER WITH...
HEY!

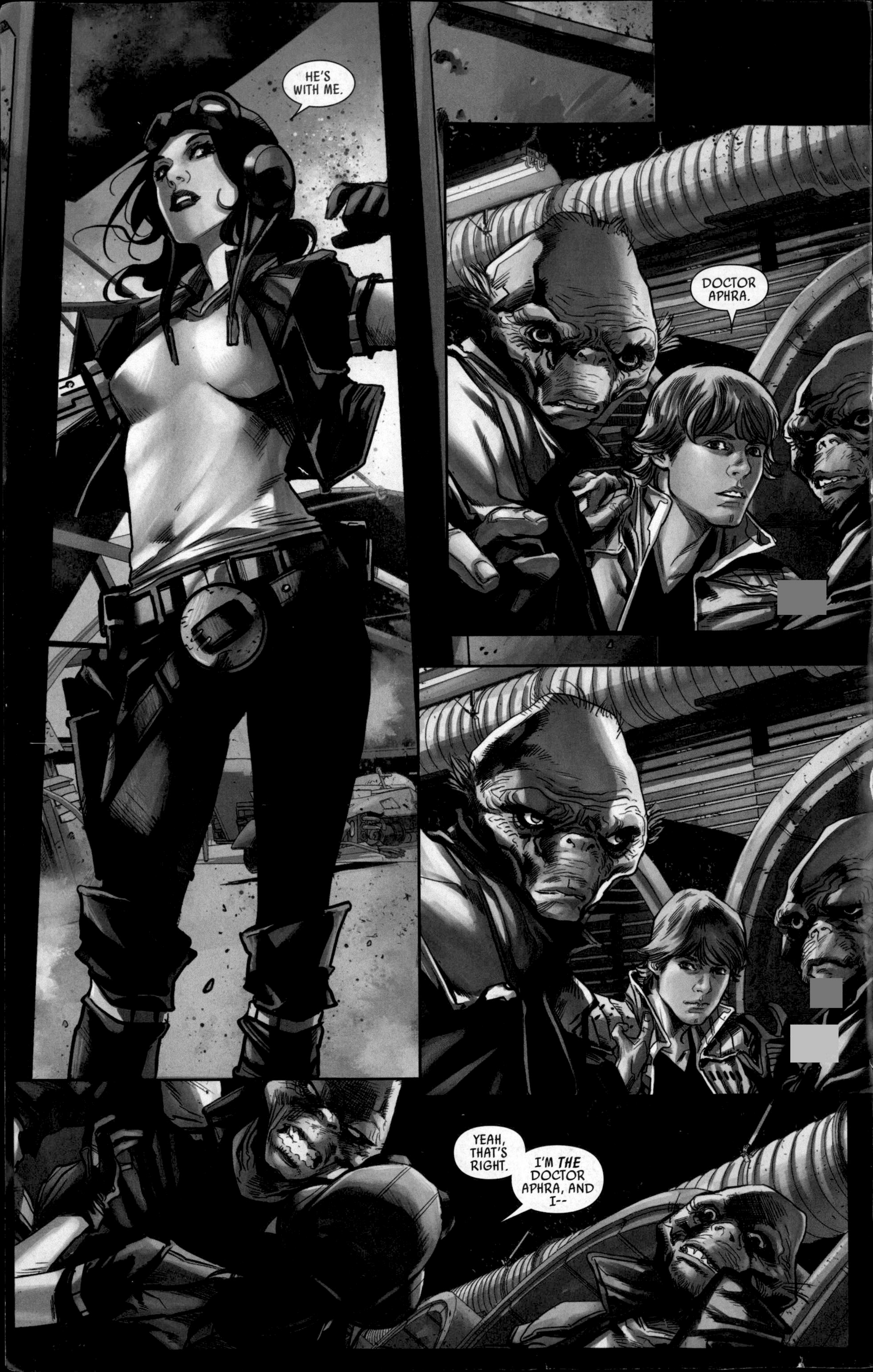
HE'S WITH ME.
DOCTOR APHRA.
YEAH, THAT'S RIGHT.
I'M THE DOCTOR APHRA, AND I--

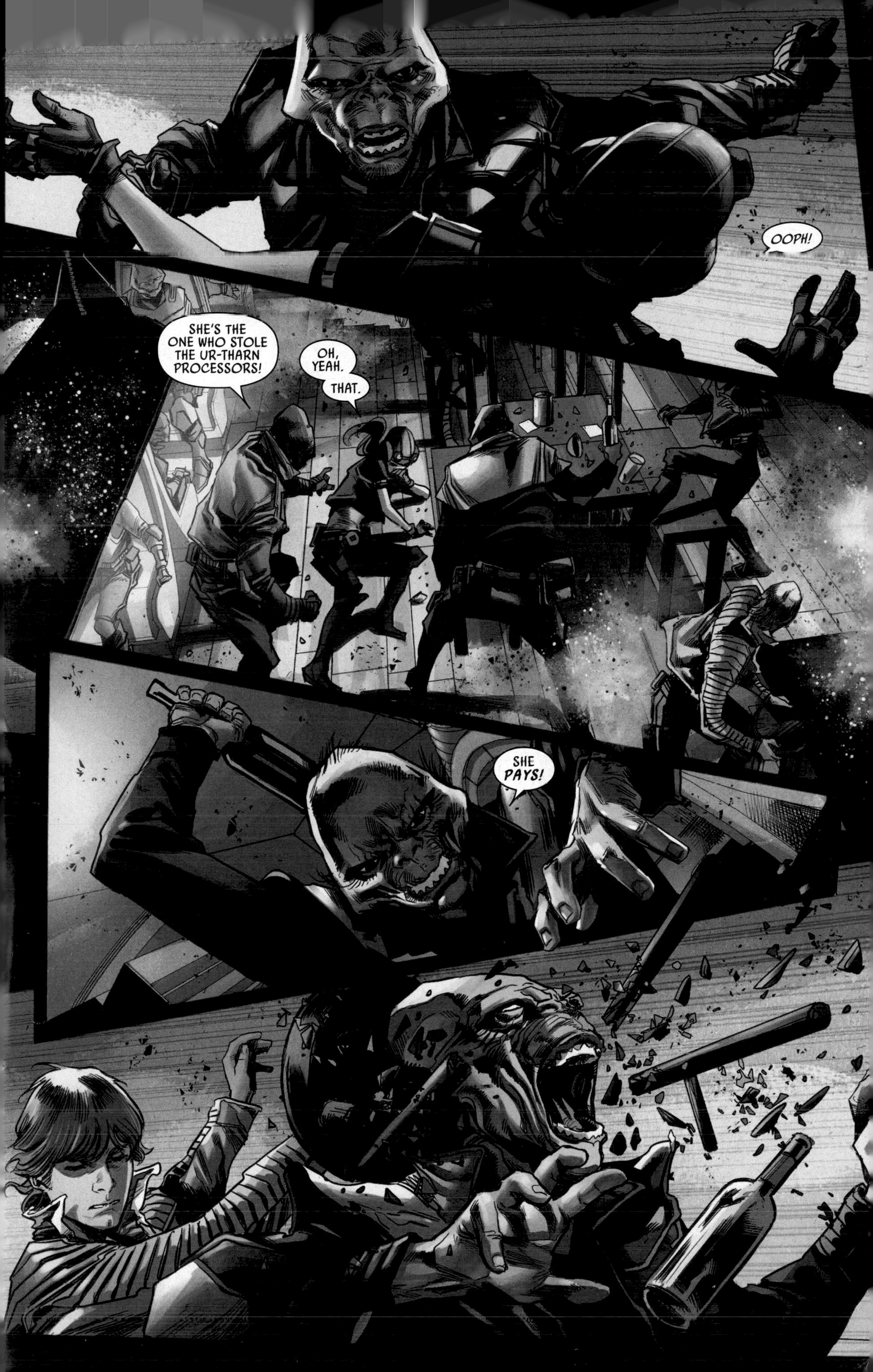
OOPH!
SHE'S THE ONE WHO STOLE THE UR-THARN PROCESSORS!
OH, YEAH.
THAT.
SHE PAYS!

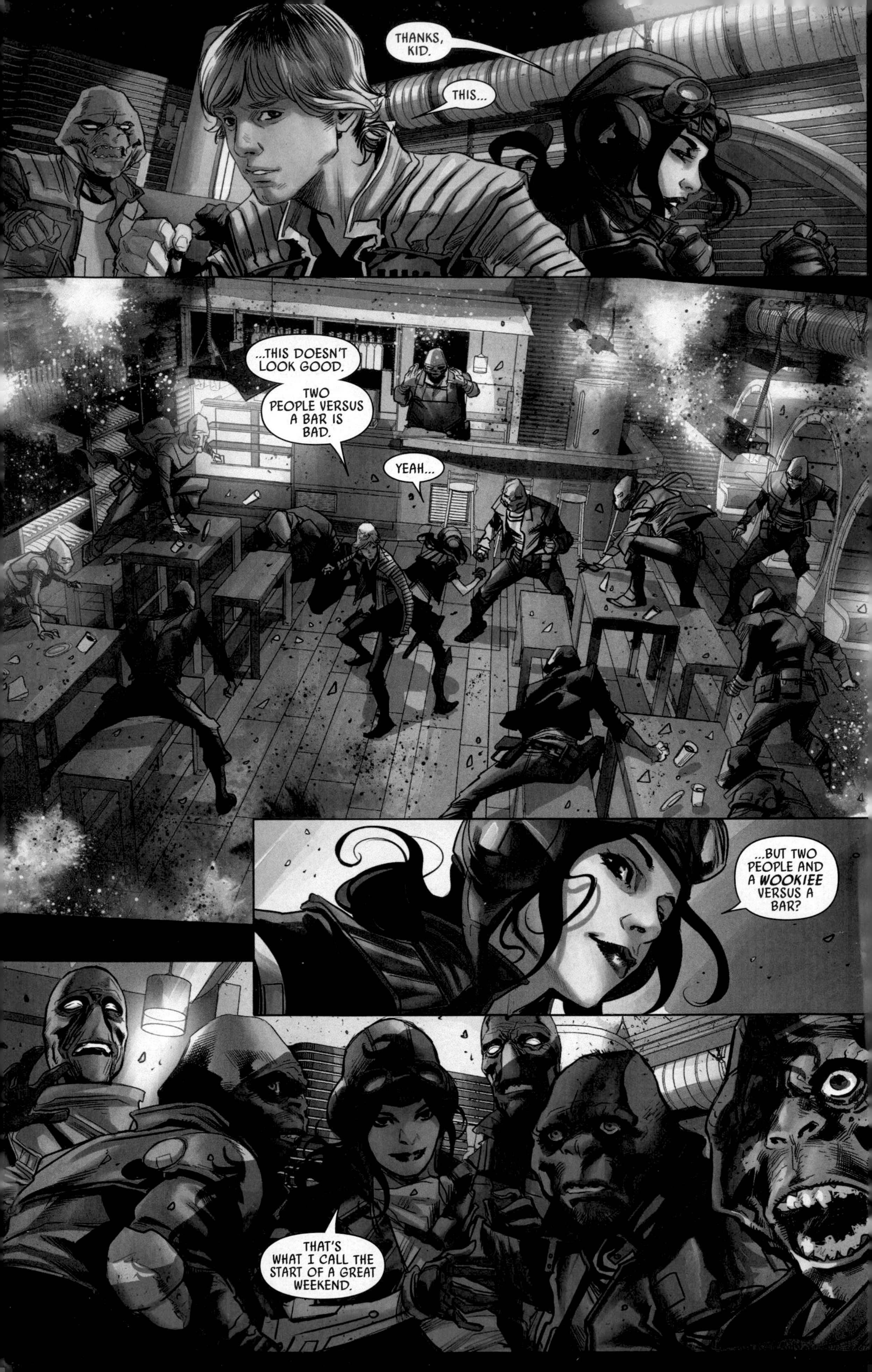
THANKS, KID.
THIS...
...THIS DOESN'T LOOK GOOD.
TWO PEOPLE VERSUS A BAR IS BAD.
YEAH...
...BUT TWO PEOPLE AND A WOOKIEE VERSUS A BAR?
THAT'S WHAT I CALL THE START OF A GREAT WEEKEND.

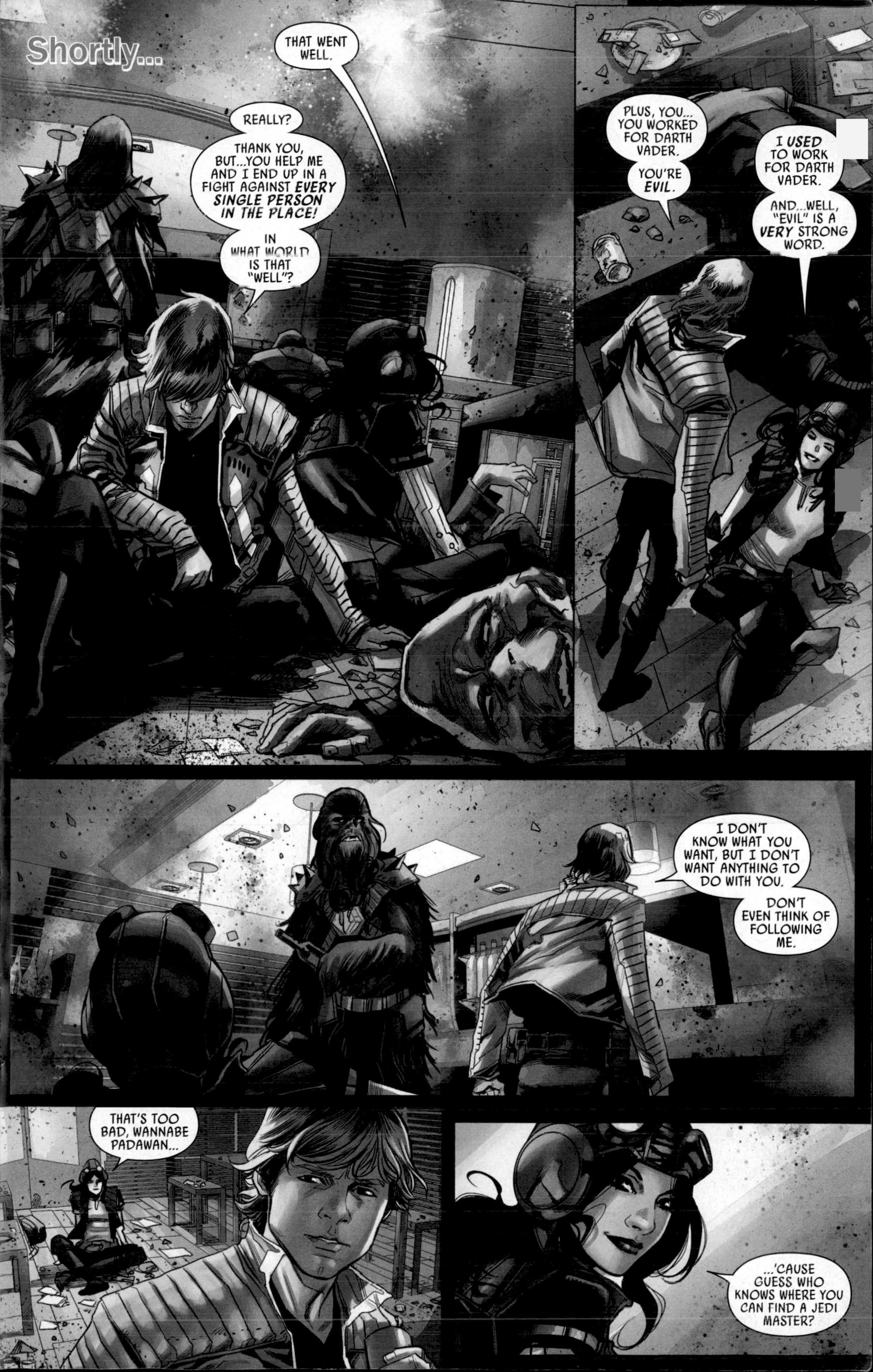
Shortly...
THAT WENT WELL.
REALLY?
THANK YOU, BUT...YOU HELP ME AND I END UP IN A FIGHT AGAINST EVERY SINGLE PERSON IN THE PLACE!
IN WHAT WORLD IS THAT "WELL"?
PLUS, YOU... YOU WORKED FOR DARTH VADER.
YOU'RE EVIL.
I USED TO WORK FOR DARTH VADER.
AND...WELL, "EVIL" IS A VERY STRONG WORD.
I DON'T KNOW WHAT YOU WANT, BUT I DON'T WANT ANYTHING TO DO WITH YOU.
DON'T EVEN THINK OF FOLLOWING ME.
THAT'S TOO BAD, WANNABE PADAWAN...
...'CAUSE GUESS WHO KNOWS WHERE YOU CAN FIND A JEDI MASTER?

STAR

SCRE

CIT

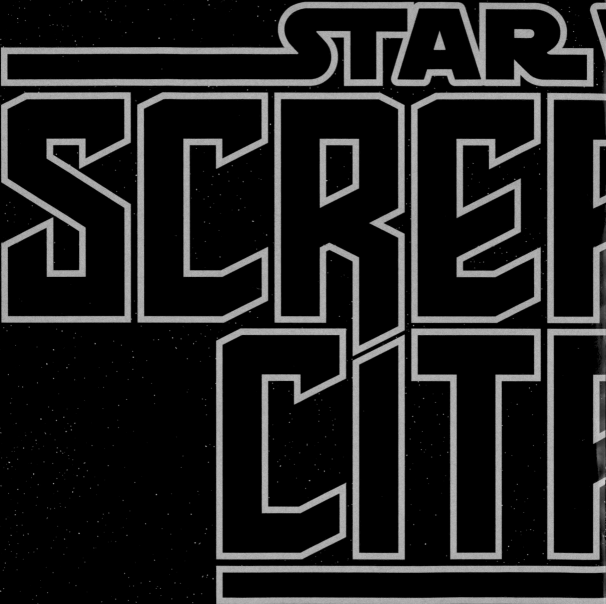

WARS

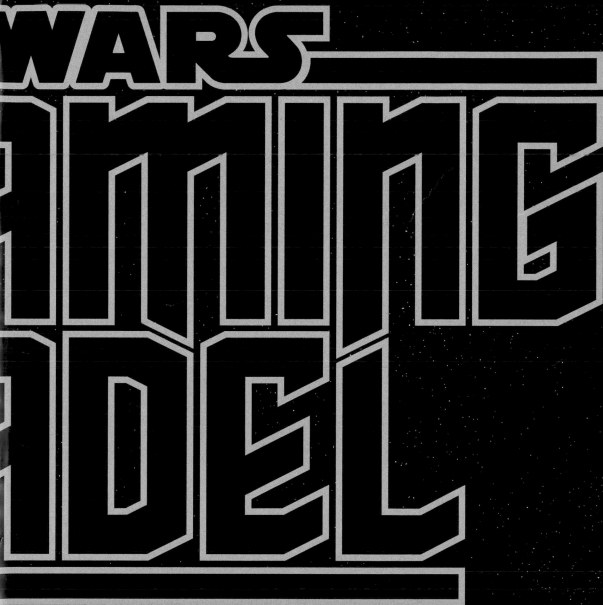

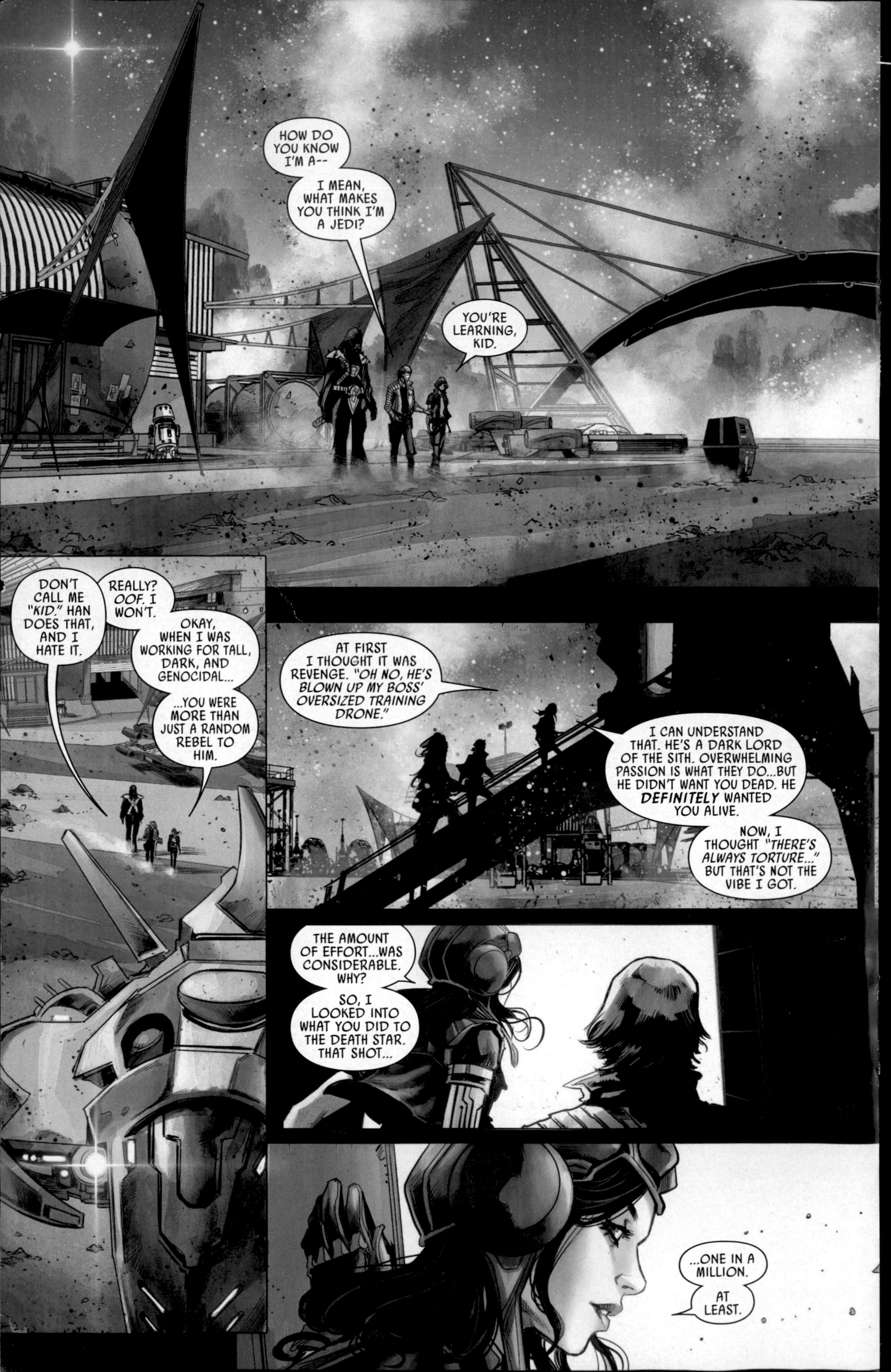
HOW DO YOU KNOW I'M A--
I MEAN, WHAT MAKES YOU THINK I'M A JEDI?
YOU'RE LEARNING, KID.
DON'T CALL ME "KID." HAN DOES THAT, AND I HATE IT.
REALLY? OOF. I WON'T.
OKAY, WHEN I WAS WORKING FOR TALL, DARK, AND GENOCIDAL...
...YOU WERE MORE THAN JUST A RANDOM REBEL TO HIM.
AT FIRST I THOUGHT IT WAS REVENGE. "OH NO, HE'S BLOWN UP MY BOSS' OVERSIZED TRAINING DRONE."
I CAN UNDERSTAND THAT. HE'S A DARK LORD OF THE SITH. OVERWHELMING PASSION IS WHAT THEY DO...BUT HE DIDN'T WANT YOU DEAD. HE DEFINITELY WANTED YOU ALIVE.
NOW, I THOUGHT "THERE'S ALWAYS TORTURE..." BUT THAT'S NOT THE VIBE I GOT.
THE AMOUNT OF EFFORT...WAS CONSIDERABLE. WHY?
SO, I LOOKED INTO WHAT YOU DID TO THE DEATH STAR. THAT SHOT...
...ONE IN A MILLION.
AT LEAST.

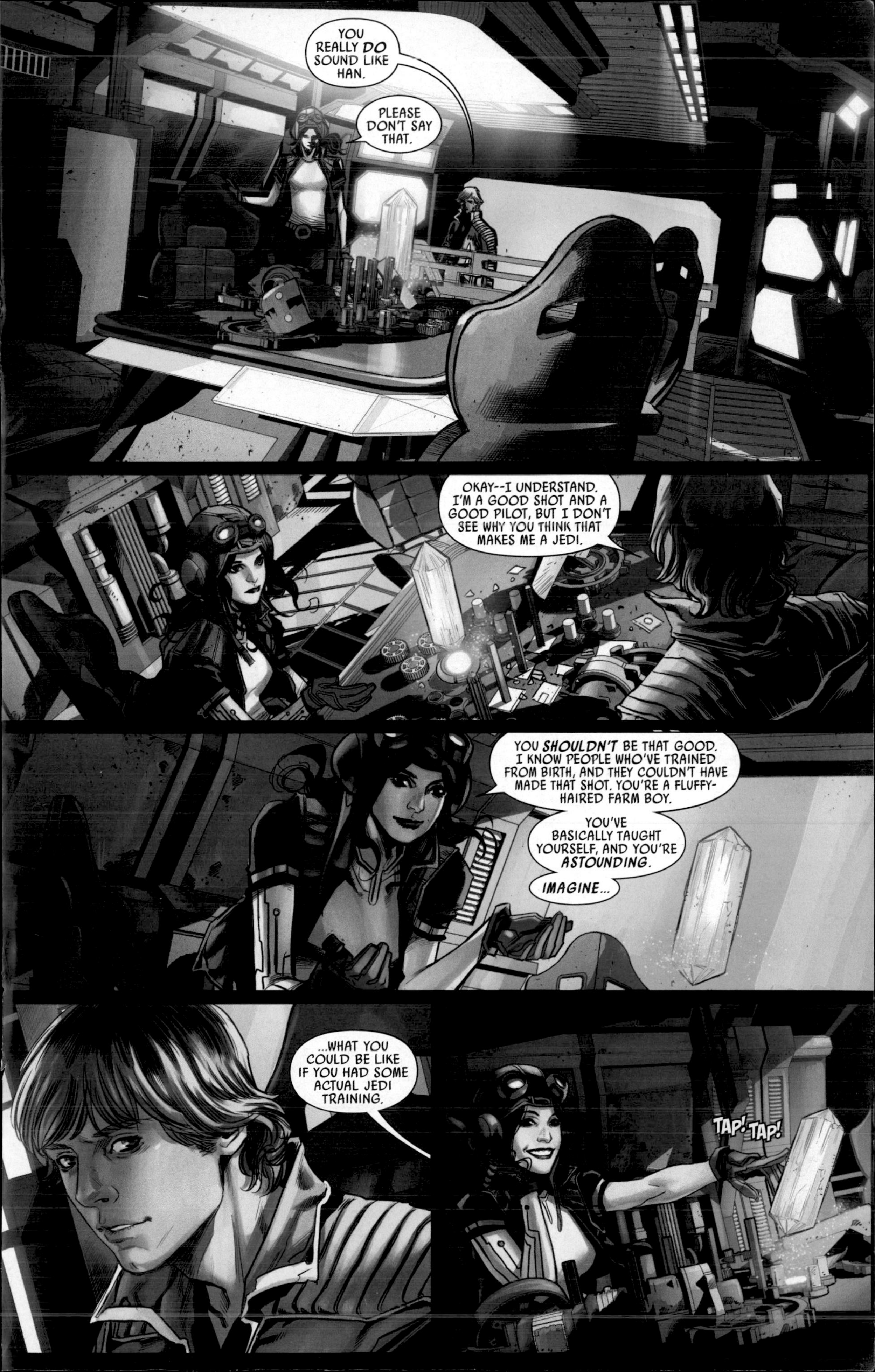
YOU REALLY DO SOUND LIKE HAN.
PLEASE DON'T SAY THAT.
OKAY--I UNDERSTAND. I'M A GOOD SHOT AND A GOOD PILOT, BUT I DON'T SEE WHY YOU THINK THAT MAKES ME A JEDI.
YOU SHOULDN'T BE THAT GOOD. I KNOW PEOPLE WHO'VE TRAINED FROM BIRTH, AND THEY COULDN'T HAVE MADE THAT SHOT. YOU'RE A FLUFFY-HAIRED FARM BOY.
YOU'VE BASICALLY TAUGHT YOURSELF, AND YOU'RE ASTOUNDING.
IMAGINE...
...WHAT YOU COULD BE LIKE IF YOU HAD SOME ACTUAL JEDI TRAINING.
TAP! TAP!

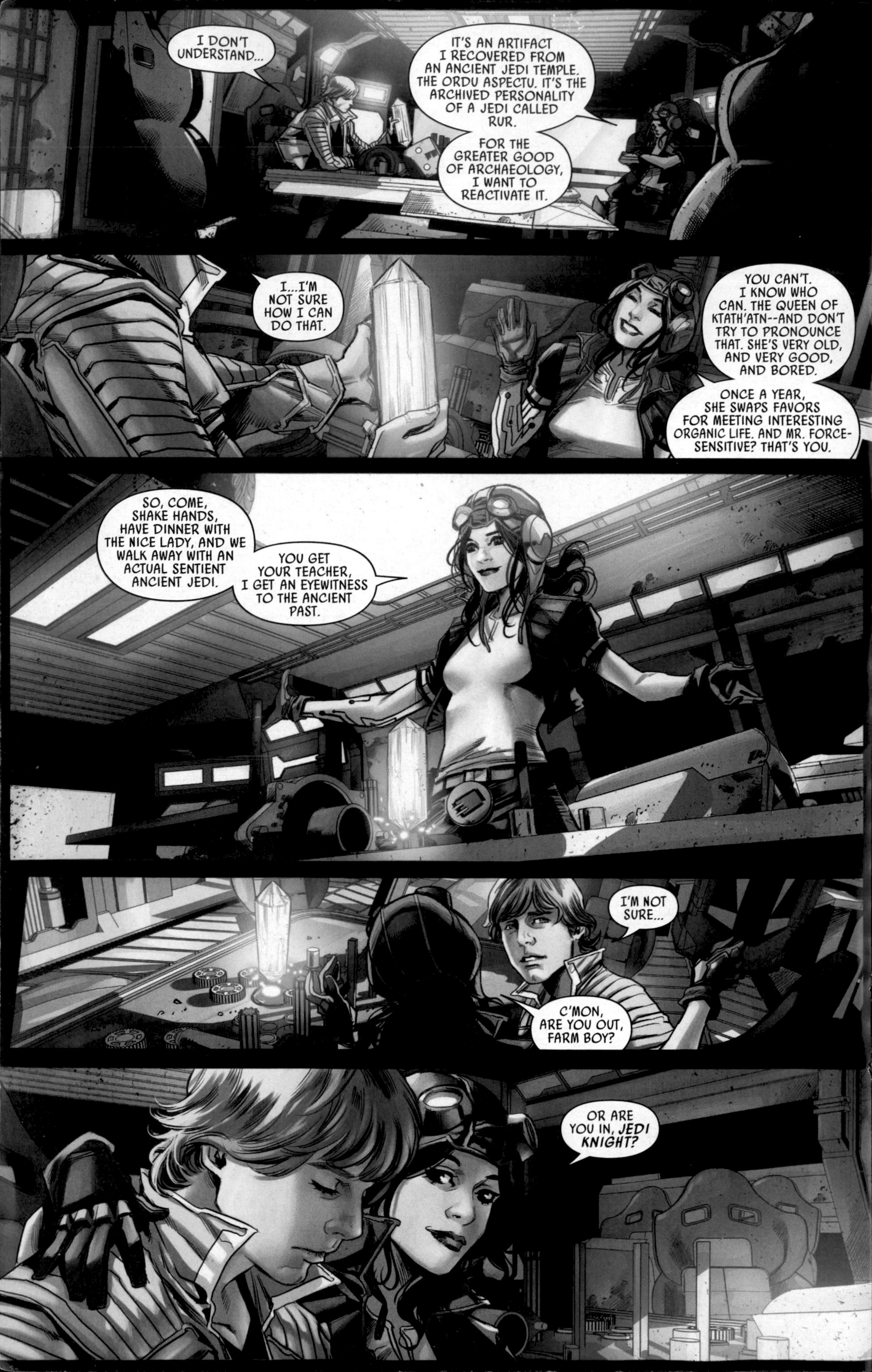
I DON'T UNDERSTAND...
IT'S AN ARTIFACT I RECOVERED FROM AN ANCIENT JEDI TEMPLE. THE ORDU ASPECTU. IT'S THE ARCHIVED PERSONALITY OF A JEDI CALLED RUR.
FOR THE GREATER GOOD OF ARCHAEOLOGY, I WANT TO REACTIVATE IT.
I...I'M NOT SURE HOW I CAN DO THAT.
YOU CAN'T. I KNOW WHO CAN. THE QUEEN OF KTATH'ATN--AND DON'T TRY TO PRONOUNCE THAT. SHE'S VERY OLD, AND VERY GOOD, AND BORED.
ONCE A YEAR, SHE SWAPS FAVORS FOR MEETING INTERESTING ORGANIC LIFE. AND MR. FORCE-SENSITIVE? THAT'S YOU.
SO, COME, SHAKE HANDS, HAVE DINNER WITH THE NICE LADY, AND WE WALK AWAY WITH AN ACTUAL SENTIENT ANCIENT JEDI.
YOU GET YOUR TEACHER, I GET AN EYEWITNESS TO THE ANCIENT PAST.
I'M NOT SURE...
C'MON, ARE YOU OUT, FARM BOY?
OR ARE YOU IN, JEDI KNIGHT?

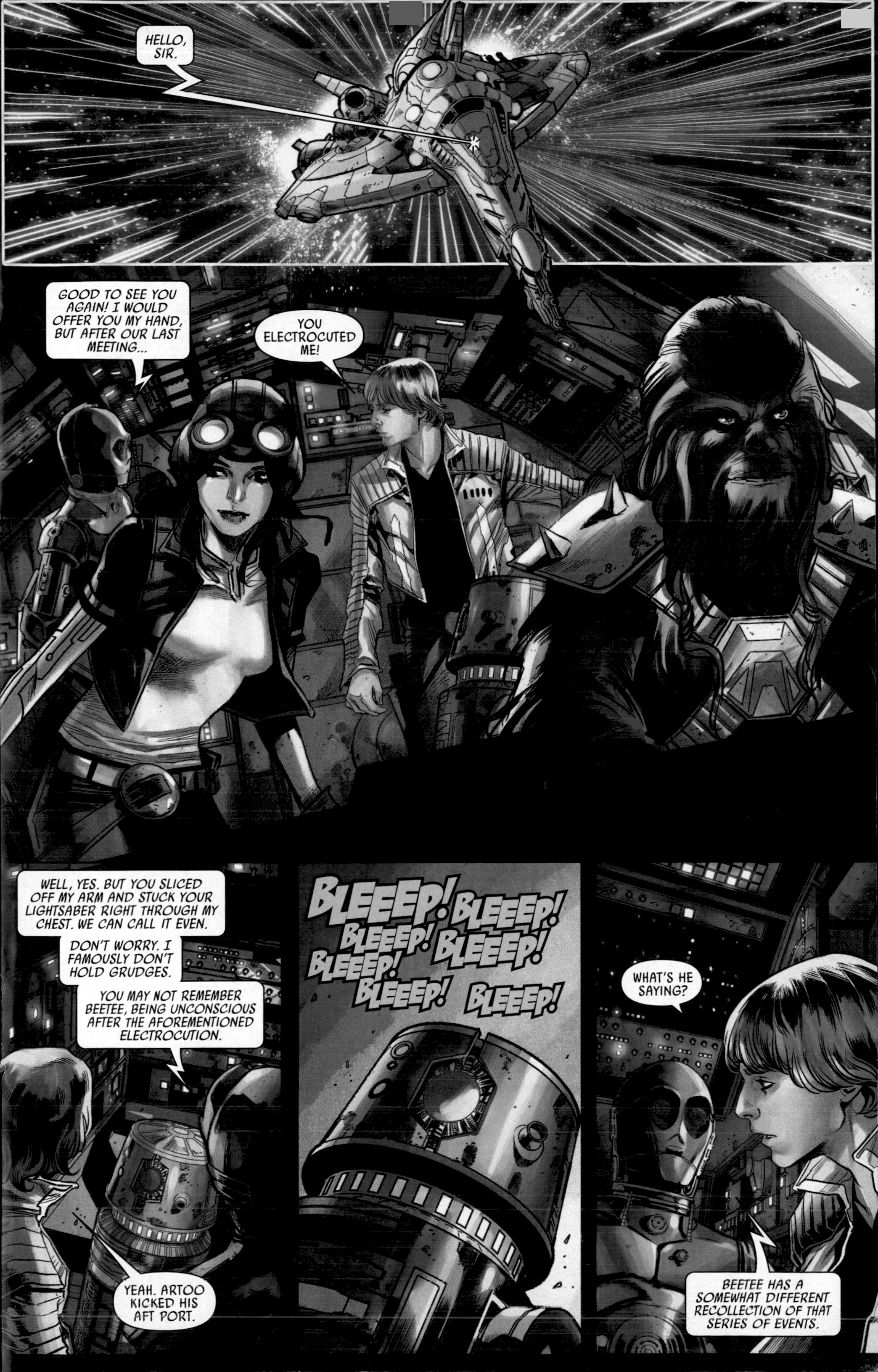
HELLO, SIR.
GOOD TO SEE YOU AGAIN! I WOULD OFFER YOU MY HAND, BUT AFTER OUR LAST MEETING...
YOU ELECTROCUTED ME!
WELL, YES. BUT YOU SLICED OFF MY ARM AND STUCK YOUR LIGHTSABER RIGHT THROUGH MY CHEST. WE CAN CALL IT EVEN.
DON'T WORRY. I FAMOUSLY DON'T HOLD GRUDGES.
YOU MAY NOT REMEMBER BEETEE, BEING UNCONSCIOUS AFTER THE AFOREMENTIONED ELECTROCUTION.
YEAH. ARTOO KICKED HIS AFT PORT.
BLEEEP! BLEEEP! BLEEEP! BLEEEP! BLEEEP! BLEEEP! BLEEEP!
WHAT'S HE SAYING?
BEETEE HAS A SOMEWHAT DIFFERENT RECOLLECTION OF THAT SERIES OF EVENTS.

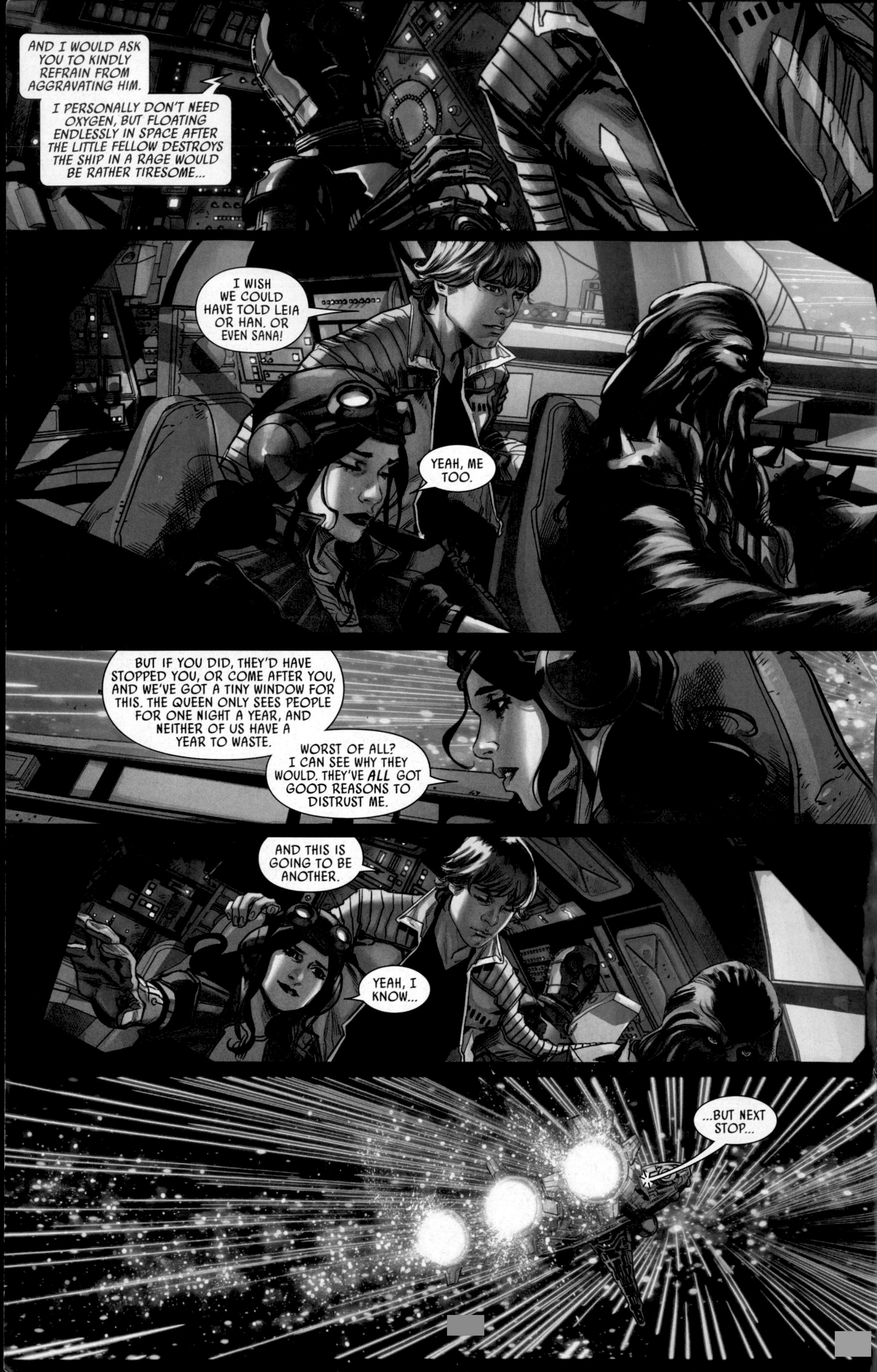
AND I WOULD ASK YOU TO KINDLY REFRAIN FROM AGGRAVATING HIM.
I PERSONALLY DON'T NEED OXYGEN, BUT FLOATING ENDLESSLY IN SPACE AFTER THE LITTLE FELLOW DESTROYS THE SHIP IN A RAGE WOULD BE RATHER TIRESOME...
I WISH WE COULD HAVE TOLD LEIA OR HAN. OR EVEN SANA!
YEAH, ME TOO.
BUT IF YOU DID, THEY'D HAVE STOPPED YOU, OR COME AFTER YOU, AND WE'VE GOT A TINY WINDOW FOR THIS. THE QUEEN ONLY SEES PEOPLE FOR ONE NIGHT A YEAR, AND NEITHER OF US HAVE A YEAR TO WASTE.
WORST OF ALL? I CAN SEE WHY THEY WOULD. THEY'VE ALL GOT GOOD REASONS TO DISTRUST ME.
AND THIS IS GOING TO BE ANOTHER.
YEAH, I KNOW...
...BUT NEXT STOP...

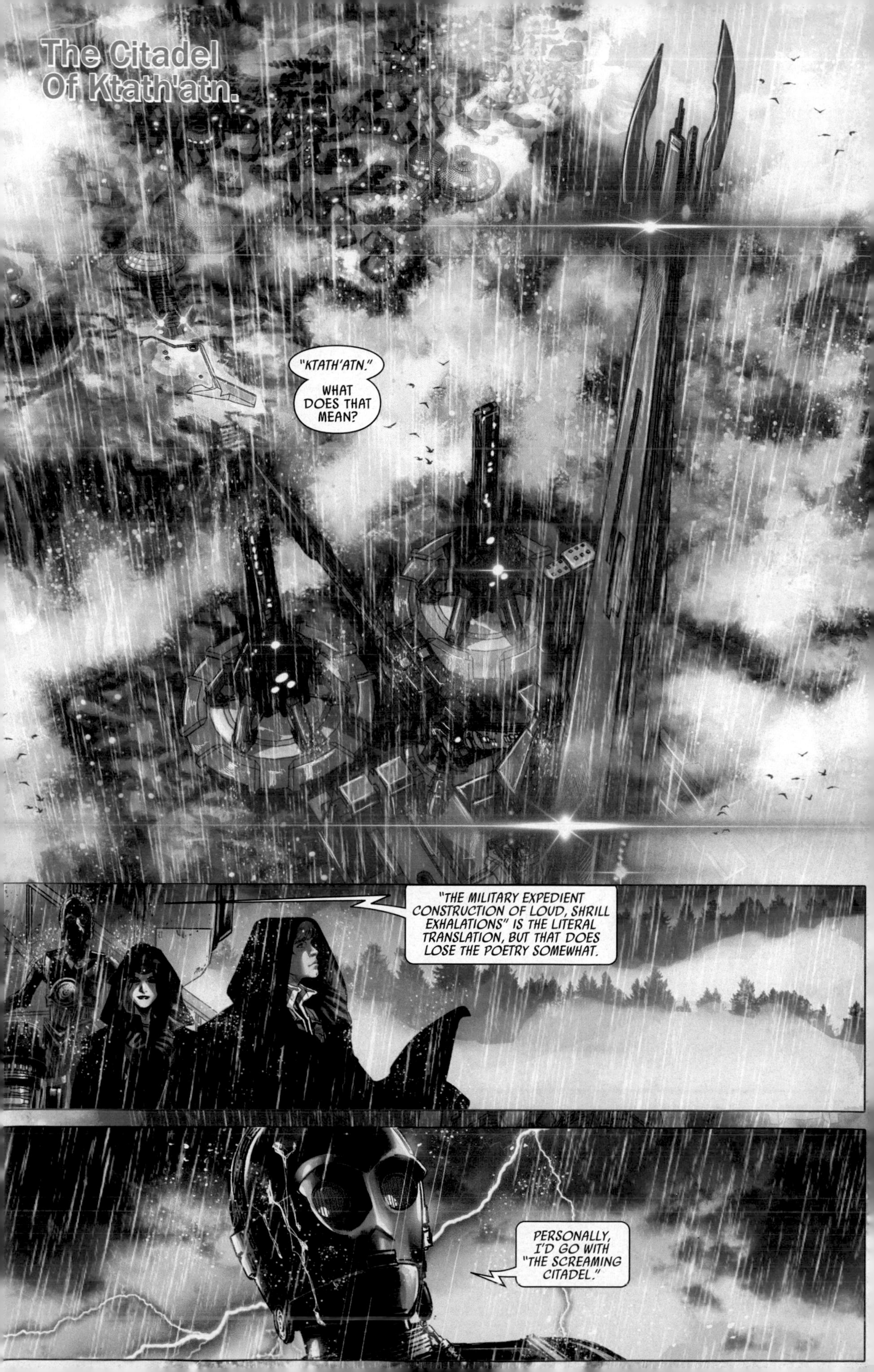
The Citadel Of Ktath'atn.
"KTATH'ATN." WHAT DOES THAT MEAN?
"THE MILITARY EXPEDIENT CONSTRUCTION OF LOUD, SHRILL EXHALATIONS" IS THE LITERAL TRANSLATION, BUT THAT DOES LOSE THE POETRY SOMEWHAT.
PERSONALLY, I'D GO WITH "THE SCREAMING CITADEL."

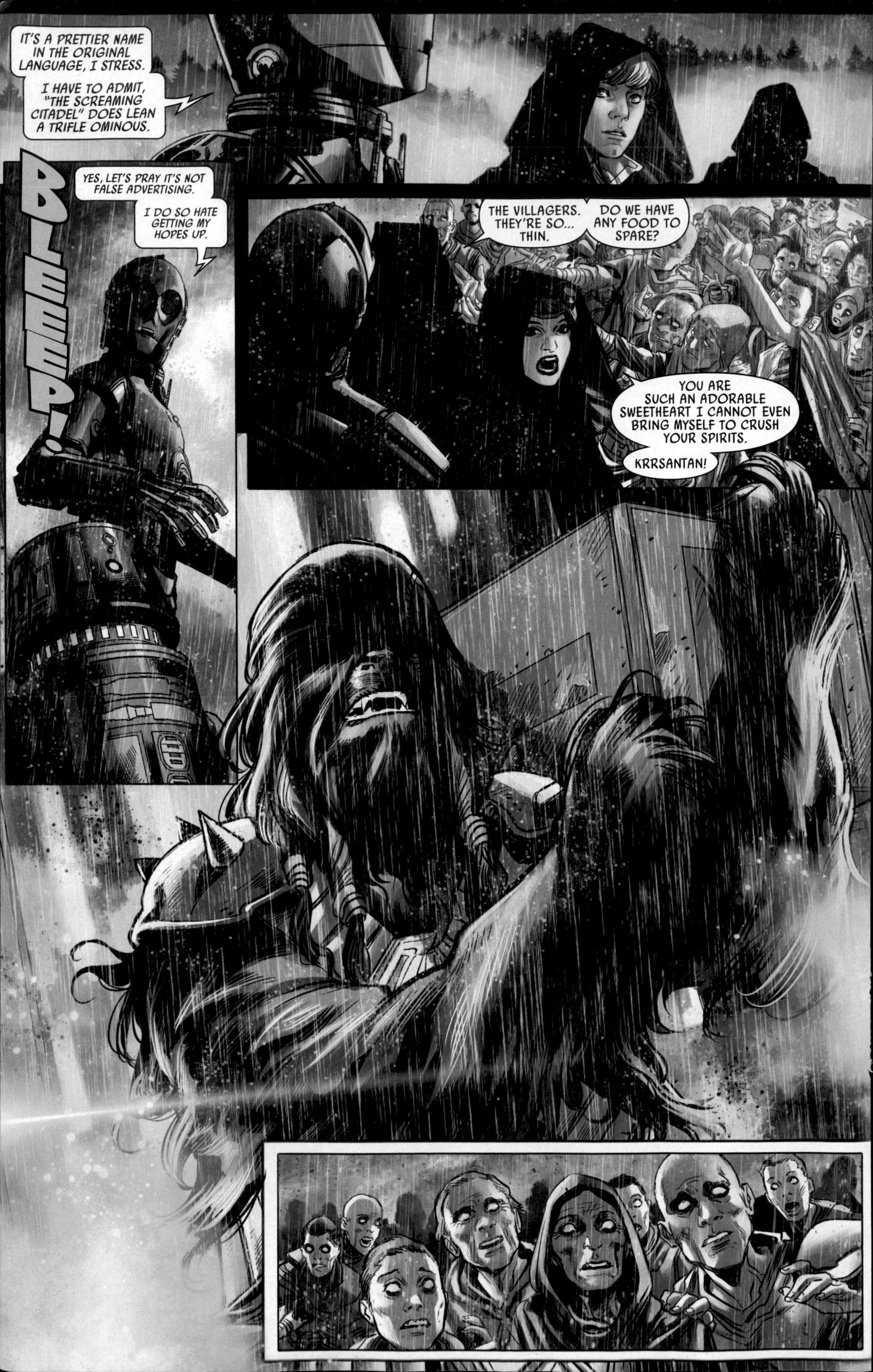
IT'S A PRETTIER NAME IN THE ORIGINAL LANGUAGE, I STRESS.
I HAVE TO ADMIT, "THE SCREAMING CITADEL" DOES LEAN A TRIFLE OMINOUS.
BLEEEP!
YES, LET'S PRAY IT'S NOT FALSE ADVERTISING.
I DO SO HATE GETTING MY HOPES UP.
THE VILLAGERS. THEY'RE SO... THIN.
DO WE HAVE ANY FOOD TO SPARE?
YOU ARE SUCH AN ADORABLE SWEETHEART I CANNOT EVEN BRING MYSELF TO CRUSH YOUR SPIRITS.
KRRSANTAN!

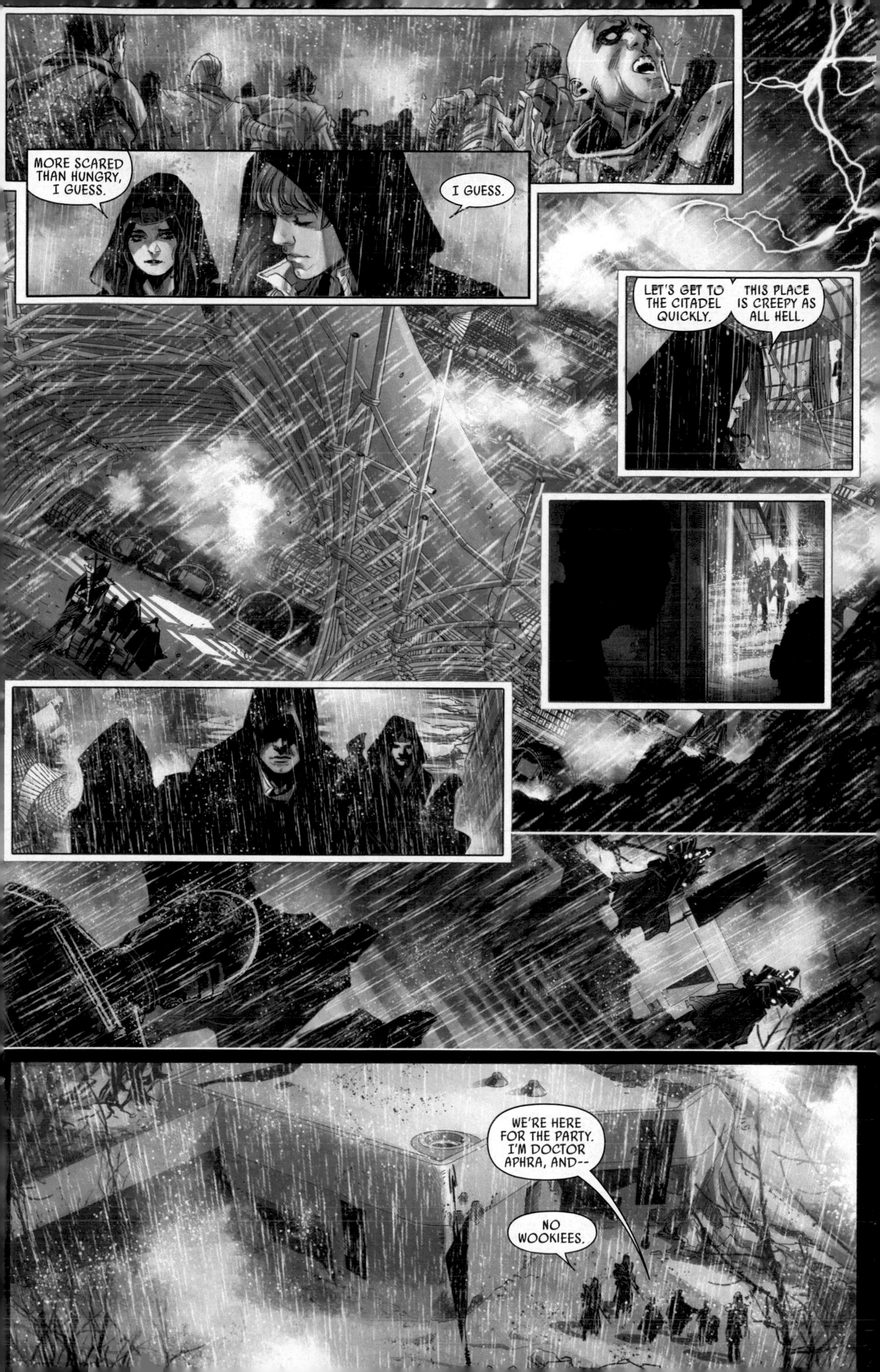
MORE SCARED THAN HUNGRY, I GUESS.
I GUESS.
LET'S GET TO THE CITADEL QUICKLY.
THIS PLACE IS CREEPY AS ALL HELL.
WE'RE HERE FOR THE PARTY. I'M DOCTOR APHRA, AND--
NO WOOKIEES.

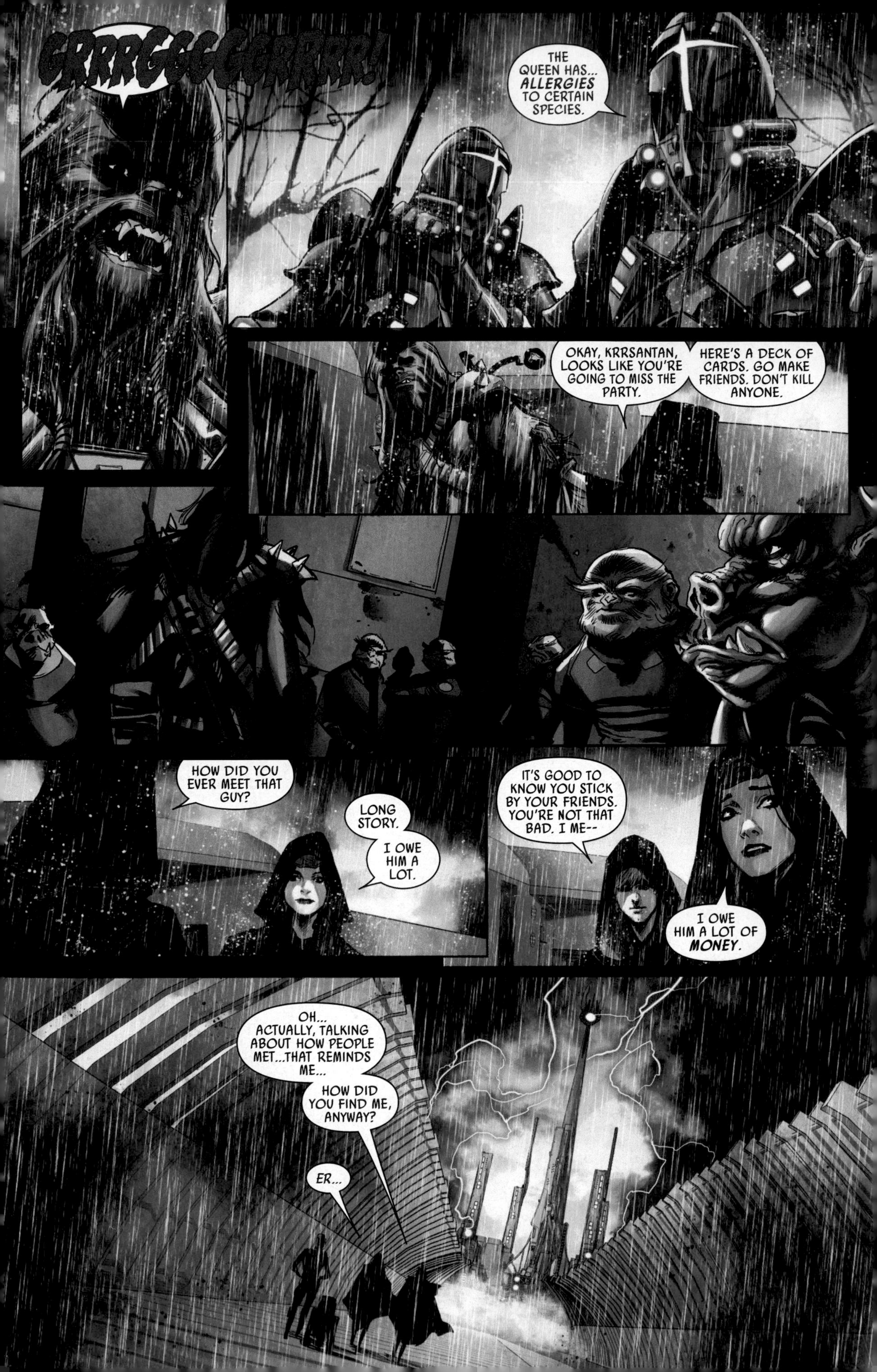
GRRRGGGGRRRR!
THE QUEEN HAS... ALLERGIES TO CERTAIN SPECIES.
OKAY, KRRSANTAN, LOOKS LIKE YOU'RE GOING TO MISS THE PARTY.
HERE'S A DECK OF CARDS. GO MAKE FRIENDS. DON'T KILL ANYONE.
HOW DID YOU EVER MEET THAT GUY?
LONG STORY.
I OWE HIM A LOT.
IT'S GOOD TO KNOW YOU STICK BY YOUR FRIENDS. YOU'RE NOT THAT BAD. I ME--
I OWE HIM A LOT OF MONEY.
OH... ACTUALLY, TALKING ABOUT HOW PEOPLE MET...THAT REMINDS ME...
HOW DID YOU FIND ME, ANYWAY?
ER...

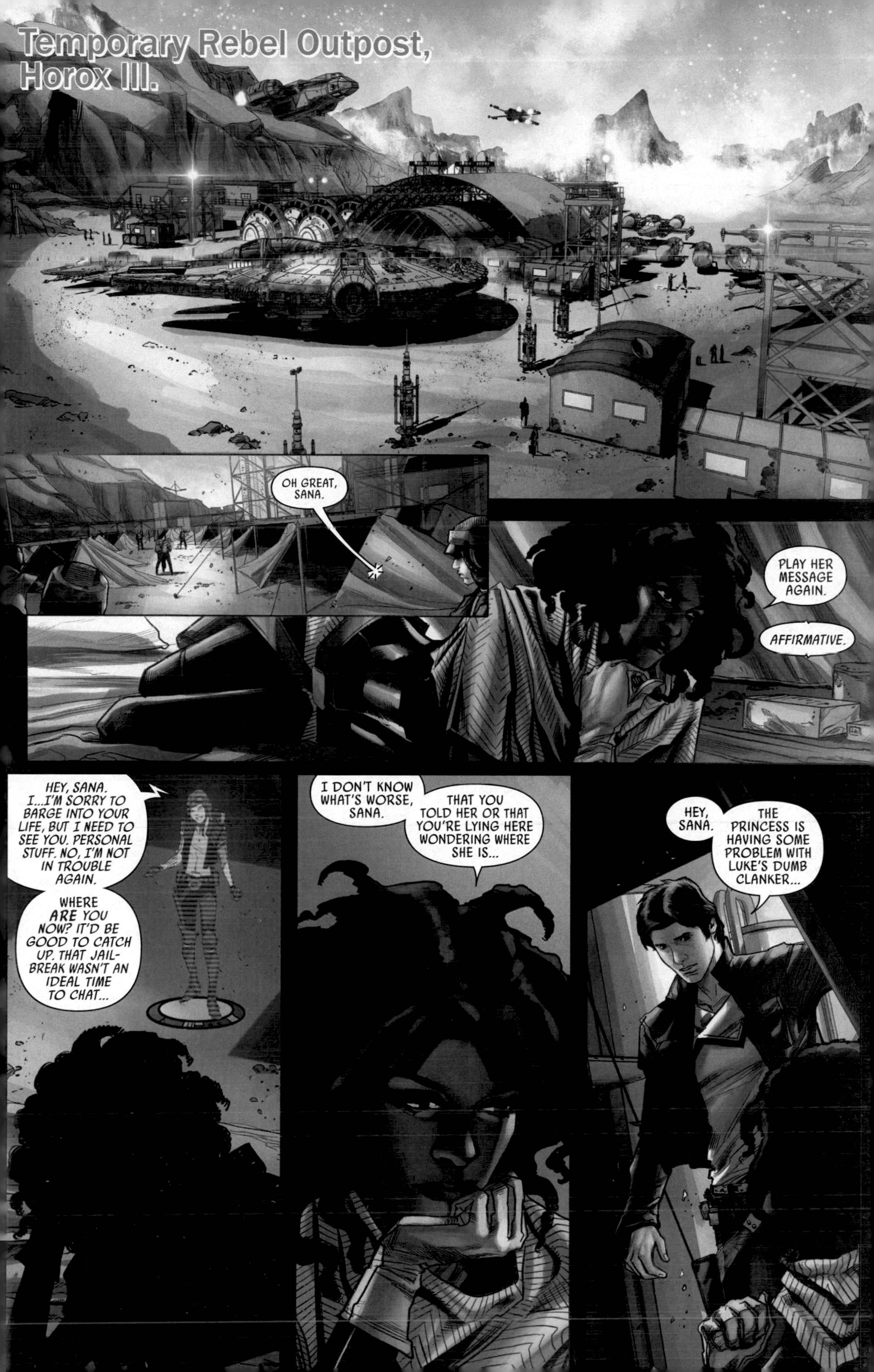
Temporary Rebel Outpost, Horox III.
OH GREAT, SANA.
PLAY HER MESSAGE AGAIN.
AFFIRMATIVE.
HEY, SANA. I...I'M SORRY TO BARGE INTO YOUR LIFE, BUT I NEED TO SEE YOU. PERSONAL STUFF. NO, I'M NOT IN TROUBLE AGAIN.
WHERE ARE YOU NOW? IT'D BE GOOD TO CATCH UP. THAT JAIL-BREAK WASN'T AN IDEAL TIME TO CHAT...
I DON'T KNOW WHAT'S WORSE, SANA.
THAT YOU TOLD HER OR THAT YOU'RE LYING HERE WONDERING WHERE SHE IS...
HEY, SANA.
THE PRINCESS IS HAVING SOME PROBLEM WITH LUKE'S DUMB CLANKER...

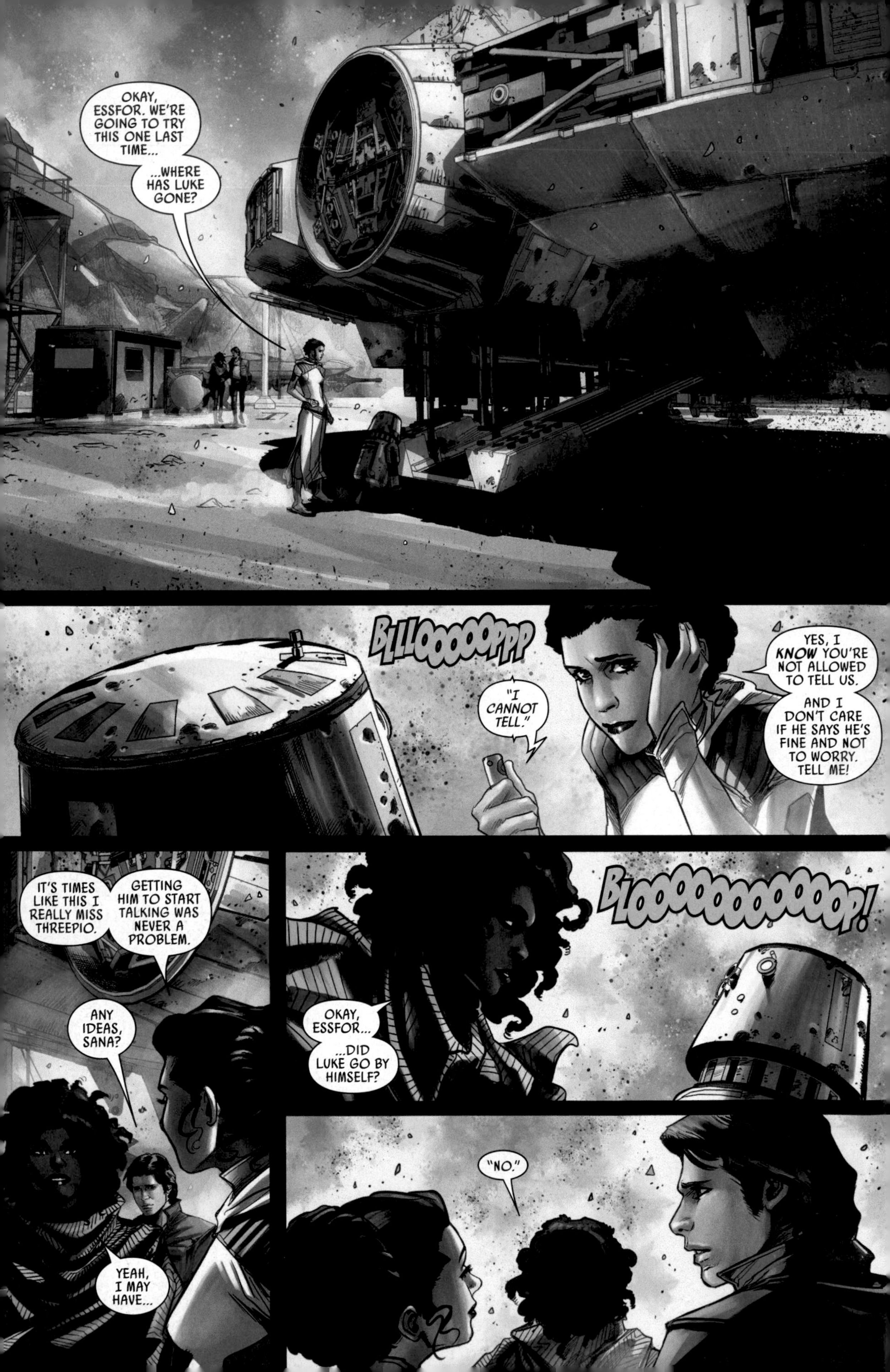
OKAY, ESSFOR. WE'RE GOING TO TRY THIS ONE LAST TIME...
...WHERE HAS LUKE GONE?
BLLLOOOOOOPPP
"I CANNOT TELL."
YES, I KNOW YOU'RE NOT ALLOWED TO TELL US.
AND I DON'T CARE IF HE SAYS HE'S FINE AND NOT TO WORRY. TELL ME!
IT'S TIMES LIKE THIS I REALLY MISS THREEPIO.
GETTING HIM TO START TALKING WAS NEVER A PROBLEM.
ANY IDEAS, SANA?
YEAH, I MAY HAVE...
OKAY, ESSFOR...
...DID LUKE GO BY HIMSELF?
BLOOOOOOOOOOOOP!
"NO."

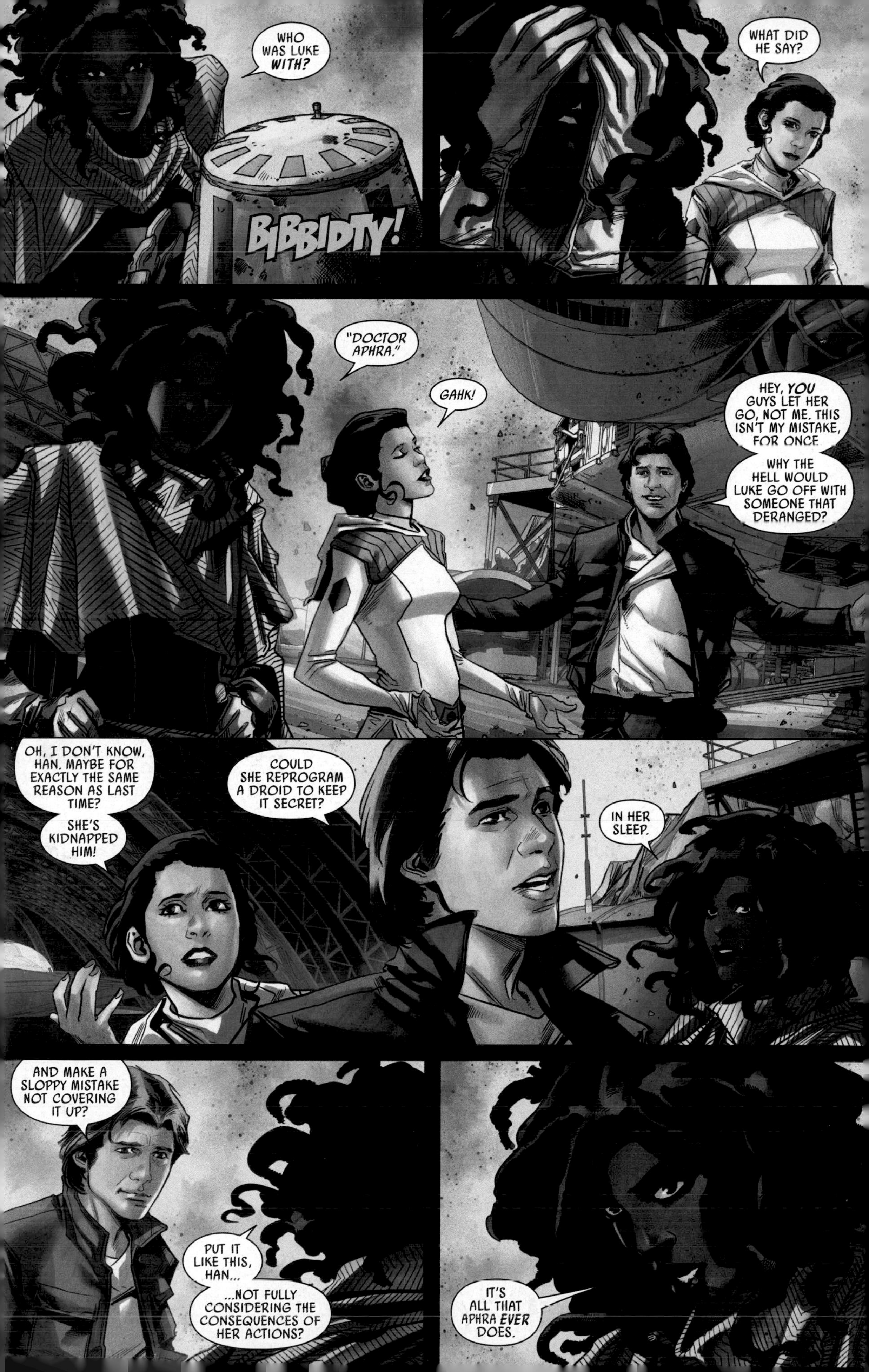
WHO WAS LUKE *WITH*?
BIBBIDTY!
WHAT DID HE SAY?
"DOCTOR APHRA."
GAHK!
HEY, *YOU* GUYS LET HER GO, NOT ME. THIS ISN'T MY MISTAKE, FOR ONCE
WHY THE HELL WOULD LUKE GO OFF WITH SOMEONE THAT DERANGED?
OH, I DON'T KNOW, HAN. MAYBE FOR EXACTLY THE SAME REASON AS LAST TIME?
SHE'S KIDNAPPED HIM!
COULD SHE REPROGRAM A DROID TO KEEP IT SECRET?
IN HER SLEEP.
AND MAKE A SLOPPY MISTAKE NOT COVERING IT UP?
PUT IT LIKE THIS, HAN...
...NOT FULLY CONSIDERING THE CONSEQUENCES OF HER ACTIONS?
IT'S ALL THAT APHRA *EVER* DOES.

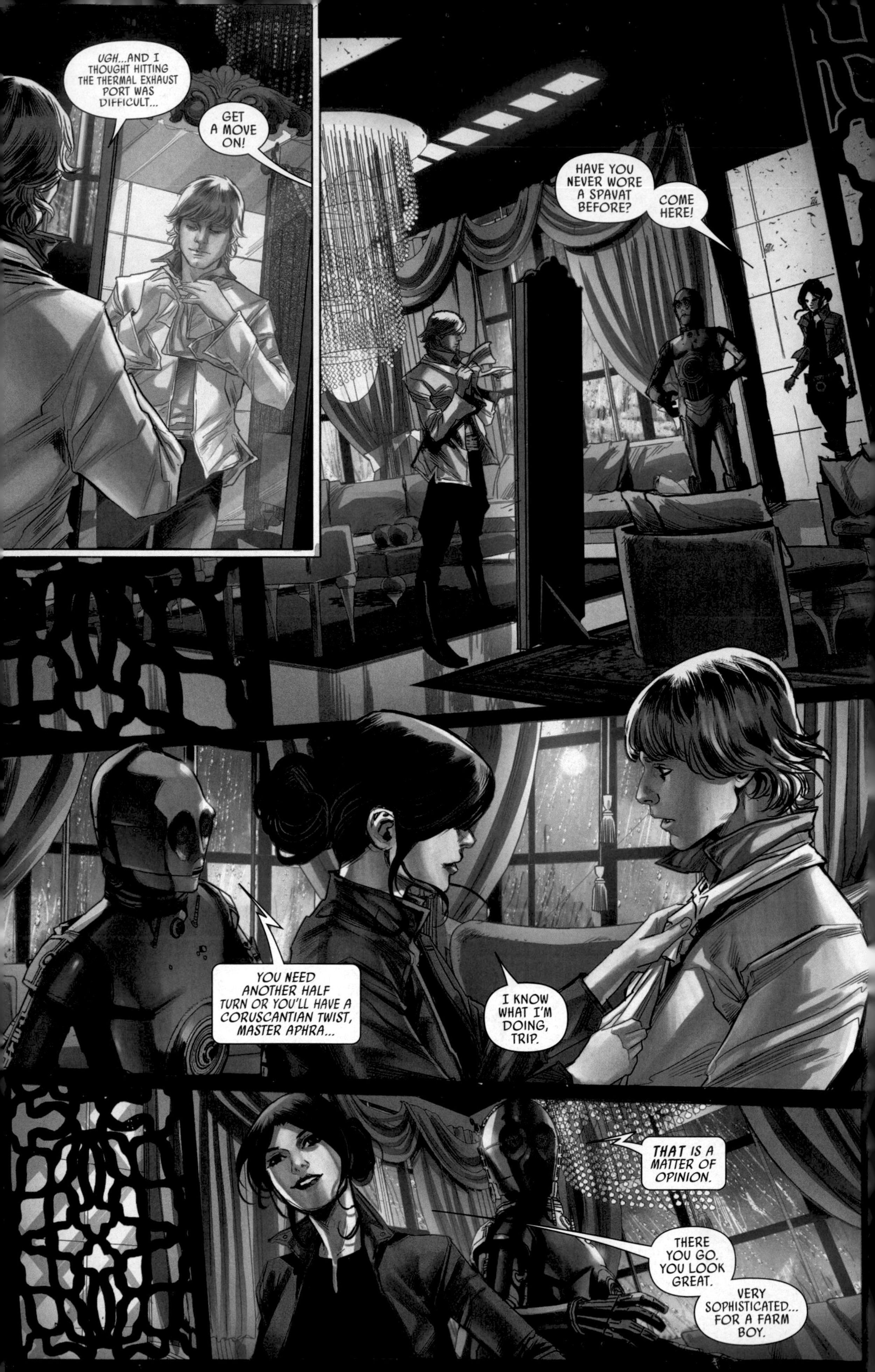
UGH...AND I THOUGHT HITTING THE THERMAL EXHAUST PORT WAS DIFFICULT...
GET A MOVE ON!
HAVE YOU NEVER WORE A SPAVAT BEFORE?
COME HERE!
YOU NEED ANOTHER HALF TURN OR YOU'LL HAVE A CORUSCANTIAN TWIST, MASTER APHRA...
I KNOW WHAT I'M DOING, TRIP.
THAT IS A MATTER OF OPINION.
THERE YOU GO. YOU LOOK GREAT.
VERY SOPHISTICATED... FOR A FARM BOY.

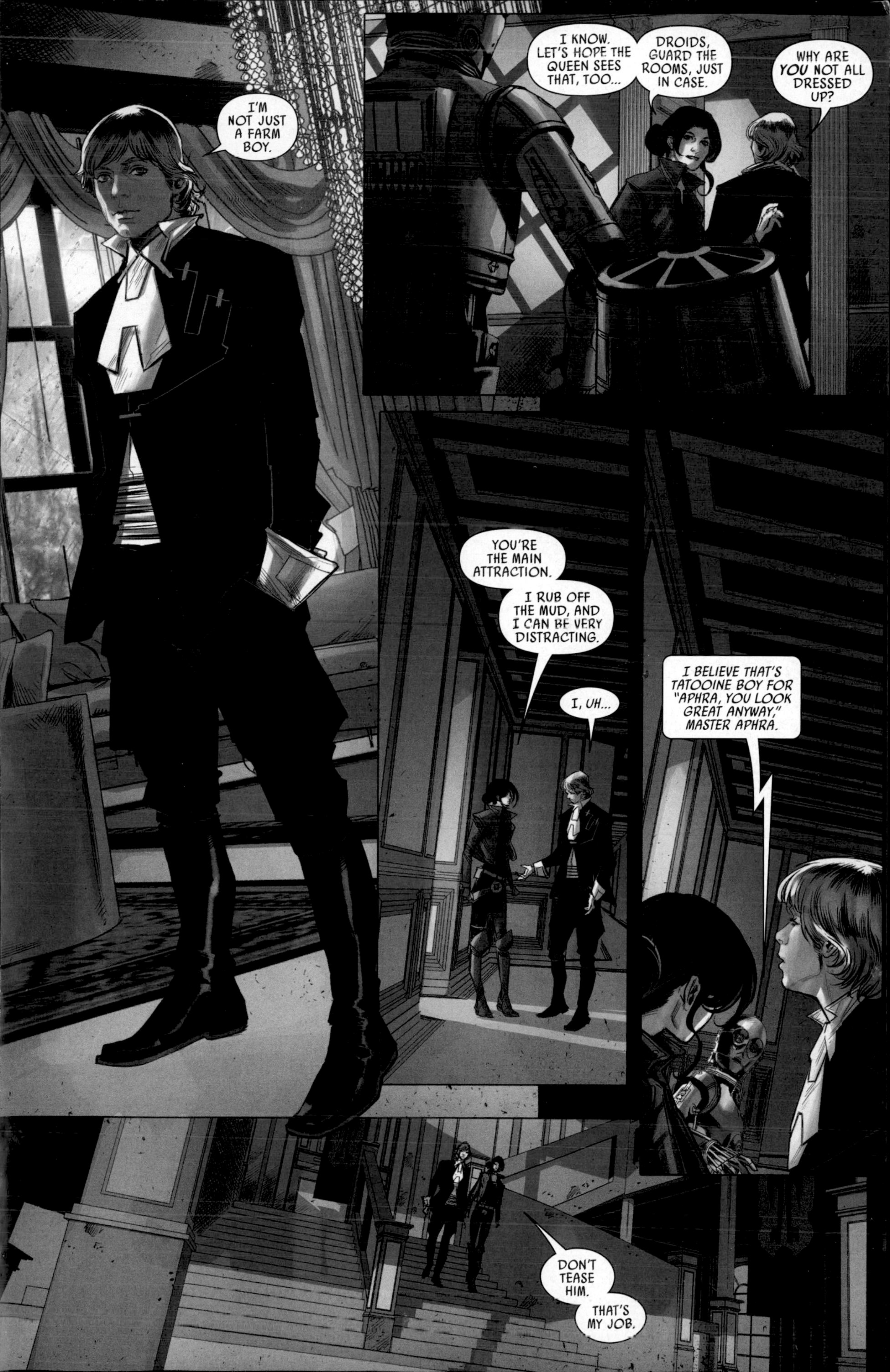
I'M NOT JUST A FARM BOY.
I KNOW. LET'S HOPE THE QUEEN SEES THAT, TOO...
DROIDS, GUARD THE ROOMS, JUST IN CASE.
WHY ARE YOU NOT ALL DRESSED UP?
YOU'RE THE MAIN ATTRACTION.
I RUB OFF THE MUD, AND I CAN BE VERY DISTRACTING.
I, UH...
I BELIEVE THAT'S TATOOINE BOY FOR "APHRA, YOU LOOK GREAT ANYWAY," MASTER APHRA.
DON'T TEASE HIM.
THAT'S MY JOB.

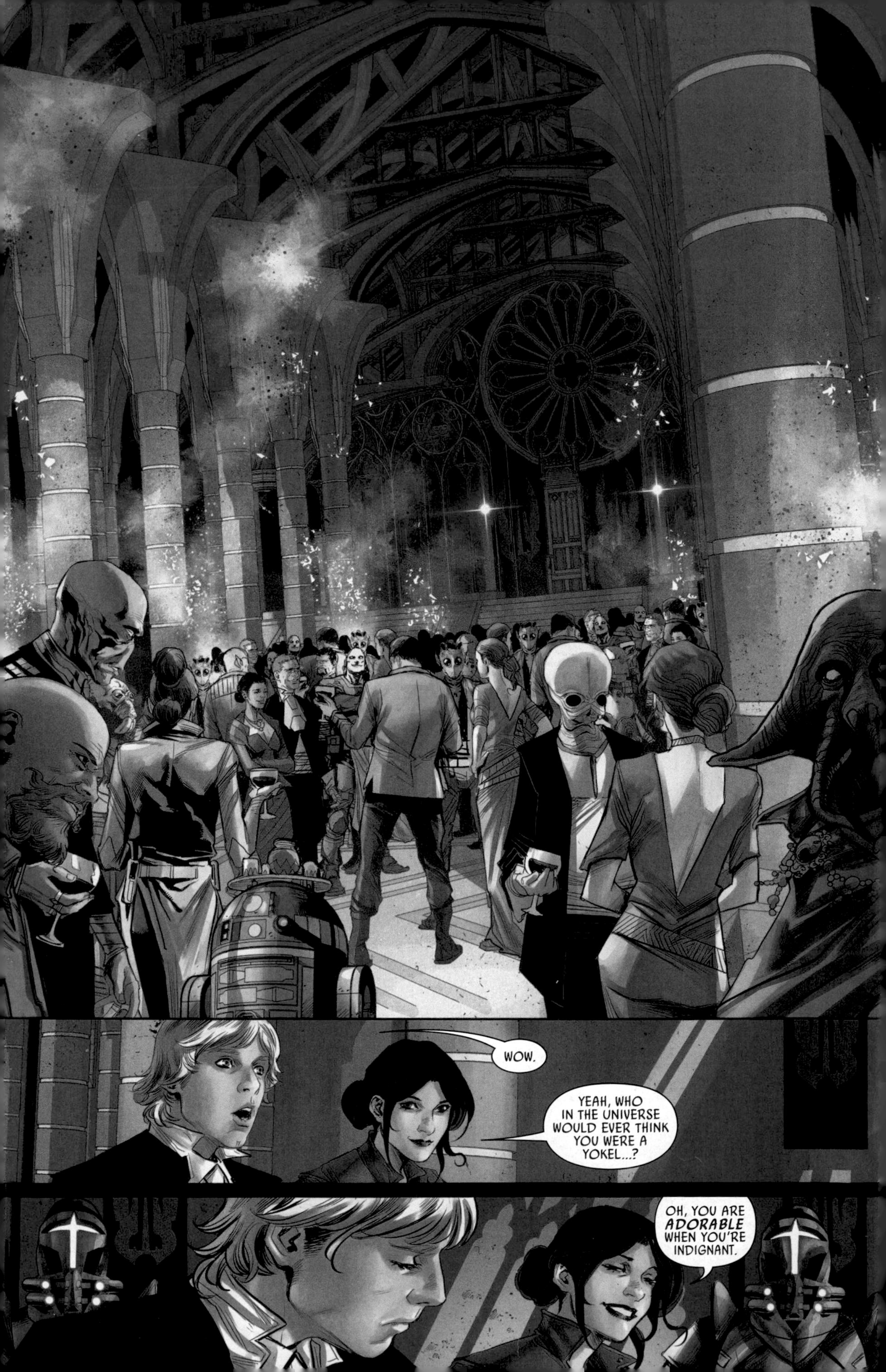
WOW.
YEAH, WHO IN THE UNIVERSE WOULD EVER THINK YOU WERE A YOKEL...?
OH, YOU ARE *ADORABLE* WHEN YOU'RE INDIGNANT.

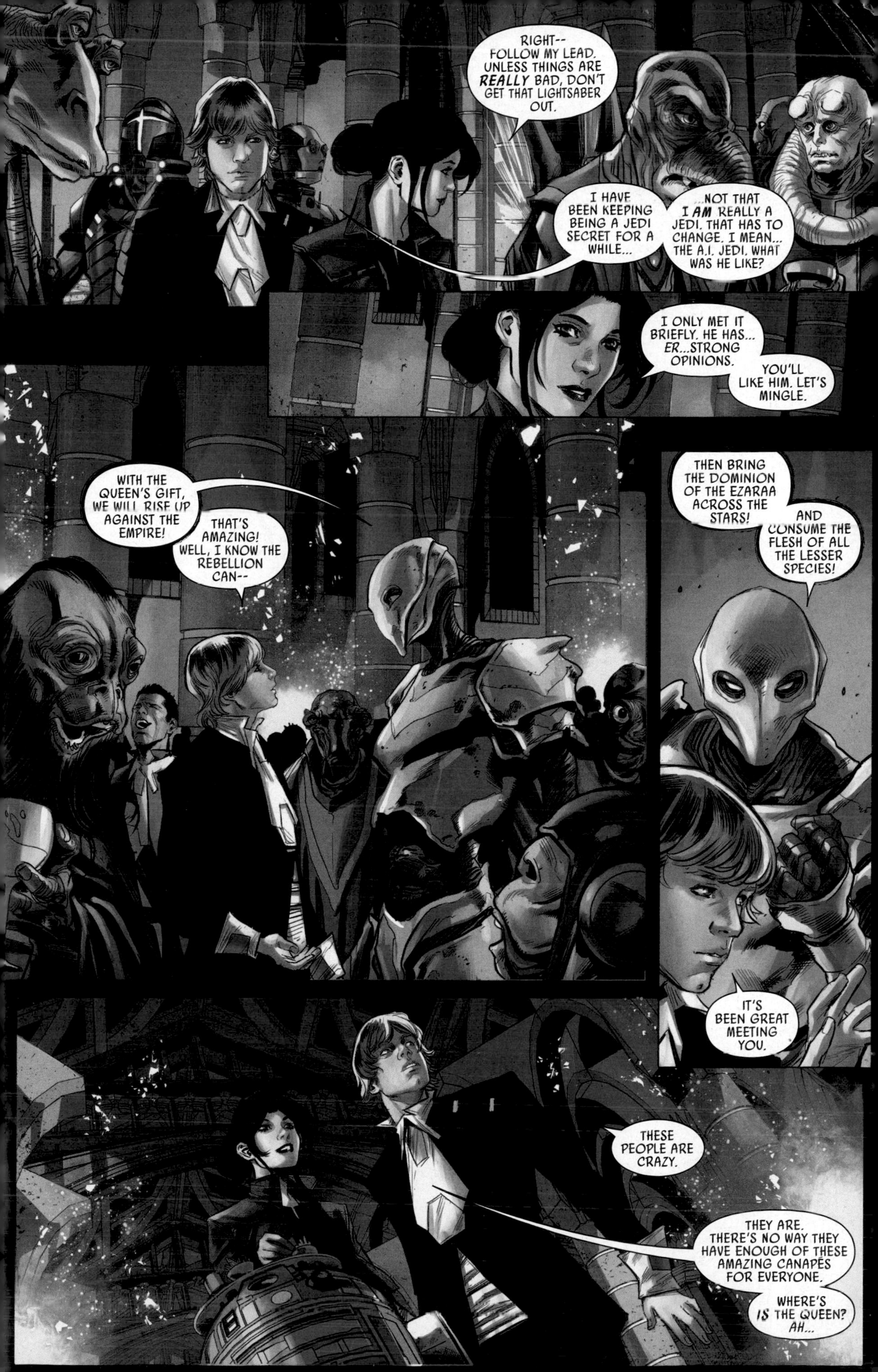
RIGHT-- FOLLOW MY LEAD. UNLESS THINGS ARE REALLY BAD, DON'T GET THAT LIGHTSABER OUT.
I HAVE BEEN KEEPING BEING A JEDI SECRET FOR A WHILE...
...NOT THAT I AM REALLY A JEDI. THAT HAS TO CHANGE. I MEAN... THE A.I. JEDI. WHAT WAS HE LIKE?
I ONLY MET IT BRIEFLY. HE HAS... ER...STRONG OPINIONS.
YOU'LL LIKE HIM. LET'S MINGLE.
WITH THE QUEEN'S GIFT, WE WILL RISE UP AGAINST THE EMPIRE!
THAT'S AMAZING! WELL, I KNOW THE REBELLION CAN--
THEN BRING THE DOMINION OF THE EZARAA ACROSS THE STARS!
AND CONSUME THE FLESH OF ALL THE LESSER SPECIES!
IT'S BEEN GREAT MEETING YOU.
THESE PEOPLE ARE CRAZY.
THEY ARE. THERE'S NO WAY THEY HAVE ENOUGH OF THESE AMAZING CANAPÉS FOR EVERYONE.
WHERE'S IS THE QUEEN? AH...

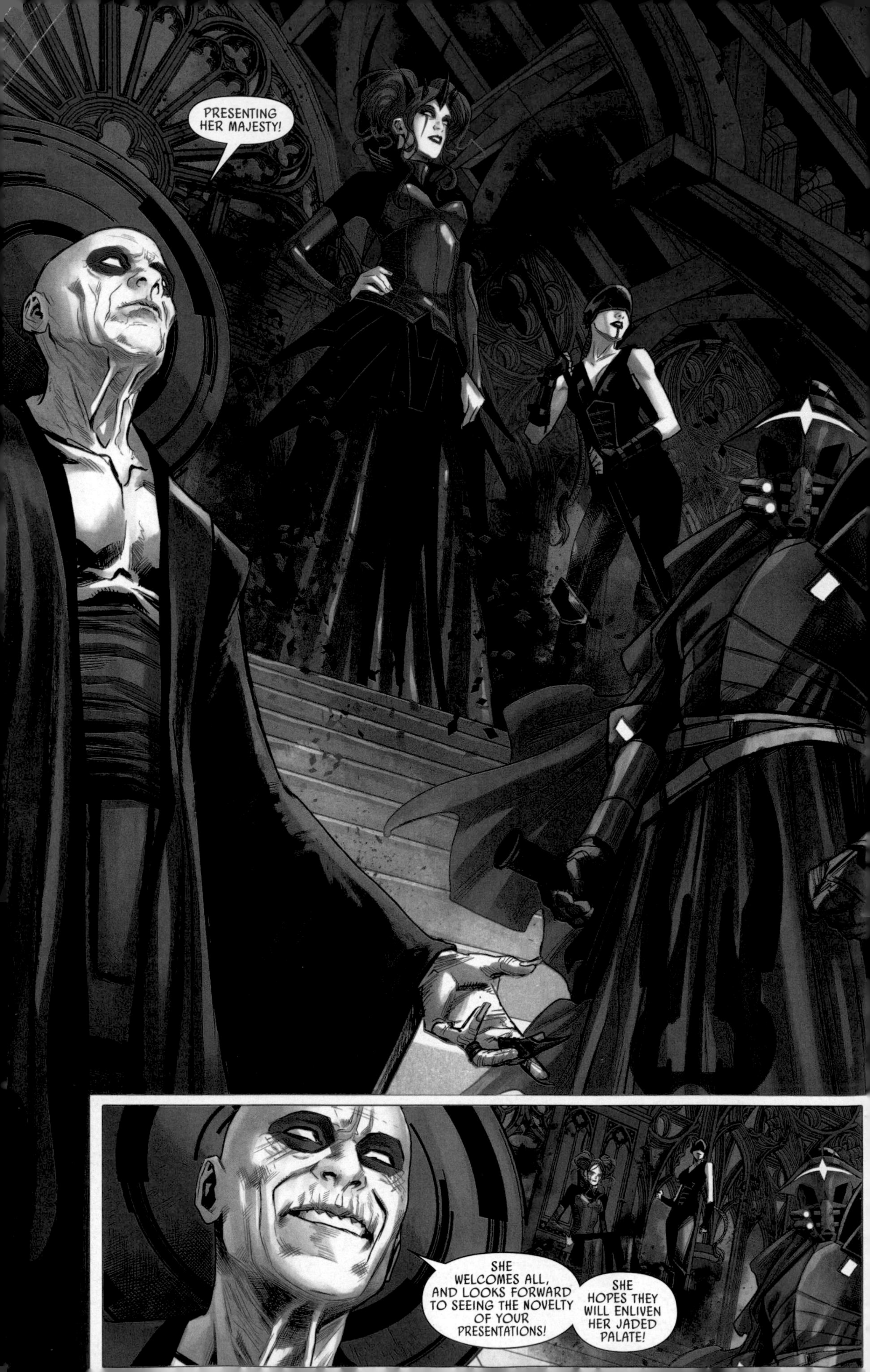
PRESENTING HER MAJESTY!
SHE WELCOMES ALL, AND LOOKS FORWARD TO SEEING THE NOVELTY OF YOUR PRESENTATIONS!
SHE HOPES THEY WILL ENLIVEN HER JADED PALATE!

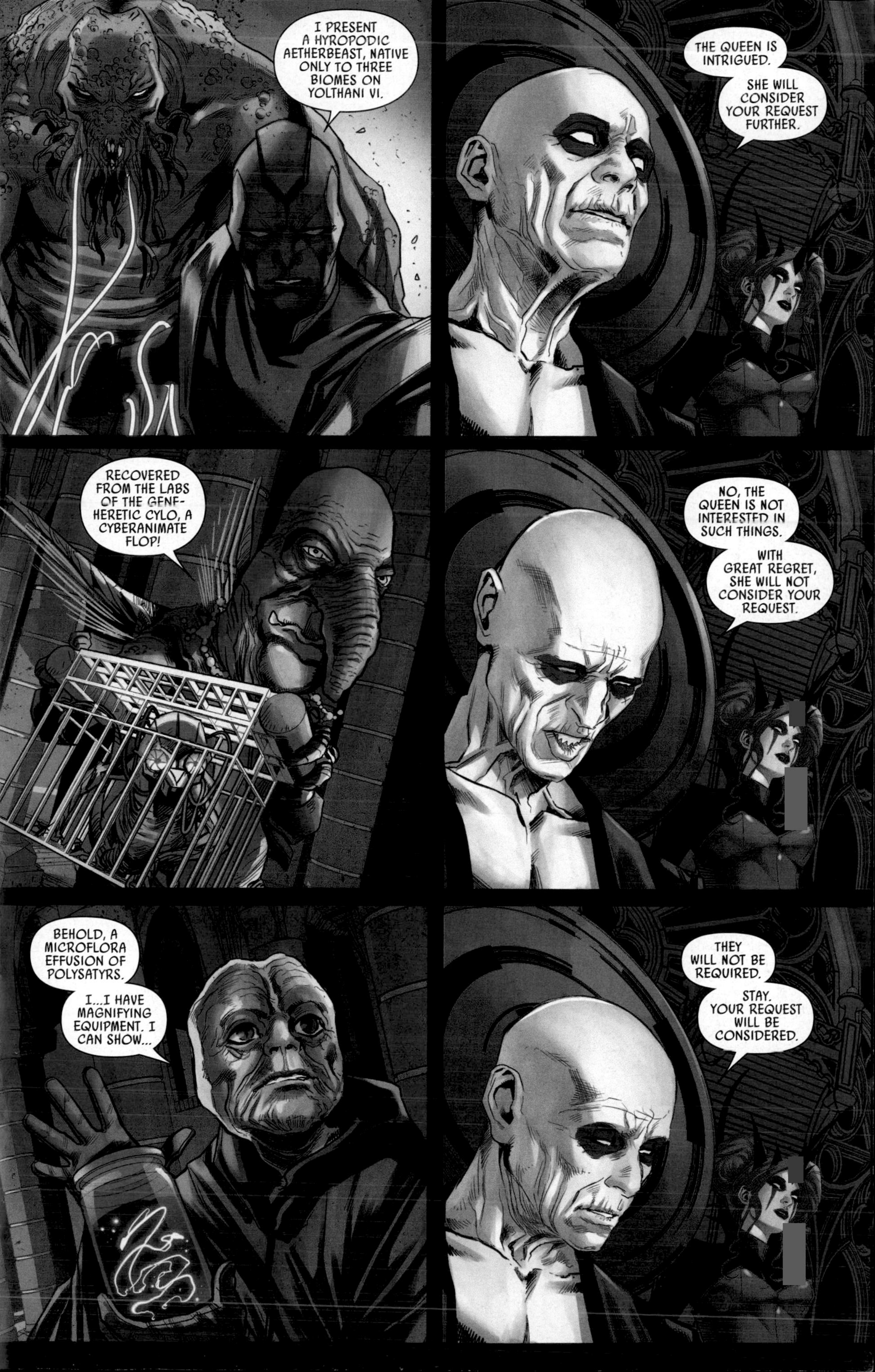
I PRESENT A HYROPODIC AETHERBEAST, NATIVE ONLY TO THREE BIOMES ON YOLTHANI VI.
THE QUEEN IS INTRIGUED.
SHE WILL CONSIDER YOUR REQUEST FURTHER.
RECOVERED FROM THE LABS OF THE GENE-HERETIC CYLO, A CYBERANIMATE FLOP!
NO, THE QUEEN IS NOT INTERESTED IN SUCH THINGS.
WITH GREAT REGRET, SHE WILL NOT CONSIDER YOUR REQUEST.
BEHOLD, A MICROFLORA EFFUSION OF POLYSATYRS.
I...I HAVE MAGNIFYING EQUIPMENT. I CAN SHOW...
THEY WILL NOT BE REQUIRED.
STAY. YOUR REQUEST WILL BE CONSIDERED.

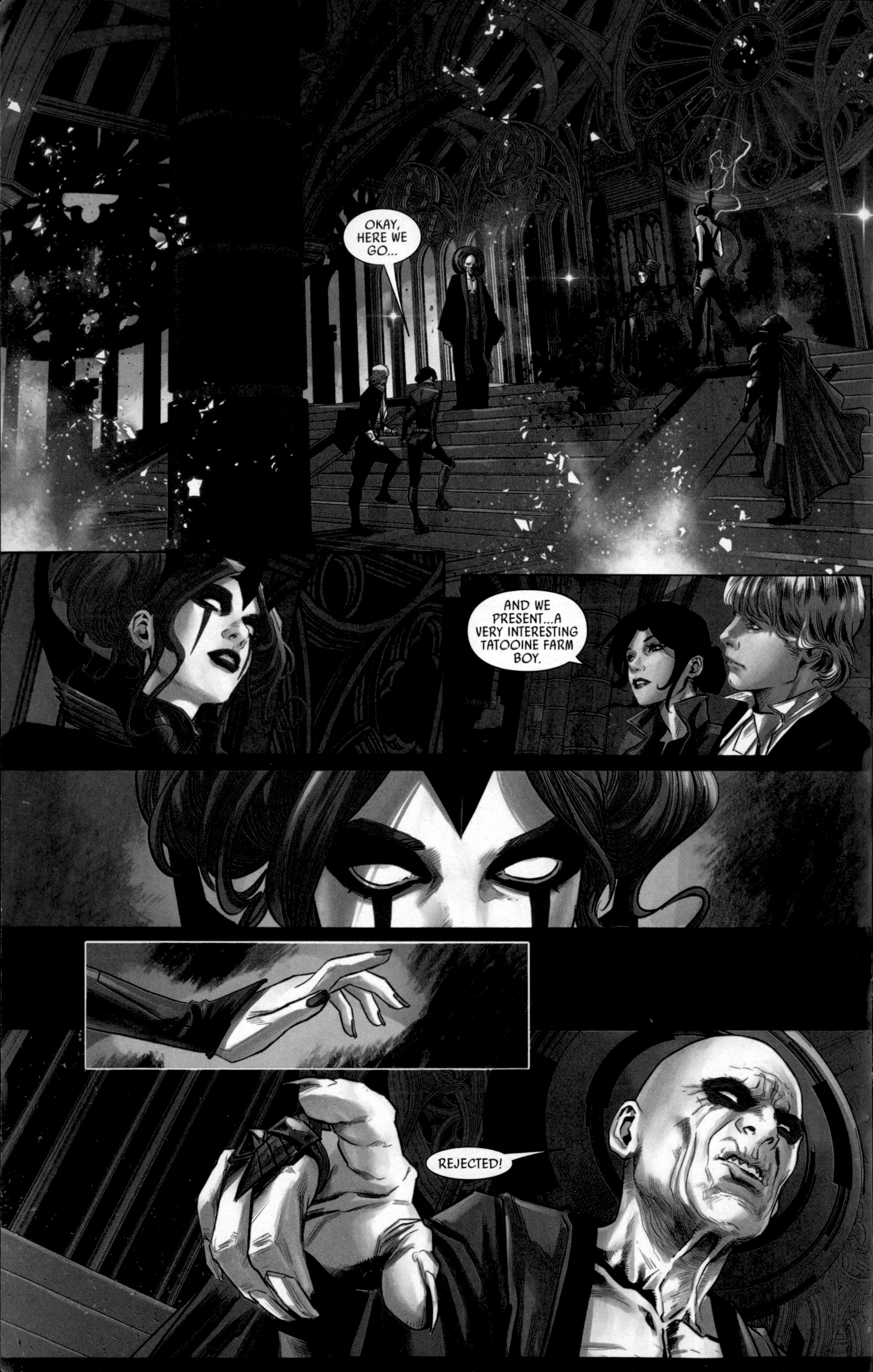
OKAY, HERE WE GO...
AND WE PRESENT...A VERY INTERESTING TATOOINE FARM BOY.
REJECTED!

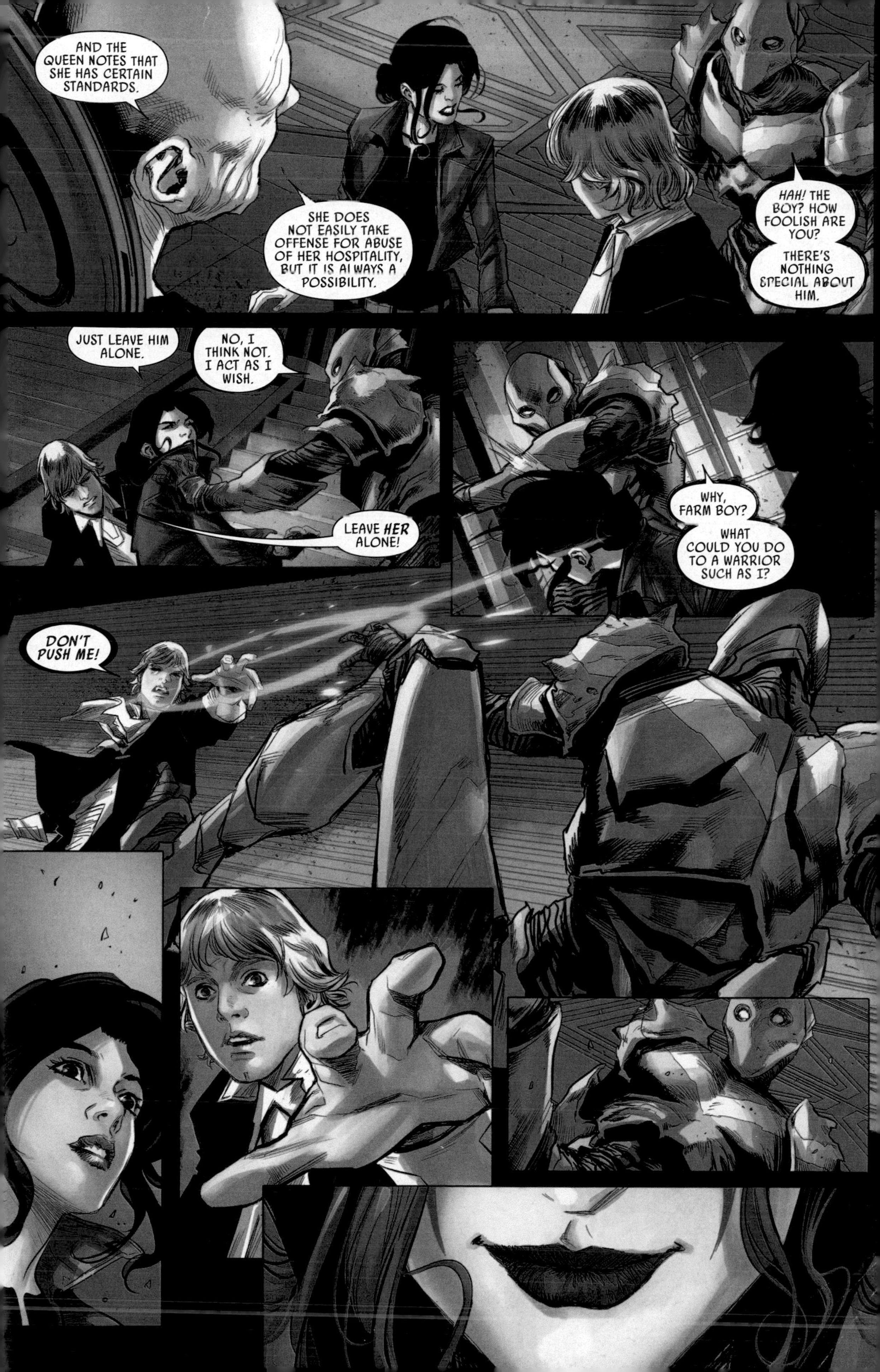
AND THE QUEEN NOTES THAT SHE HAS CERTAIN STANDARDS.
SHE DOES NOT EASILY TAKE OFFENSE FOR ABUSE OF HER HOSPITALITY, BUT IT IS ALWAYS A POSSIBILITY.
HAH! THE BOY? HOW FOOLISH ARE YOU?
THERE'S NOTHING SPECIAL ABOUT HIM.
JUST LEAVE HIM ALONE.
NO, I THINK NOT. I ACT AS I WISH.
LEAVE HER ALONE!
WHY, FARM BOY?
WHAT COULD YOU DO TO A WARRIOR SUCH AS I?
DON'T PUSH ME!

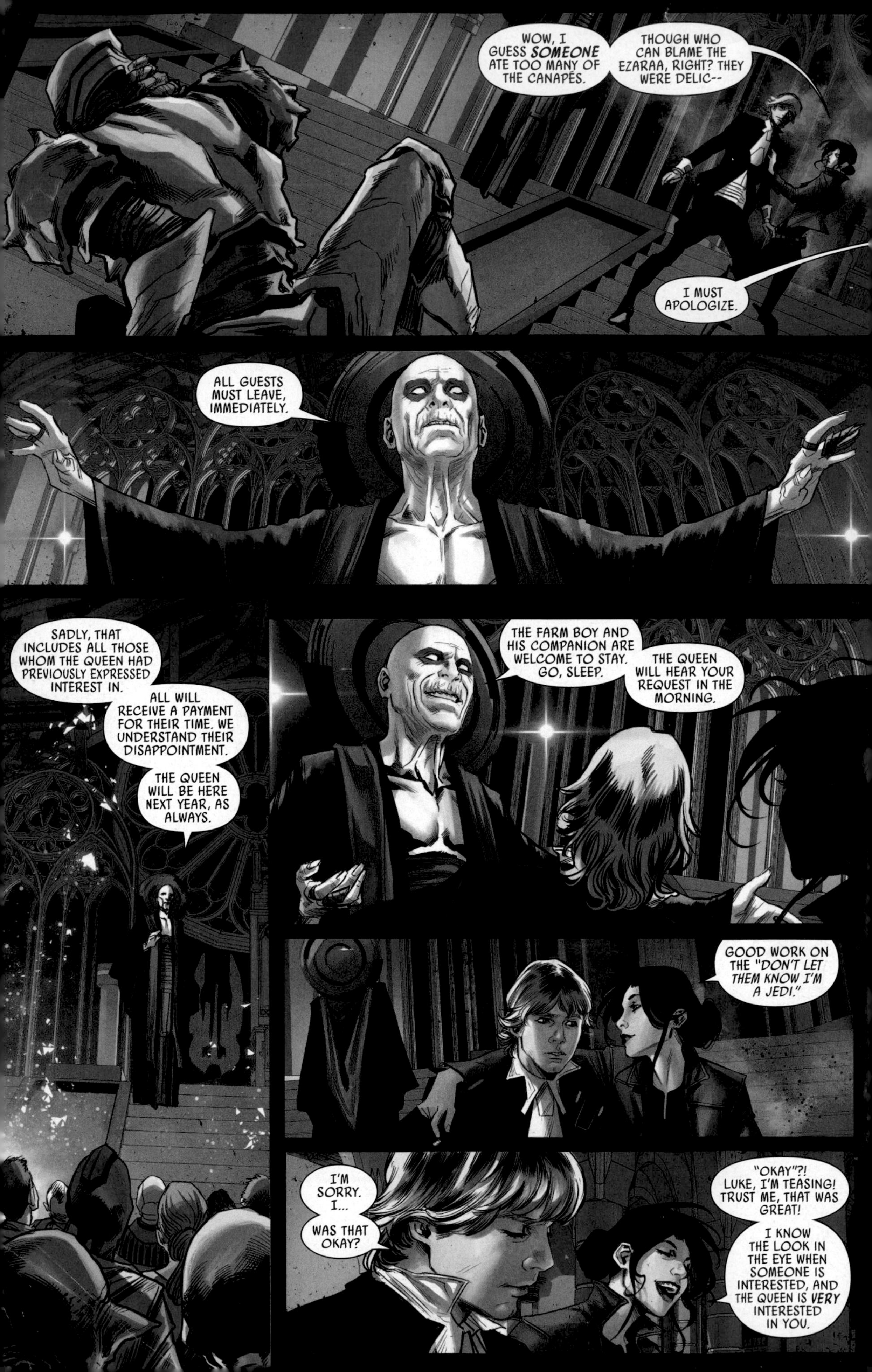
WOW, I GUESS *SOMEONE* ATE TOO MANY OF THE CANAPÉS.
THOUGH WHO CAN BLAME THE EZARAA, RIGHT? THEY WERE DELIC--
I MUST APOLOGIZE.
ALL GUESTS MUST LEAVE, IMMEDIATELY.
SADLY, THAT INCLUDES ALL THOSE WHOM THE QUEEN HAD PREVIOUSLY EXPRESSED INTEREST IN.
ALL WILL RECEIVE A PAYMENT FOR THEIR TIME. WE UNDERSTAND THEIR DISAPPOINTMENT.
THE QUEEN WILL BE HERE NEXT YEAR, AS ALWAYS.
THE FARM BOY AND HIS COMPANION ARE WELCOME TO STAY. GO, SLEEP.
THE QUEEN WILL HEAR YOUR REQUEST IN THE MORNING.
GOOD WORK ON THE *"DON'T LET THEM KNOW I'M A JEDI."*
I'M SORRY. I...
WAS THAT OKAY?
"OKAY"?! LUKE, I'M TEASING! TRUST ME, THAT WAS GREAT!
I KNOW THE LOOK IN THE EYE WHEN SOMEONE IS INTERESTED, AND THE QUEEN IS *VERY* INTERESTED IN YOU.

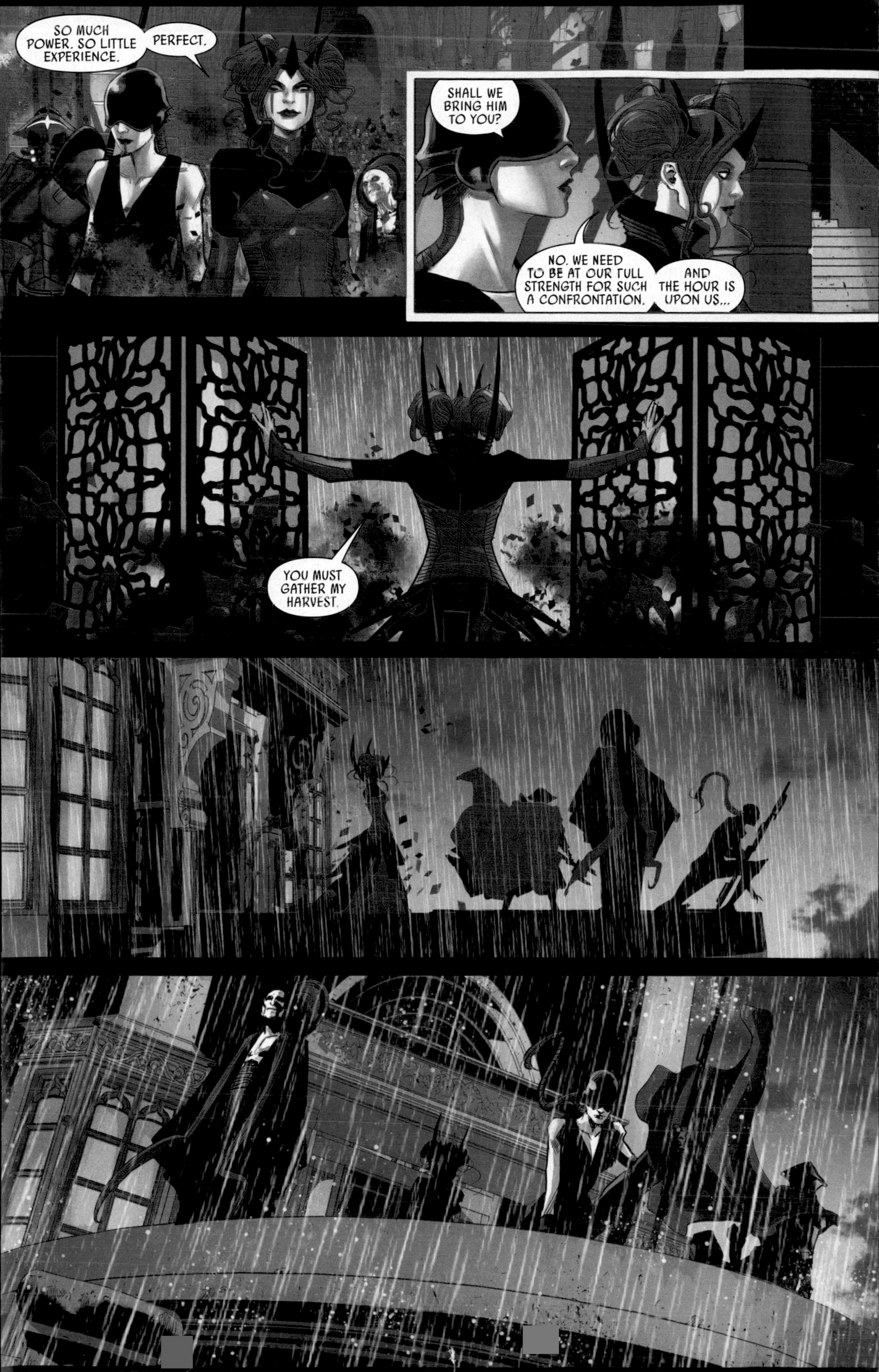
SO MUCH POWER. SO LITTLE EXPERIENCE.
PERFECT.
SHALL WE BRING HIM TO YOU?
NO. WE NEED TO BE AT OUR FULL STRENGTH FOR SUCH A CONFRONTATION.
AND THE HOUR IS UPON US...
YOU MUST GATHER MY HARVEST.

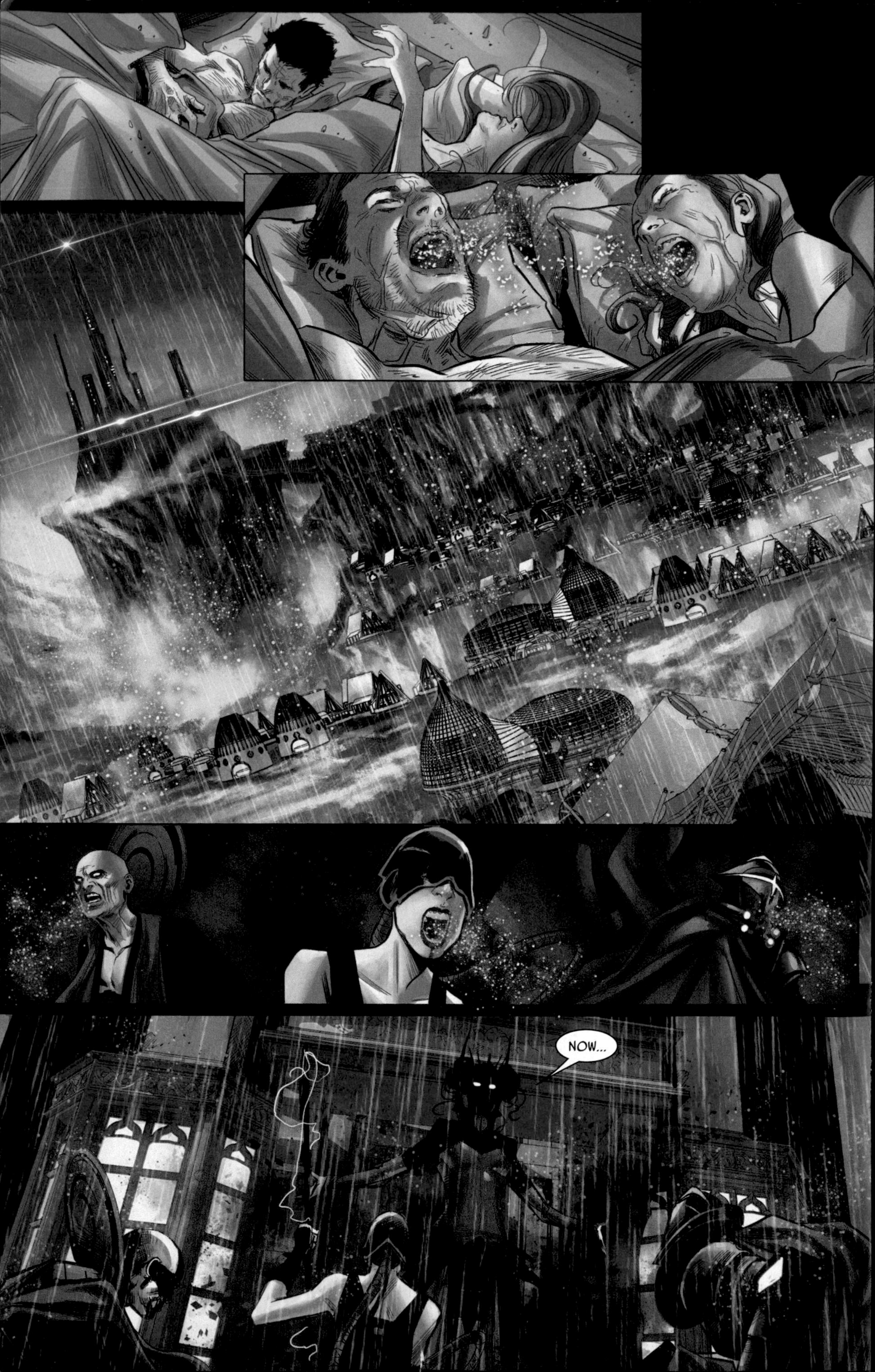
NOW...

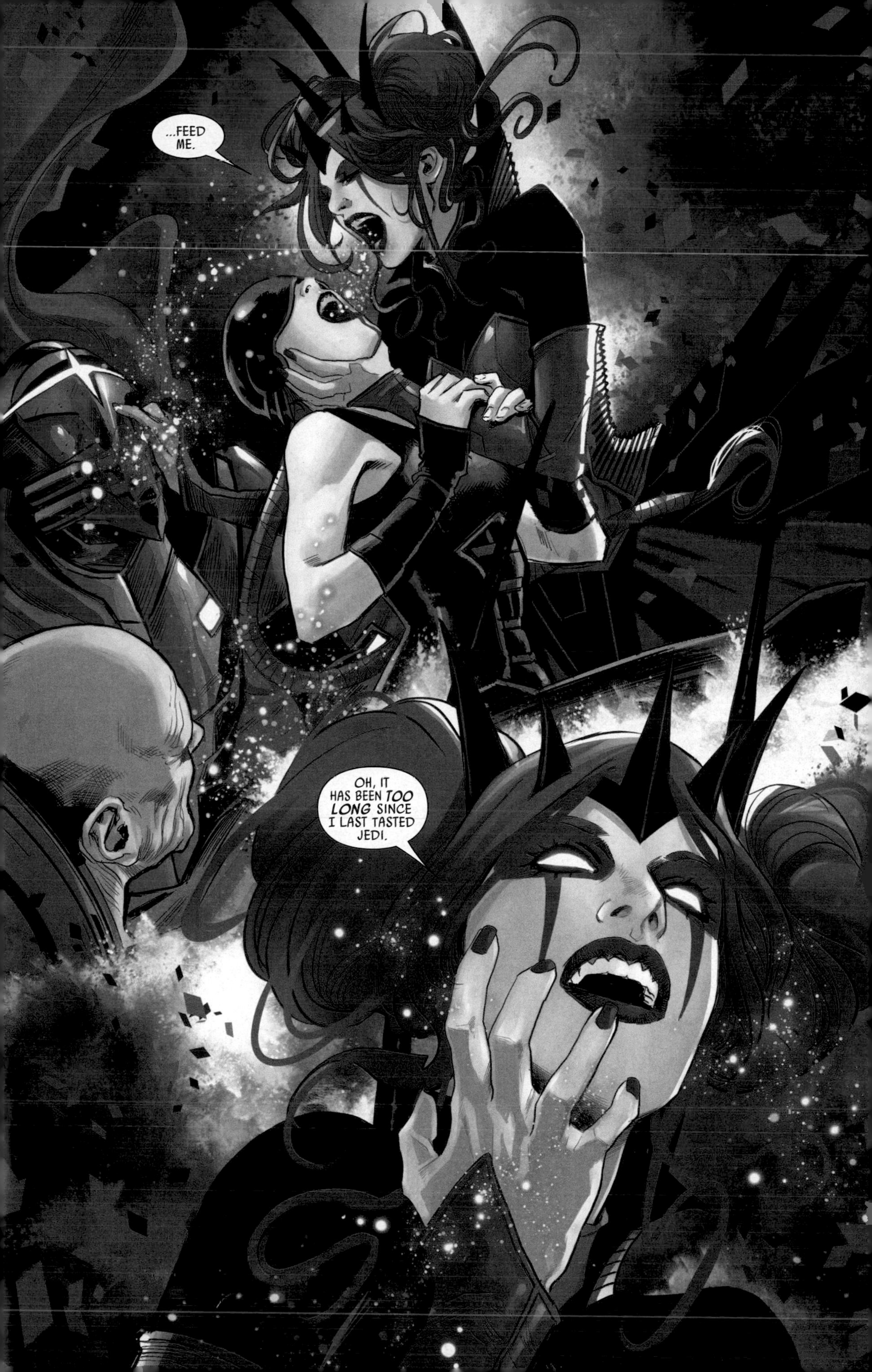
...FEED ME.
OH, IT HAS BEEN TOO LONG SINCE I LAST TASTED JEDI.

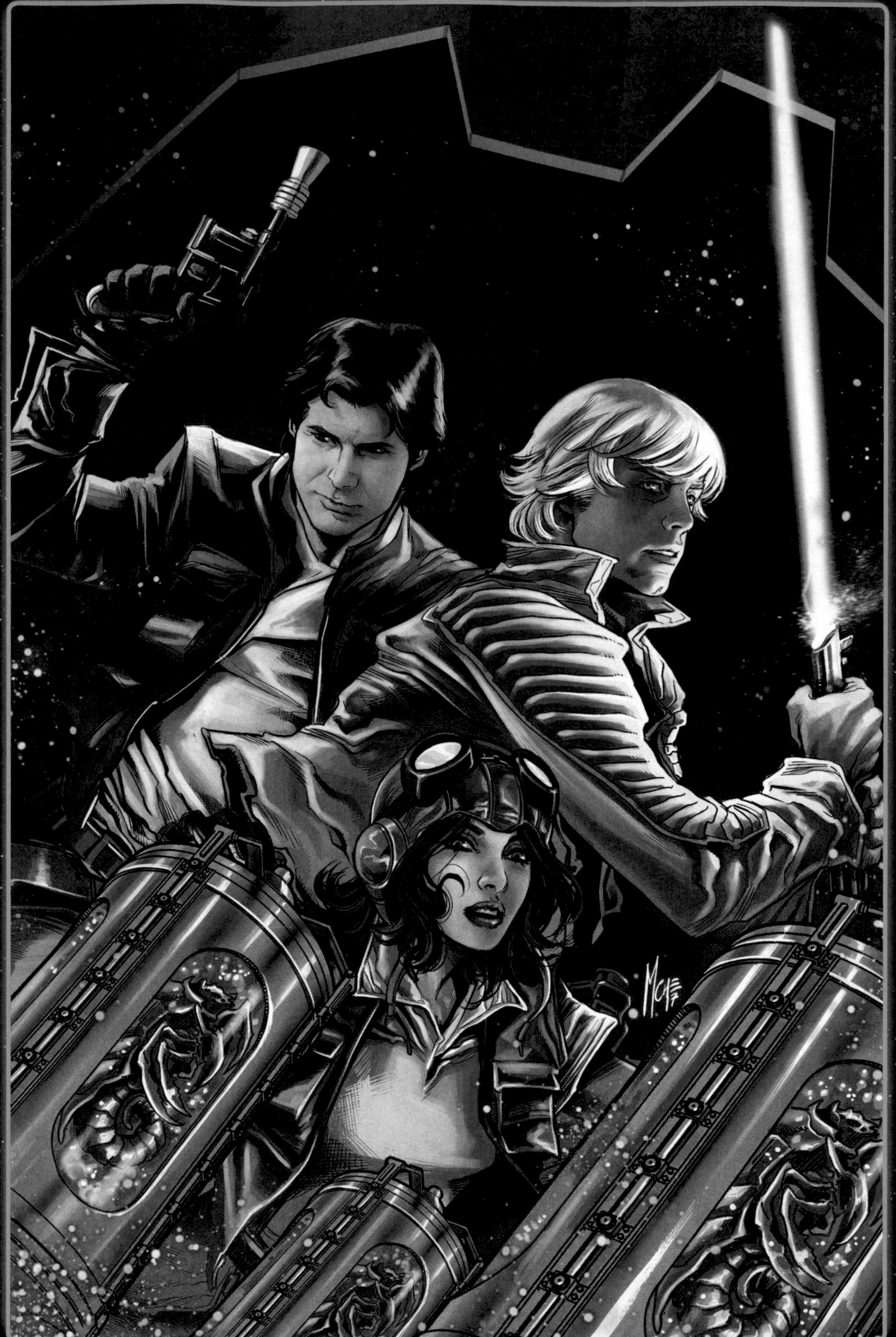

STAR WARS 31

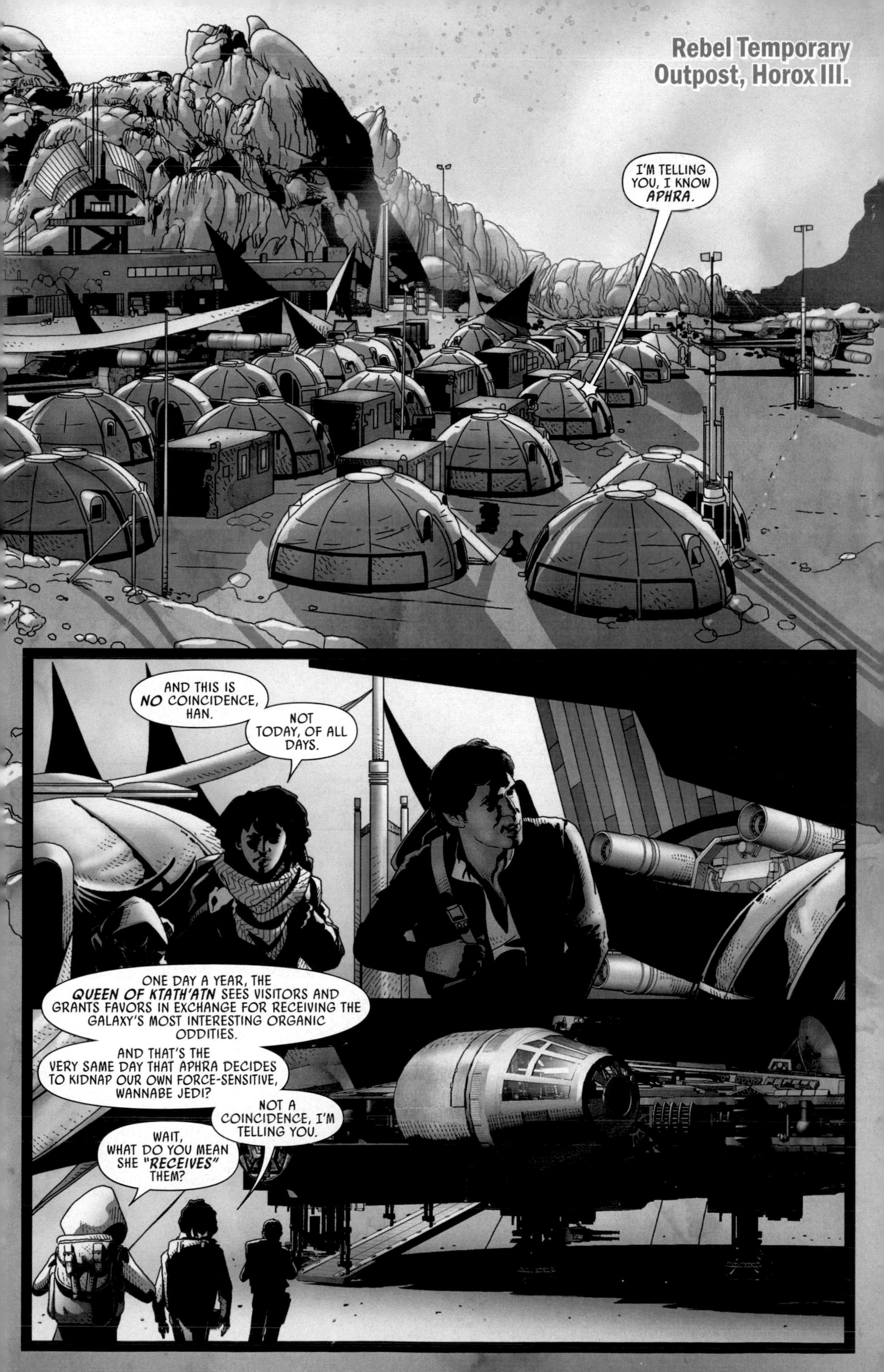
Rebel Temporary Outpost, Horox III.
I'M TELLING YOU, I KNOW APHRA.
AND THIS IS NO COINCIDENCE, HAN.
NOT TODAY, OF ALL DAYS.
ONE DAY A YEAR, THE QUEEN OF KTATH'ATN SEES VISITORS AND GRANTS FAVORS IN EXCHANGE FOR RECEIVING THE GALAXY'S MOST INTERESTING ORGANIC ODDITIES.
AND THAT'S THE VERY SAME DAY THAT APHRA DECIDES TO KIDNAP OUR OWN FORCE-SENSITIVE, WANNABE JEDI?
NOT A COINCIDENCE, I'M TELLING YOU.
WAIT, WHAT DO YOU MEAN SHE "RECEIVES" THEM?

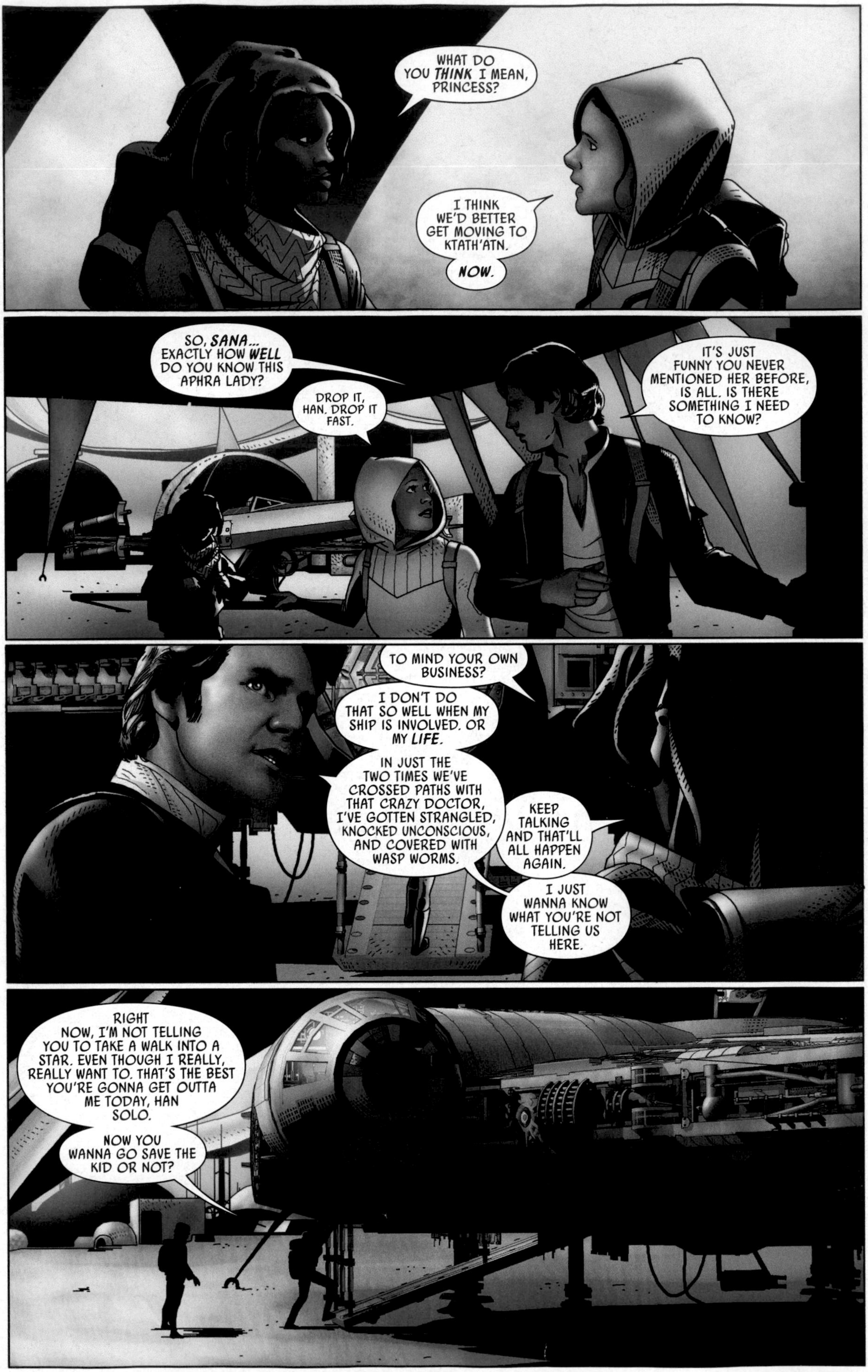
WHAT DO YOU THINK I MEAN, PRINCESS?
I THINK WE'D BETTER GET MOVING TO KTATH'ATN.
NOW.
SO, SANA... EXACTLY HOW WELL DO YOU KNOW THIS APHRA LADY?
DROP IT, HAN. DROP IT FAST.
IT'S JUST FUNNY YOU NEVER MENTIONED HER BEFORE, IS ALL. IS THERE SOMETHING I NEED TO KNOW?
TO MIND YOUR OWN BUSINESS?
I DON'T DO THAT SO WELL WHEN MY SHIP IS INVOLVED. OR MY LIFE.
IN JUST THE TWO TIMES WE'VE CROSSED PATHS WITH THAT CRAZY DOCTOR, I'VE GOTTEN STRANGLED, KNOCKED UNCONSCIOUS, AND COVERED WITH WASP WORMS.
KEEP TALKING AND THAT'LL ALL HAPPEN AGAIN.
I JUST WANNA KNOW WHAT YOU'RE NOT TELLING US HERE.
RIGHT NOW, I'M NOT TELLING YOU TO TAKE A WALK INTO A STAR. EVEN THOUGH I REALLY, REALLY WANT TO. THAT'S THE BEST YOU'RE GONNA GET OUTTA ME TODAY, HAN SOLO.
NOW YOU WANNA GO SAVE THE KID OR NOT?

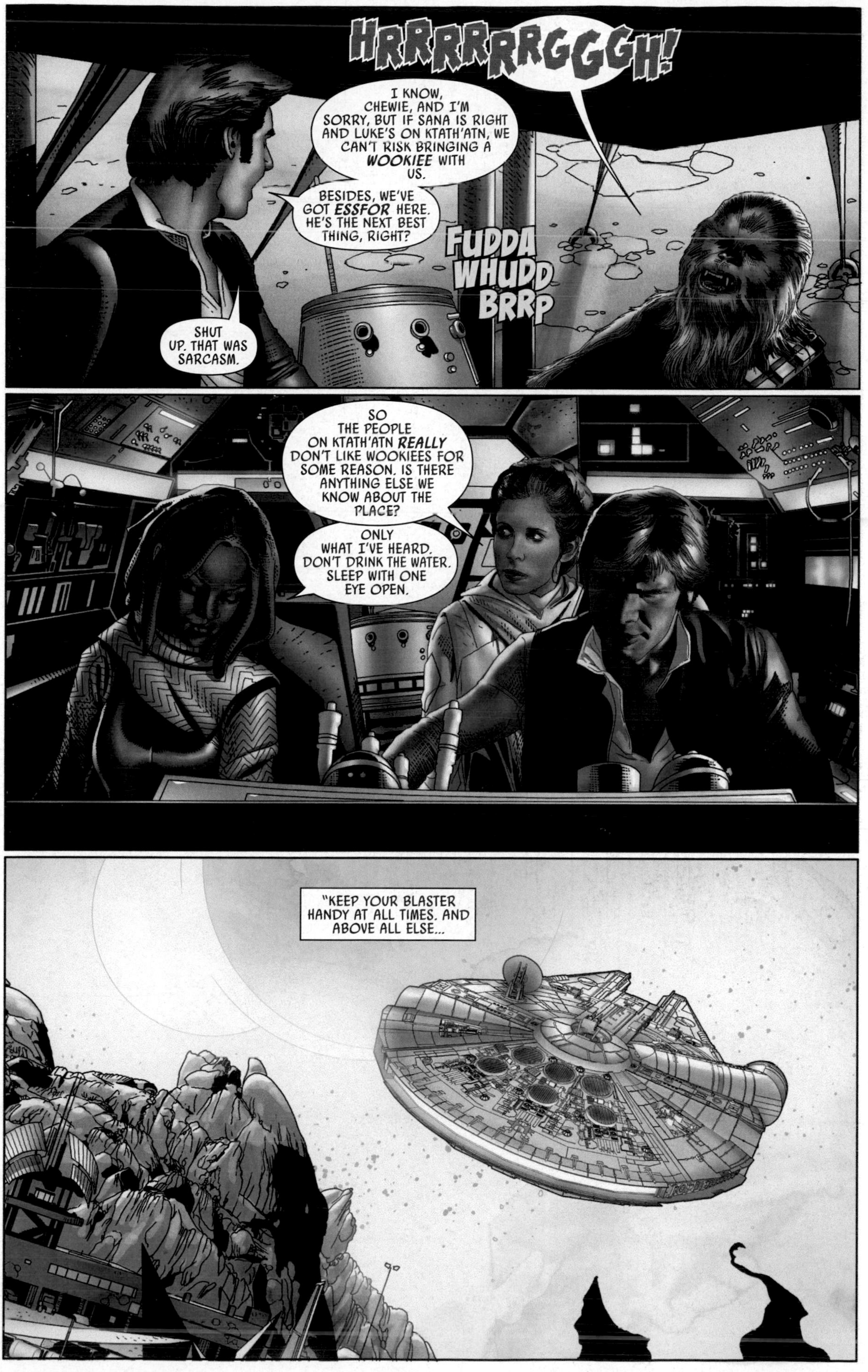
HRRRRRRGGGH!
I KNOW, CHEWIE, AND I'M SORRY, BUT IF SANA IS RIGHT AND LUKE'S ON KTATH'ATN, WE CAN'T RISK BRINGING A WOOKIEE WITH US.
BESIDES, WE'VE GOT ESSFOR HERE. HE'S THE NEXT BEST THING, RIGHT?
FUDDA WHUDD BRRP
SHUT UP. THAT WAS SARCASM.
SO THE PEOPLE ON KTATH'ATN REALLY DON'T LIKE WOOKIEES FOR SOME REASON. IS THERE ANYTHING ELSE WE KNOW ABOUT THE PLACE?
ONLY WHAT I'VE HEARD. DON'T DRINK THE WATER. SLEEP WITH ONE EYE OPEN.
"KEEP YOUR BLASTER HANDY AT ALL TIMES. AND ABOVE ALL ELSE...

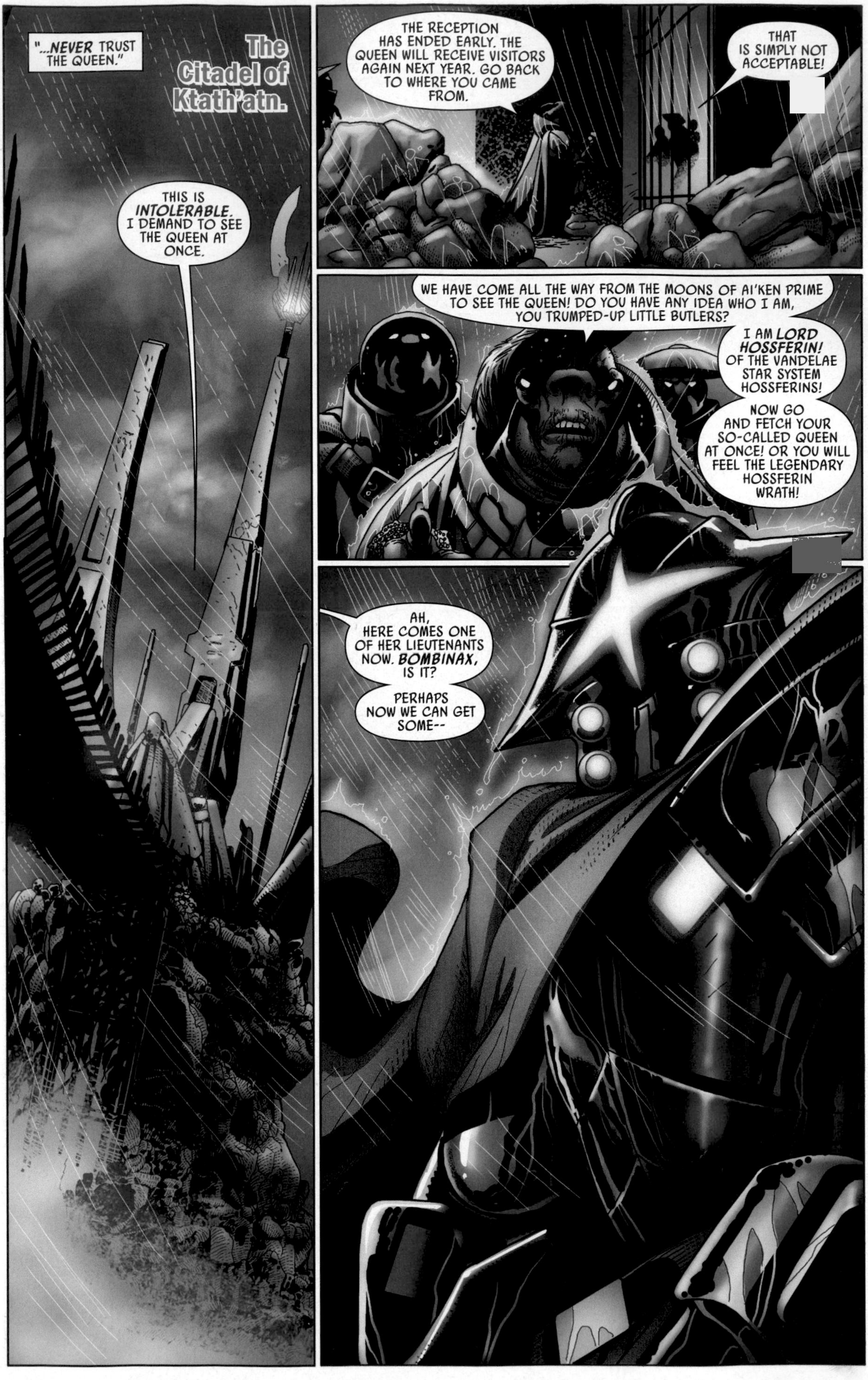
"...NEVER TRUST THE QUEEN."
The Citadel of Ktath'atn.
THIS IS INTOLERABLE. I DEMAND TO SEE THE QUEEN AT ONCE.
THE RECEPTION HAS ENDED EARLY. THE QUEEN WILL RECEIVE VISITORS AGAIN NEXT YEAR. GO BACK TO WHERE YOU CAME FROM.
THAT IS SIMPLY NOT ACCEPTABLE!
WE HAVE COME ALL THE WAY FROM THE MOONS OF AI'KEN PRIME TO SEE THE QUEEN! DO YOU HAVE ANY IDEA WHO I AM, YOU TRUMPED-UP LITTLE BUTLERS?
I AM LORD HOSSFERIN! OF THE VANDELAE STAR SYSTEM HOSSFERINS!
NOW GO AND FETCH YOUR SO-CALLED QUEEN AT ONCE! OR YOU WILL FEEL THE LEGENDARY HOSSFERIN WRATH!
AH, HERE COMES ONE OF HER LIEUTENANTS NOW. BOMBINAX, IS IT?
PERHAPS NOW WE CAN GET SOME--

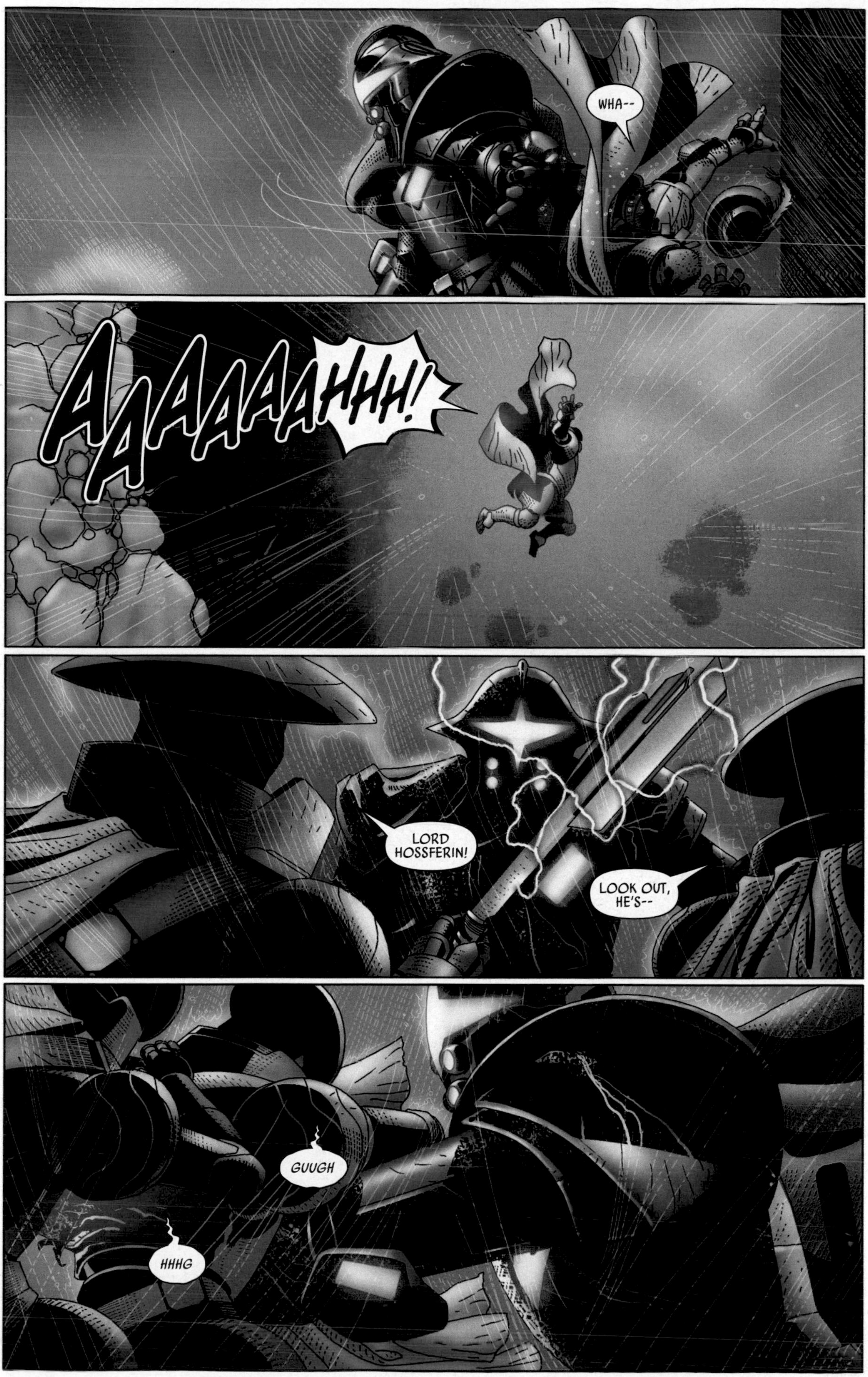
WHA--
AAAAAAAHHH!
LORD HOSSFERIN!
LOOK OUT, HE'S--
GUUGH
HHHG

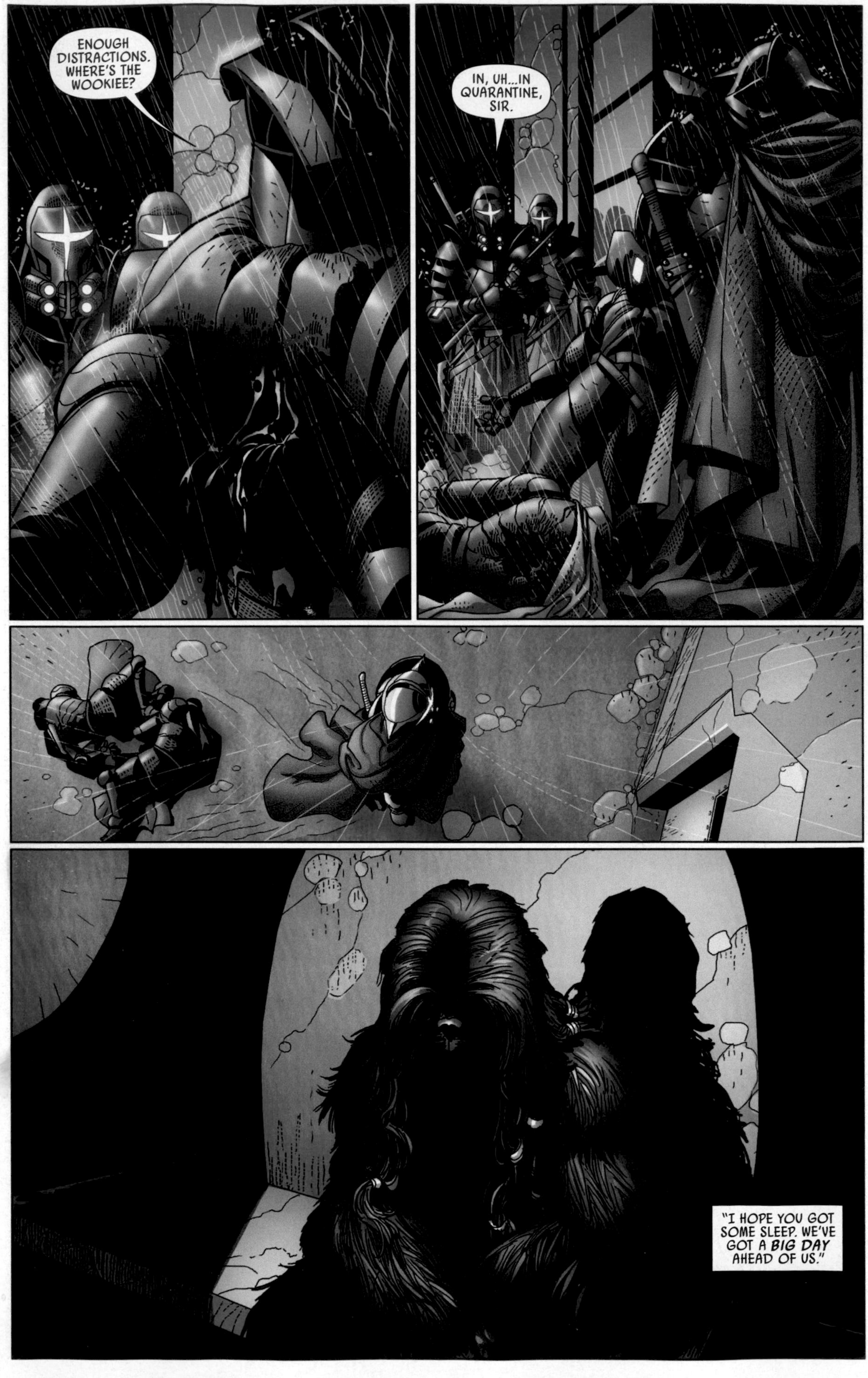
ENOUGH DISTRACTIONS. WHERE'S THE WOOKIEE?
IN, UH...IN QUARANTINE, SIR.
"I HOPE YOU GOT SOME SLEEP. WE'VE GOT A *BIG DAY* AHEAD OF US."

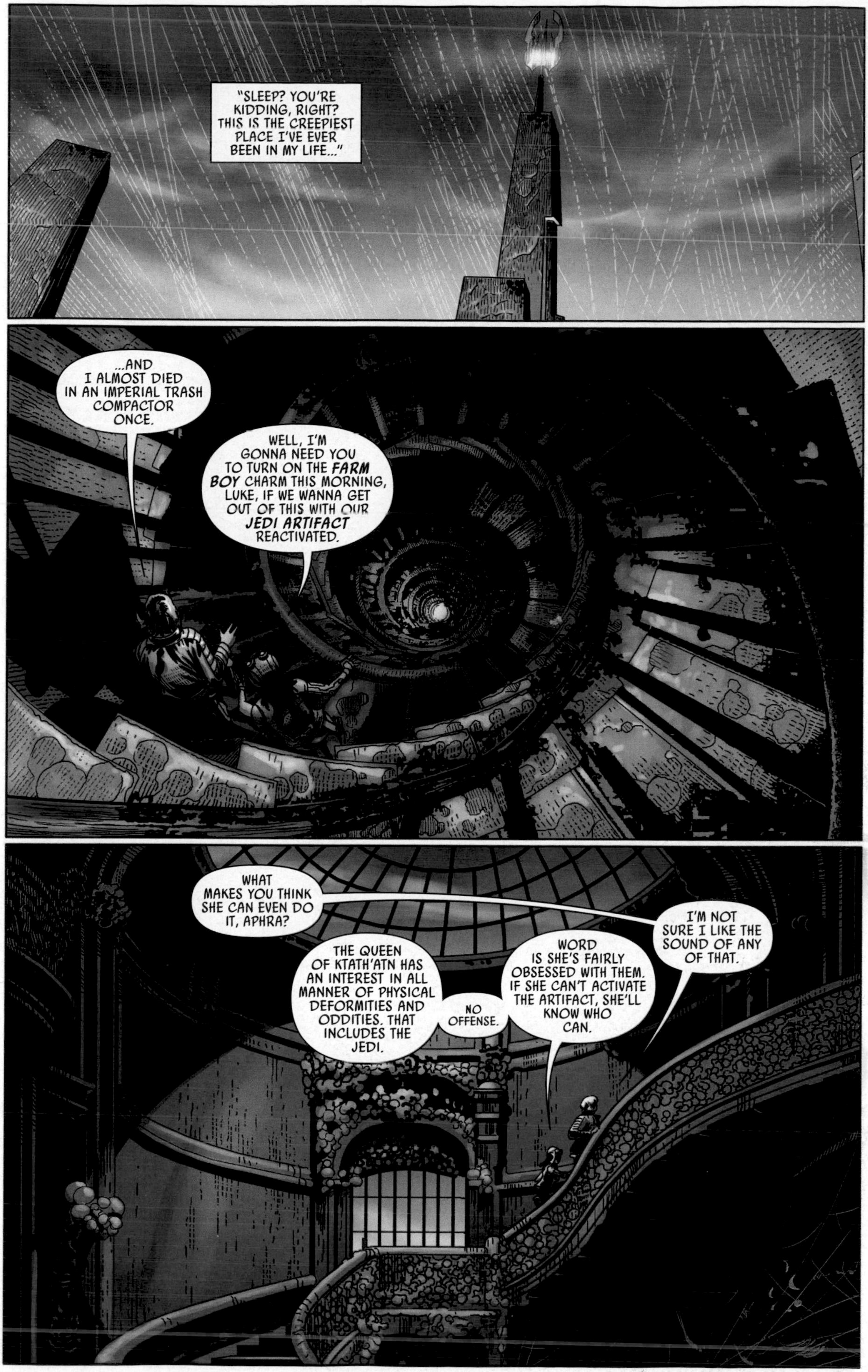
"SLEEP? YOU'RE KIDDING, RIGHT? THIS IS THE CREEPIEST PLACE I'VE EVER BEEN IN MY LIFE..."
...AND I ALMOST DIED IN AN IMPERIAL TRASH COMPACTOR ONCE.
WELL, I'M GONNA NEED YOU TO TURN ON THE FARM BOY CHARM THIS MORNING, LUKE, IF WE WANNA GET OUT OF THIS WITH OUR JEDI ARTIFACT REACTIVATED.
WHAT MAKES YOU THINK SHE CAN EVEN DO IT, APHRA?
THE QUEEN OF KTATH'ATN HAS AN INTEREST IN ALL MANNER OF PHYSICAL DEFORMITIES AND ODDITIES. THAT INCLUDES THE JEDI.
NO OFFENSE.
WORD IS SHE'S FAIRLY OBSESSED WITH THEM. IF SHE CAN'T ACTIVATE THE ARTIFACT, SHE'LL KNOW WHO CAN.
I'M NOT SURE I LIKE THE SOUND OF ANY OF THAT.

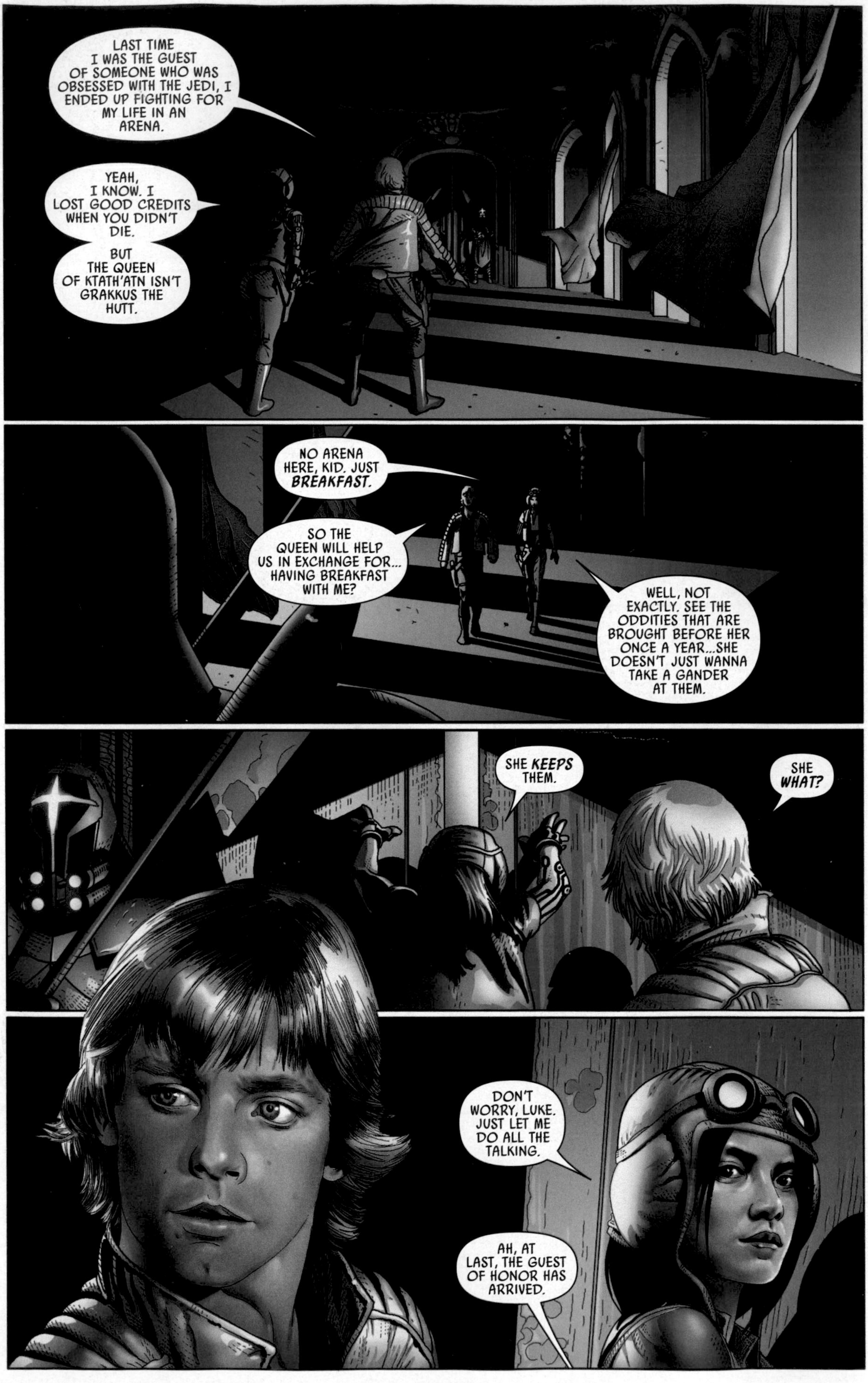
LAST TIME I WAS THE GUEST OF SOMEONE WHO WAS OBSESSED WITH THE JEDI, I ENDED UP FIGHTING FOR MY LIFE IN AN ARENA.
YEAH, I KNOW. I LOST GOOD CREDITS WHEN YOU DIDN'T DIE.
BUT THE QUEEN OF KTATH'ATN ISN'T GRAKKUS THE HUTT.
NO ARENA HERE, KID. JUST *BREAKFAST.*
SO THE QUEEN WILL HELP US IN EXCHANGE FOR... HAVING BREAKFAST WITH ME?
WELL, NOT EXACTLY. SEE THE ODDITIES THAT ARE BROUGHT BEFORE HER ONCE A YEAR...SHE DOESN'T JUST WANNA TAKE A GANDER AT THEM.
SHE *KEEPS* THEM.
SHE *WHAT?*
DON'T WORRY, LUKE. JUST LET ME DO ALL THE TALKING.
AH, AT LAST, THE GUEST OF HONOR HAS ARRIVED.

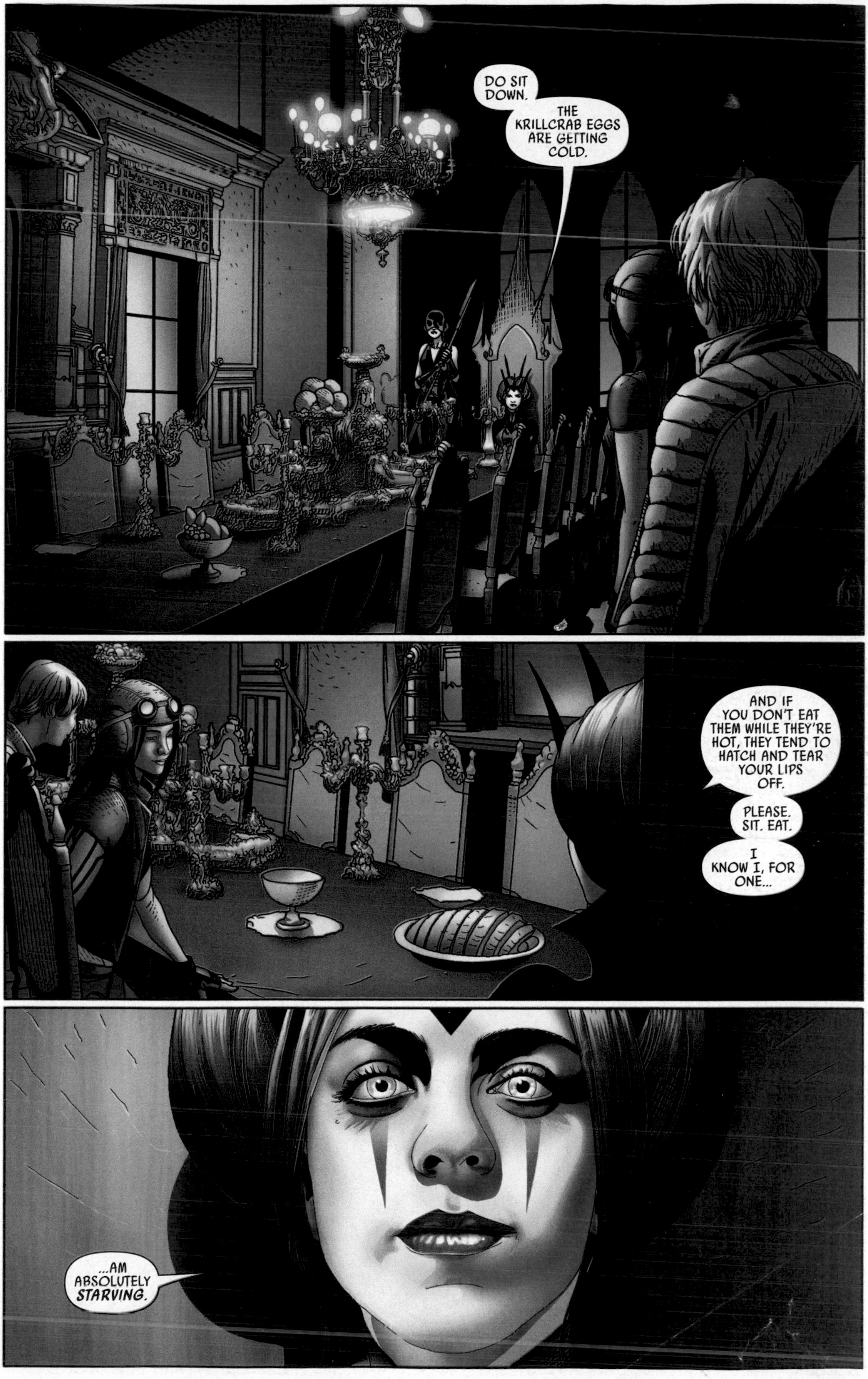
DO SIT DOWN.
THE KRILLCRAB EGGS ARE GETTING COLD.
AND IF YOU DON'T EAT THEM WHILE THEY'RE HOT, THEY TEND TO HATCH AND TEAR YOUR LIPS OFF.
PLEASE. SIT. EAT.
I KNOW I, FOR ONE...
...AM ABSOLUTELY *STARVING.*

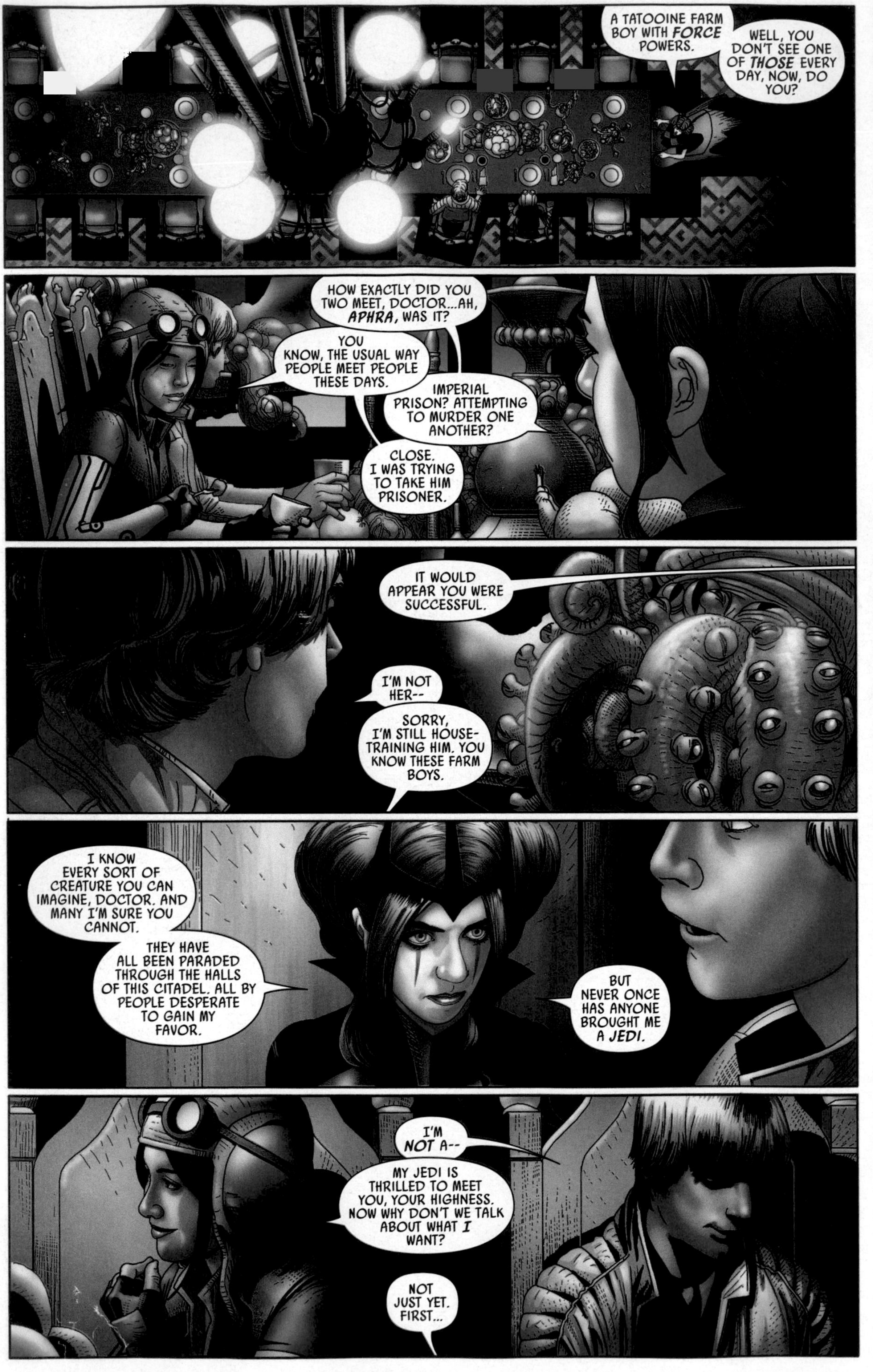
A TATOOINE FARM BOY WITH FORCE POWERS.
WELL, YOU DON'T SEE ONE OF THOSE EVERY DAY, NOW, DO YOU?
HOW EXACTLY DID YOU TWO MEET, DOCTOR...AH, APHRA, WAS IT?
YOU KNOW, THE USUAL WAY PEOPLE MEET PEOPLE THESE DAYS.
IMPERIAL PRISON? ATTEMPTING TO MURDER ONE ANOTHER?
CLOSE. I WAS TRYING TO TAKE HIM PRISONER.
IT WOULD APPEAR YOU WERE SUCCESSFUL.
I'M NOT HER--
SORRY, I'M STILL HOUSE-TRAINING HIM. YOU KNOW THESE FARM BOYS.
I KNOW EVERY SORT OF CREATURE YOU CAN IMAGINE, DOCTOR. AND MANY I'M SURE YOU CANNOT.
THEY HAVE ALL BEEN PARADED THROUGH THE HALLS OF THIS CITADEL. ALL BY PEOPLE DESPERATE TO GAIN MY FAVOR.
BUT NEVER ONCE HAS ANYONE BROUGHT ME A JEDI.
I'M NOT A--
MY JEDI IS THRILLED TO MEET YOU, YOUR HIGHNESS. NOW WHY DON'T WE TALK ABOUT WHAT I WANT?
NOT JUST YET. FIRST...

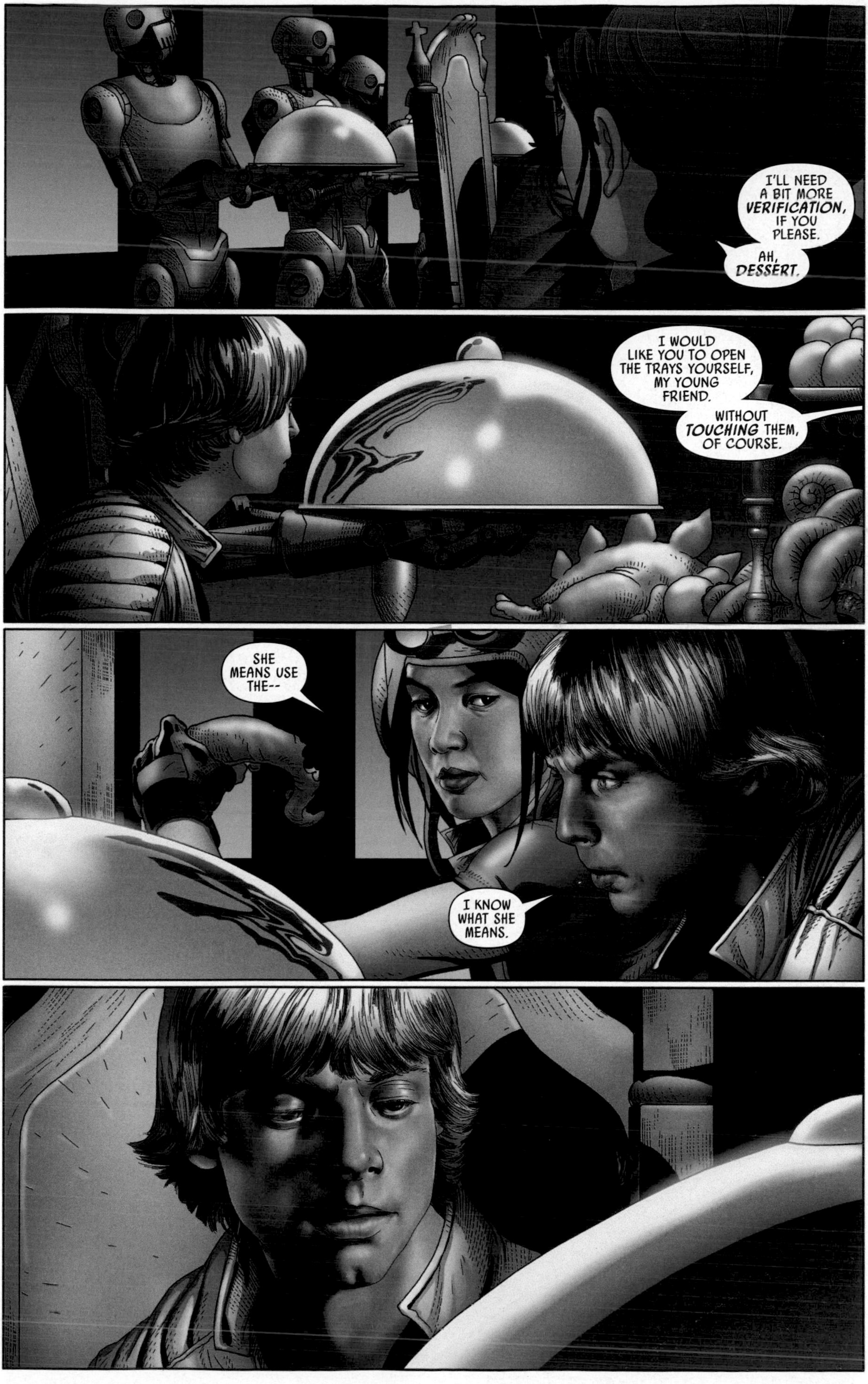
I'LL NEED A BIT MORE VERIFICATION, IF YOU PLEASE.
AH, DESSERT.
I WOULD LIKE YOU TO OPEN THE TRAYS YOURSELF, MY YOUNG FRIEND.
WITHOUT TOUCHING THEM, OF COURSE.
SHE MEANS USE THE--
I KNOW WHAT SHE MEANS.

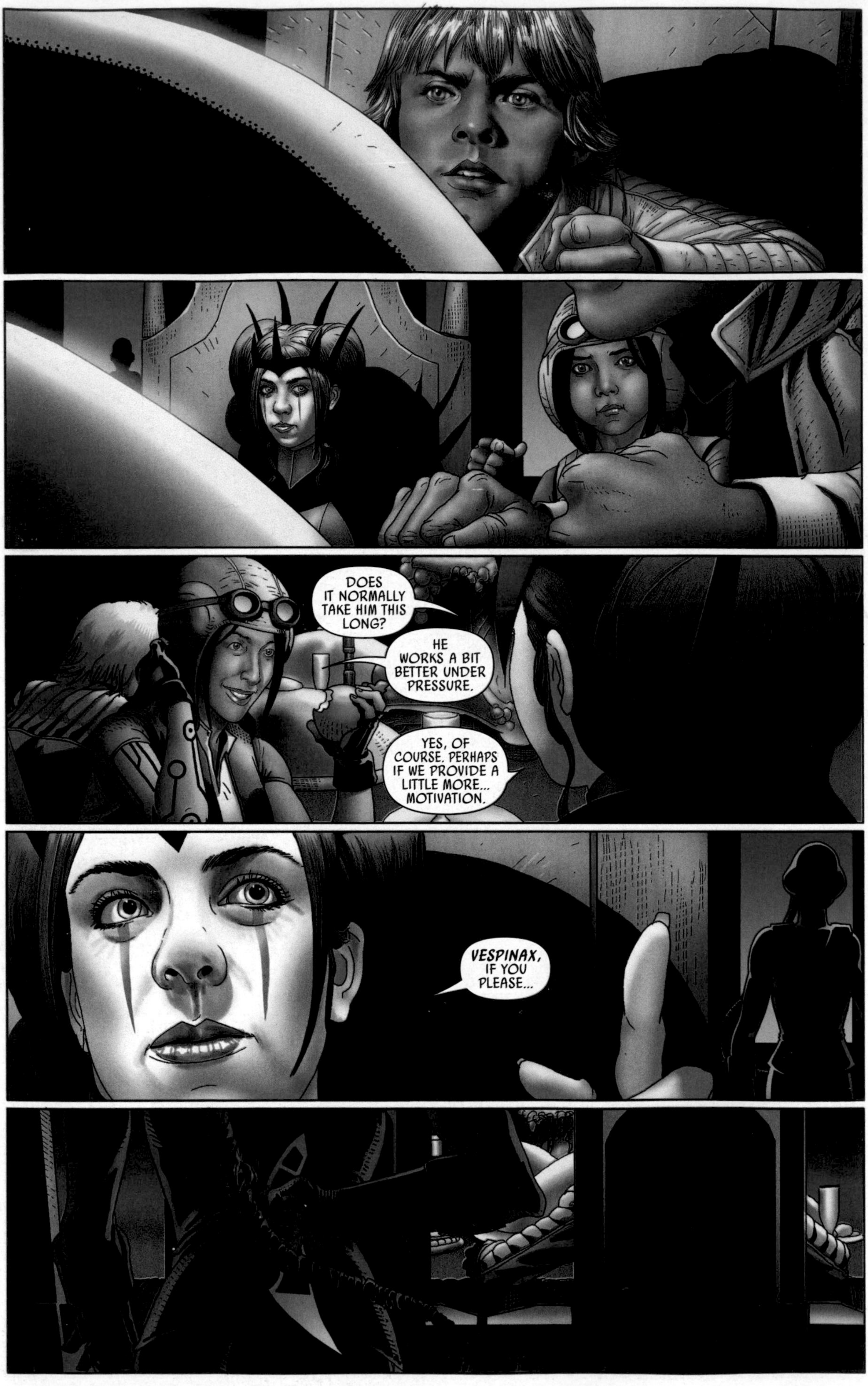
DOES IT NORMALLY TAKE HIM THIS LONG?
HE WORKS A BIT BETTER UNDER PRESSURE.
YES, OF COURSE. PERHAPS IF WE PROVIDE A LITTLE MORE... MOTIVATION.
VESPINAX, IF YOU PLEASE...

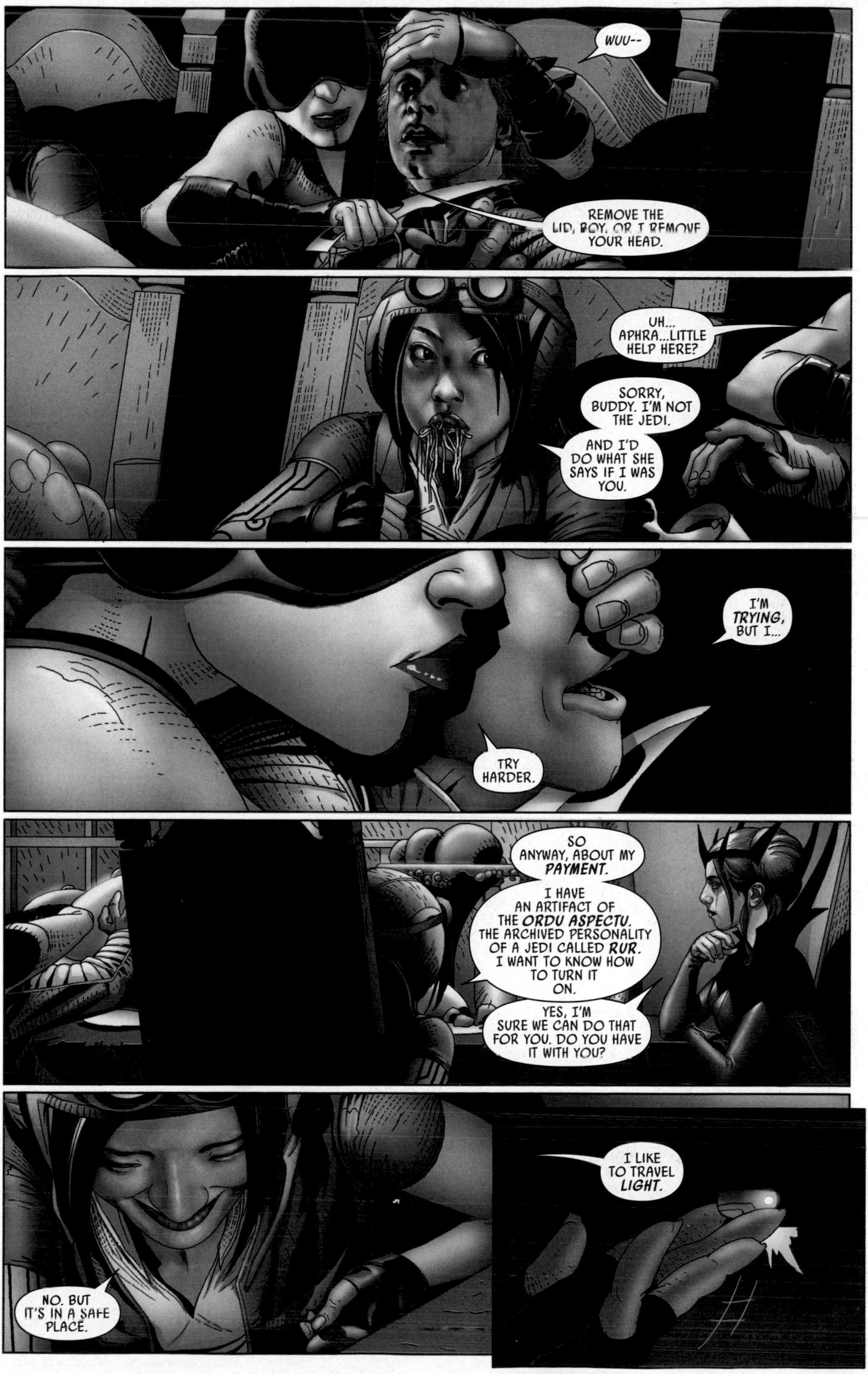
WUU--
REMOVE THE LID, BOY, OR I REMOVE YOUR HEAD.
UH... APHRA...LITTLE HELP HERE?
SORRY, BUDDY. I'M NOT THE JEDI.
AND I'D DO WHAT SHE SAYS IF I WAS YOU.
I'M TRYING, BUT I...
TRY HARDER.
SO ANYWAY, ABOUT MY PAYMENT.
I HAVE AN ARTIFACT OF THE ORDU ASPECTU. THE ARCHIVED PERSONALITY OF A JEDI CALLED RUR. I WANT TO KNOW HOW TO TURN IT ON.
YES, I'M SURE WE CAN DO THAT FOR YOU. DO YOU HAVE IT WITH YOU?
NO. BUT IT'S IN A SAFE PLACE.
I LIKE TO TRAVEL LIGHT.

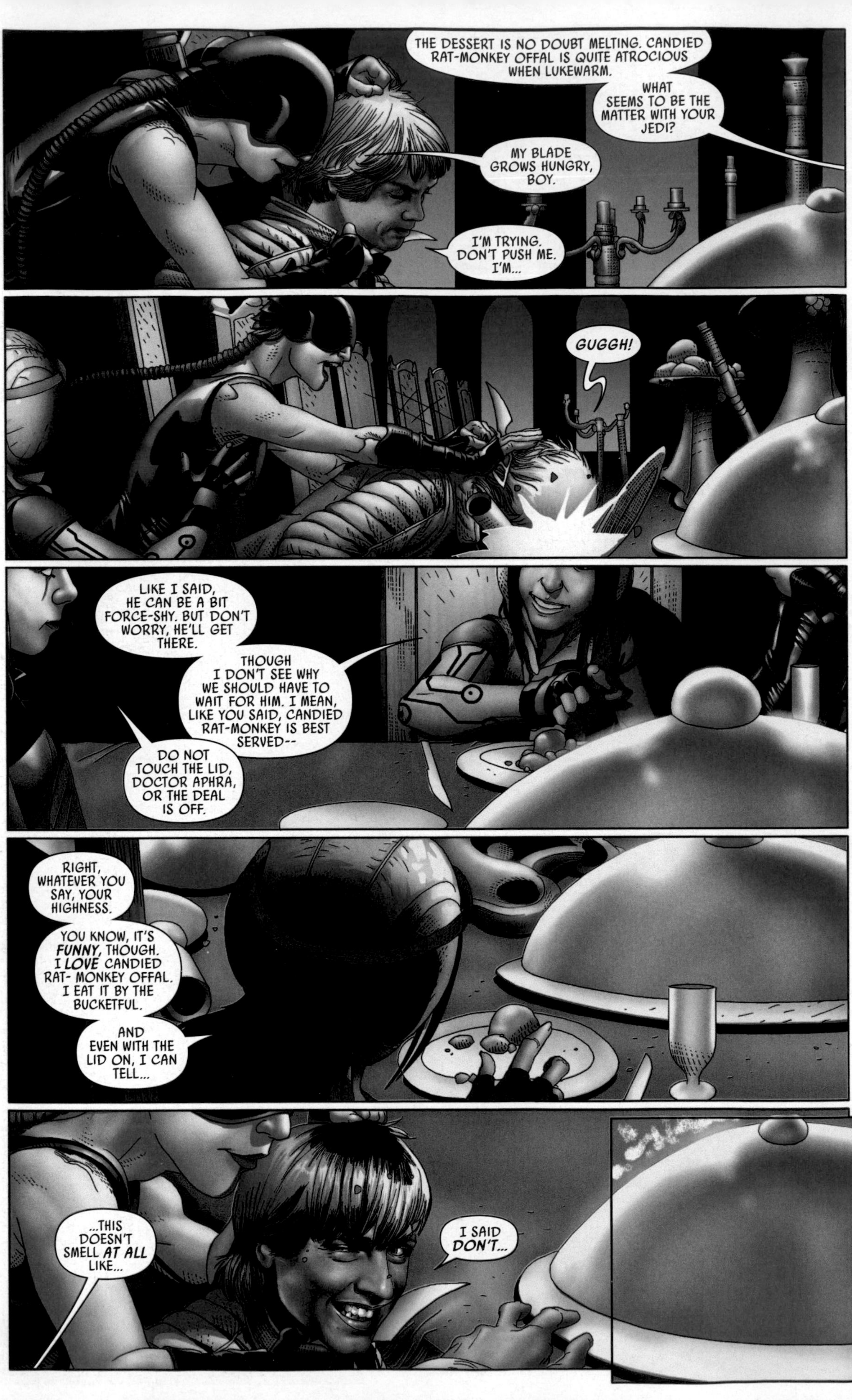

THE DESSERT IS NO DOUBT MELTING. CANDIED RAT-MONKEY OFFAL IS QUITE ATROCIOUS WHEN LUKEWARM.
WHAT SEEMS TO BE THE MATTER WITH YOUR JEDI?
MY BLADE GROWS HUNGRY, BOY.
I'M TRYING. DON'T PUSH ME. I'M...
GUGGH!
LIKE I SAID, HE CAN BE A BIT FORCE-SHY. BUT DON'T WORRY, HE'LL GET THERE.
THOUGH I DON'T SEE WHY WE SHOULD HAVE TO WAIT FOR HIM. I MEAN, LIKE YOU SAID, CANDIED RAT-MONKEY IS BEST SERVED--
DO NOT TOUCH THE LID, DOCTOR APHRA, OR THE DEAL IS OFF.
RIGHT, WHATEVER YOU SAY, YOUR HIGHNESS.
YOU KNOW, IT'S *FUNNY*, THOUGH. I *LOVE* CANDIED RAT- MONKEY OFFAL. I EAT IT BY THE BUCKETFUL.
AND EVEN WITH THE LID ON, I CAN TELL...
...THIS DOESN'T SMELL *AT ALL* LIKE...
I SAID *DON'T*...

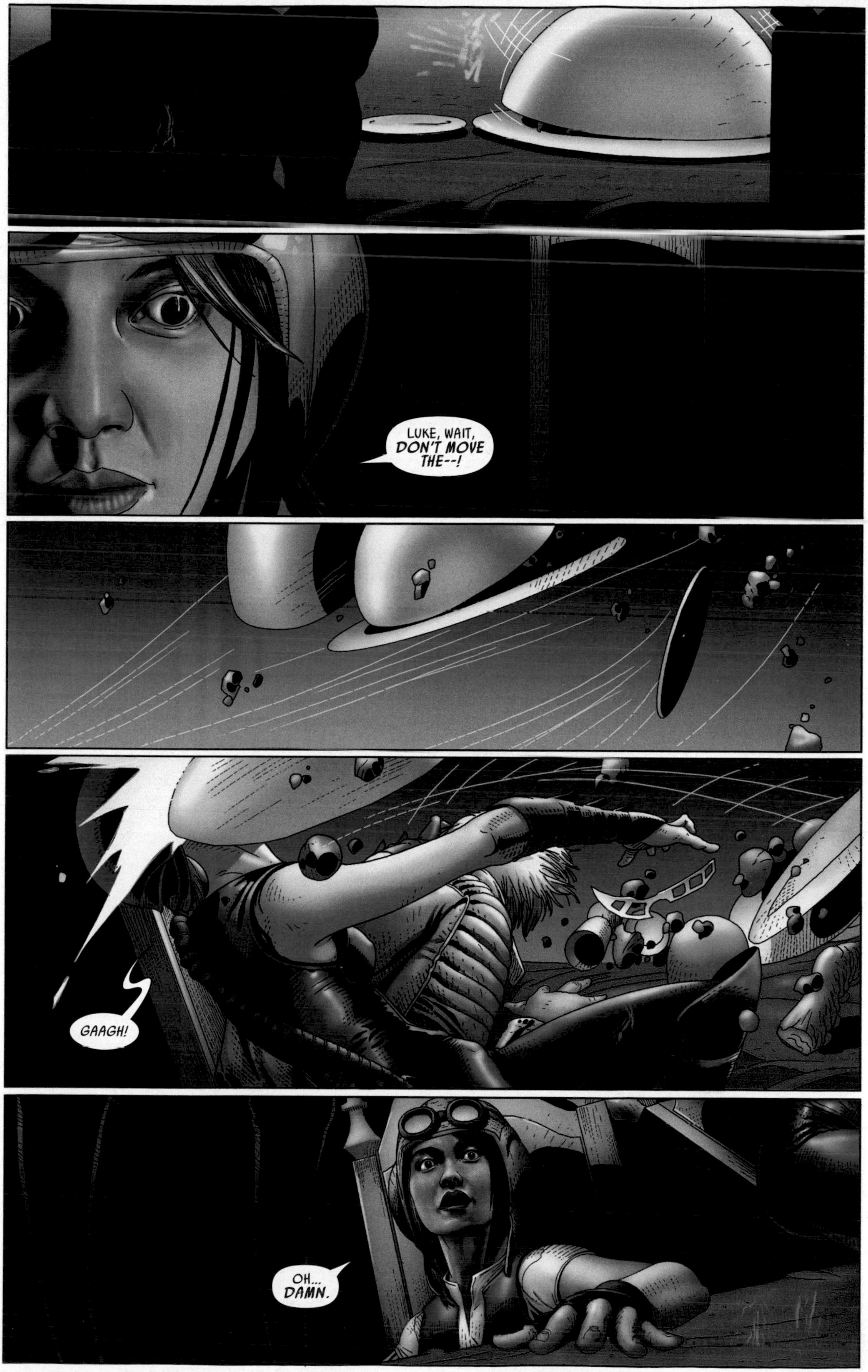
LUKE, WAIT, DON'T MOVE THE--!
GAAGH!
OH... DAMN.

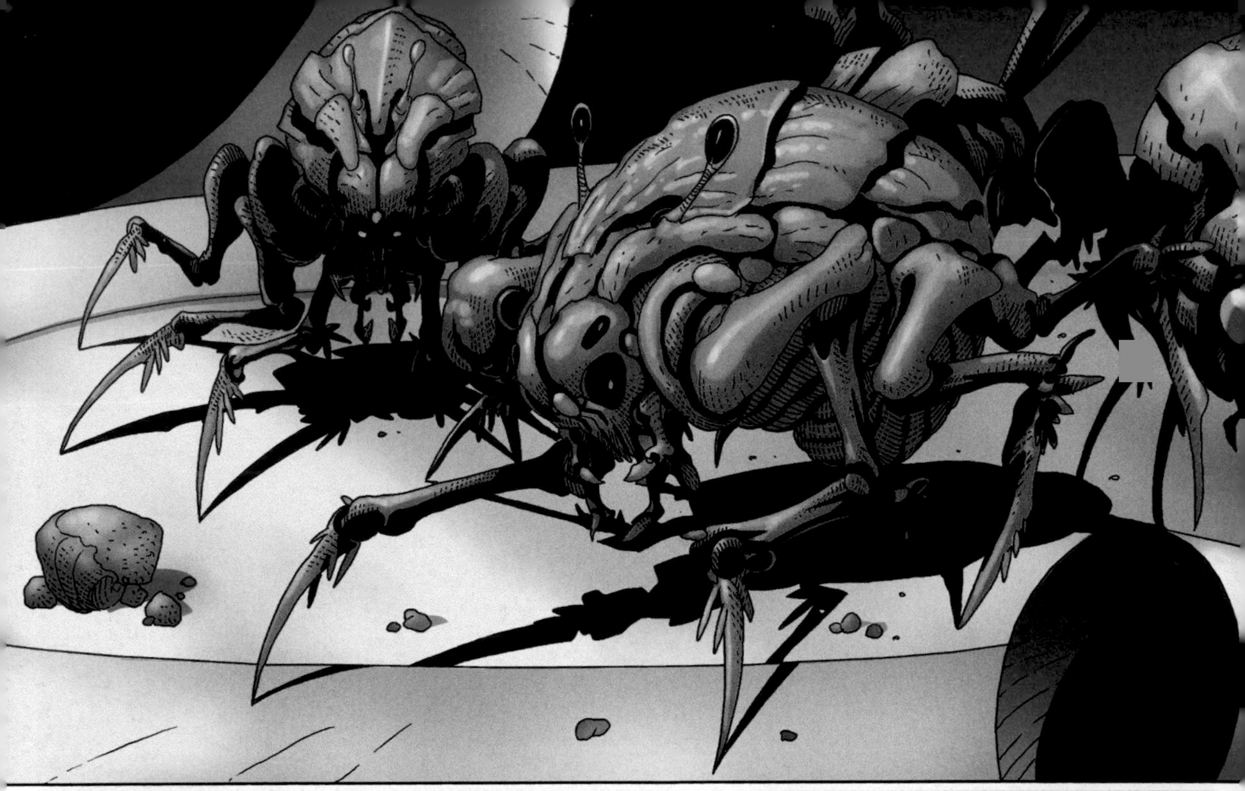

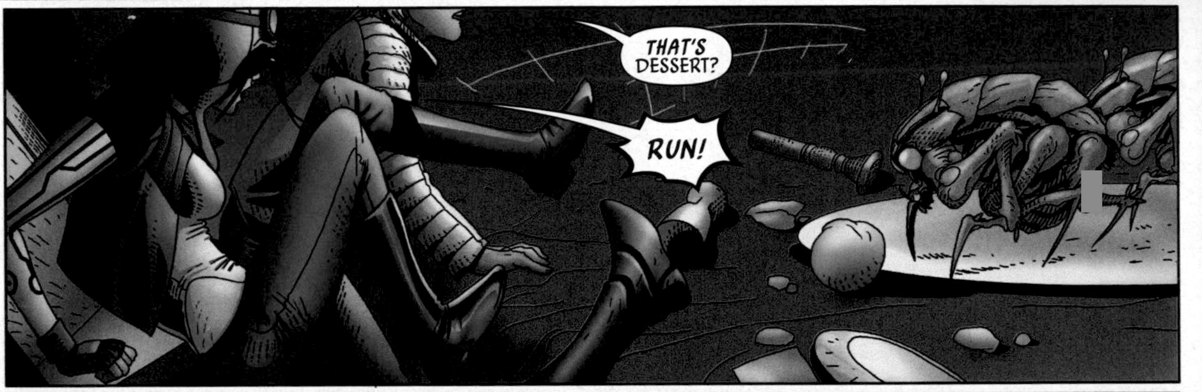
THAT'S DESSERT?
RUN!

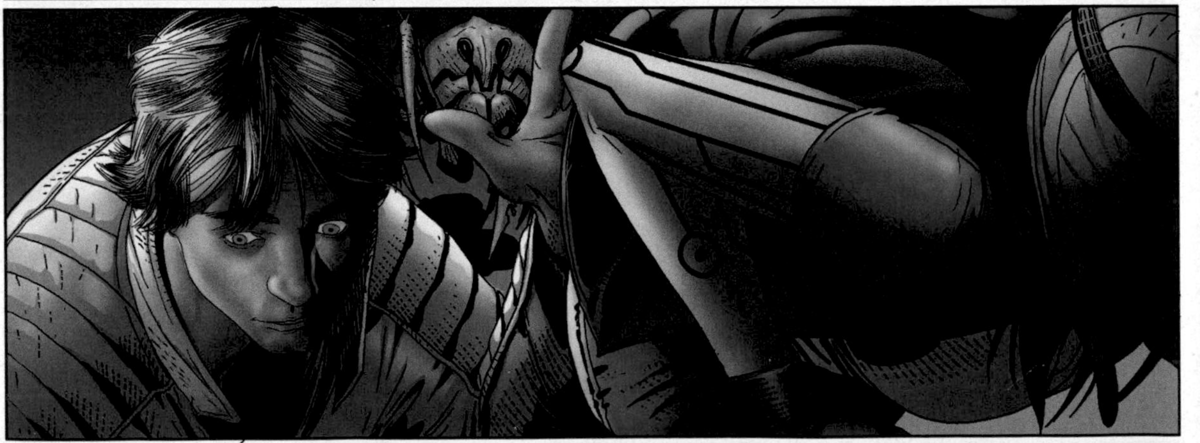

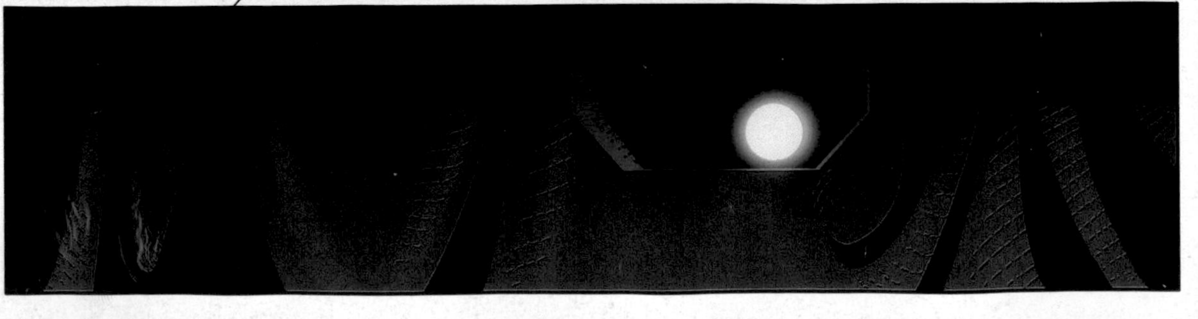

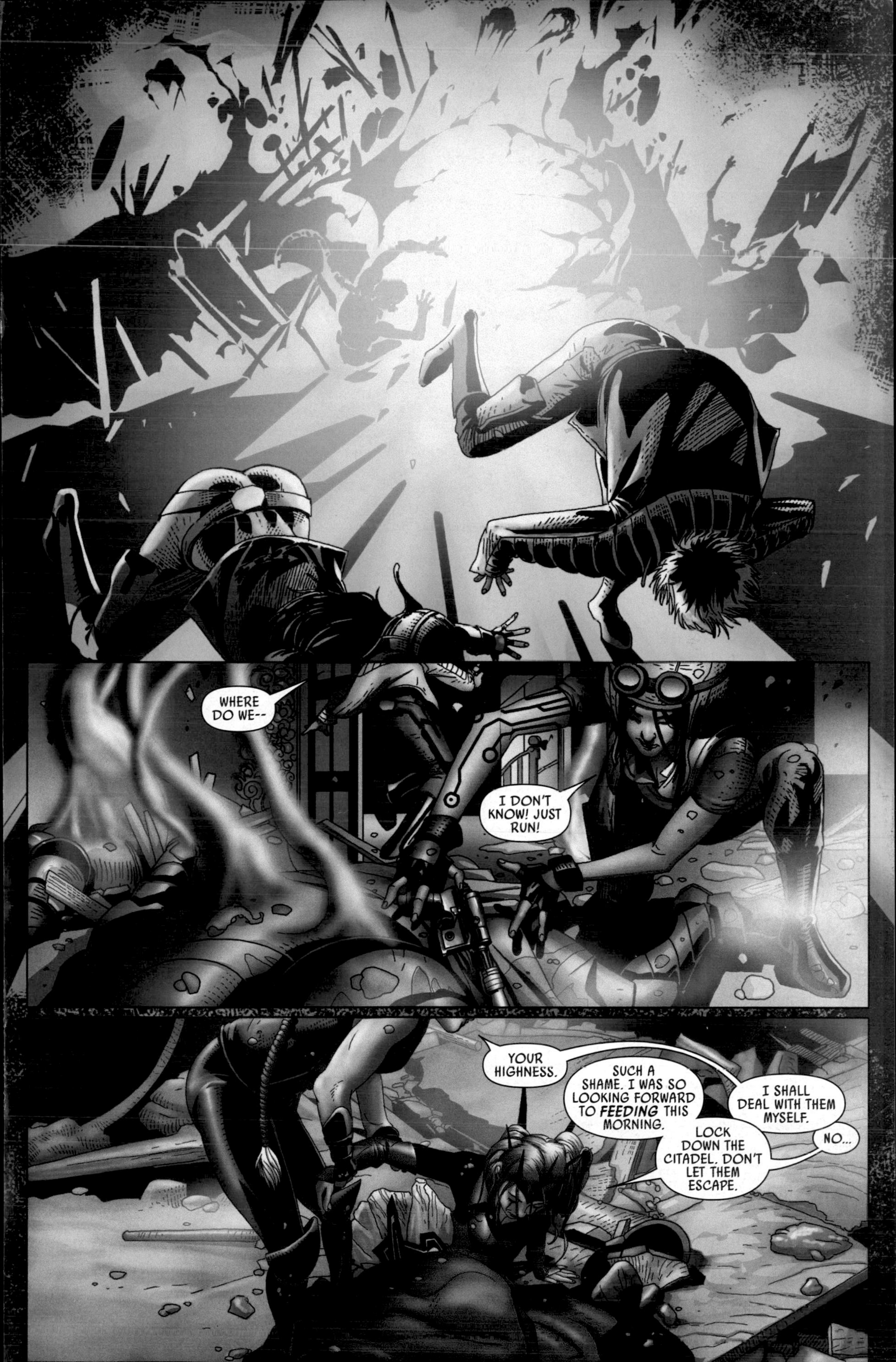
WHERE DO WE--
I DON'T KNOW! JUST RUN!
YOUR HIGHNESS.
SUCH A SHAME. I WAS SO LOOKING FORWARD TO *FEEDING* THIS MORNING.
LOCK DOWN THE CITADEL. DON'T LET THEM ESCAPE.
I SHALL DEAL WITH THEM MYSELF.
NO...

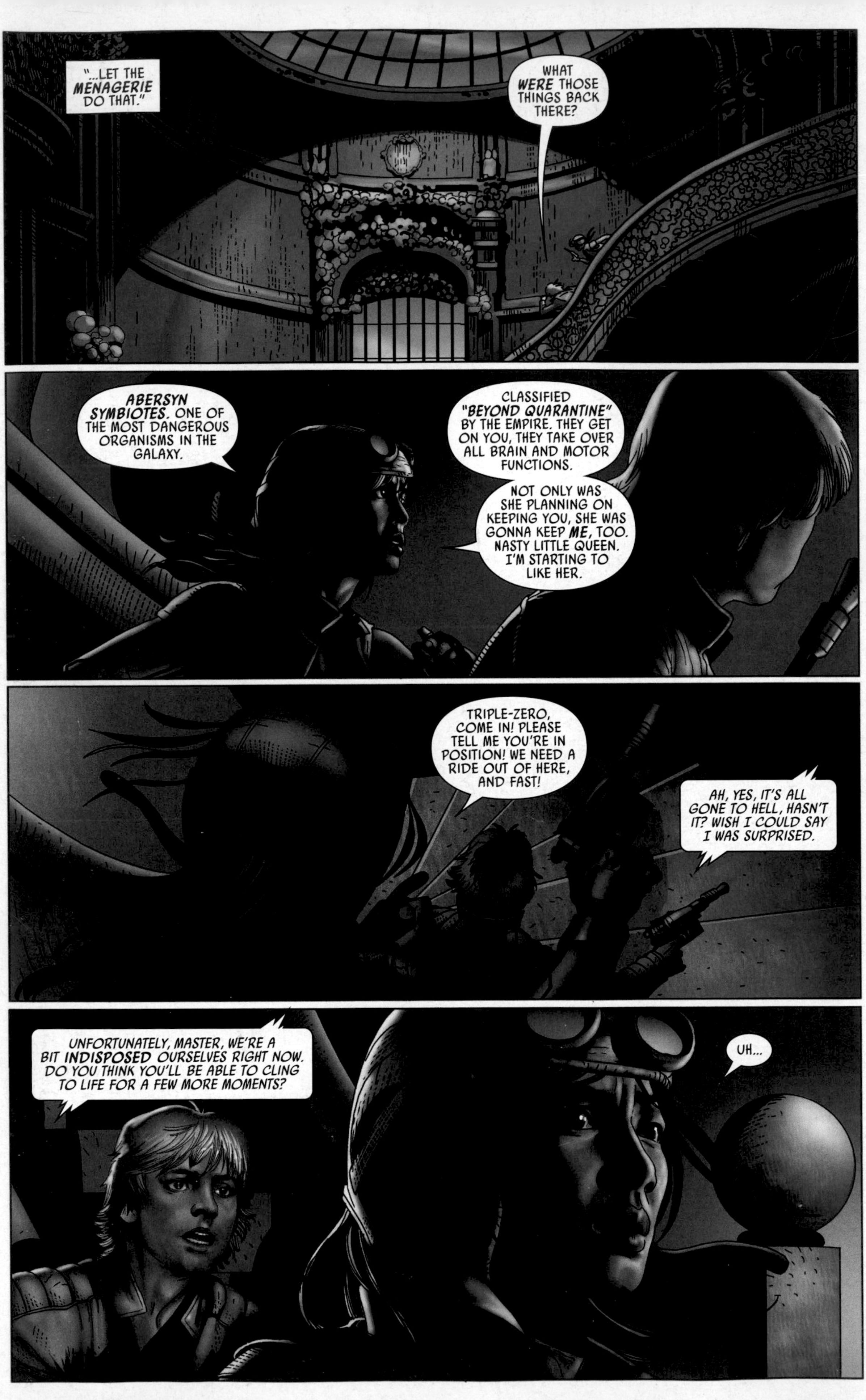
"...LET THE MENAGERIE DO THAT."
WHAT WERE THOSE THINGS BACK THERE?
ABERSYN SYMBIOTES. ONE OF THE MOST DANGEROUS ORGANISMS IN THE GALAXY.
CLASSIFIED "BEYOND QUARANTINE" BY THE EMPIRE. THEY GET ON YOU, THEY TAKE OVER ALL BRAIN AND MOTOR FUNCTIONS.
NOT ONLY WAS SHE PLANNING ON KEEPING YOU, SHE WAS GONNA KEEP ME, TOO. NASTY LITTLE QUEEN. I'M STARTING TO LIKE HER.
TRIPLE-ZERO, COME IN! PLEASE TELL ME YOU'RE IN POSITION! WE NEED A RIDE OUT OF HERE, AND FAST!
AH, YES, IT'S ALL GONE TO HELL, HASN'T IT? WISH I COULD SAY I WAS SURPRISED.
UNFORTUNATELY, MASTER, WE'RE A BIT INDISPOSED OURSELVES RIGHT NOW. DO YOU THINK YOU'LL BE ABLE TO CLING TO LIFE FOR A FEW MORE MOMENTS?
UH...

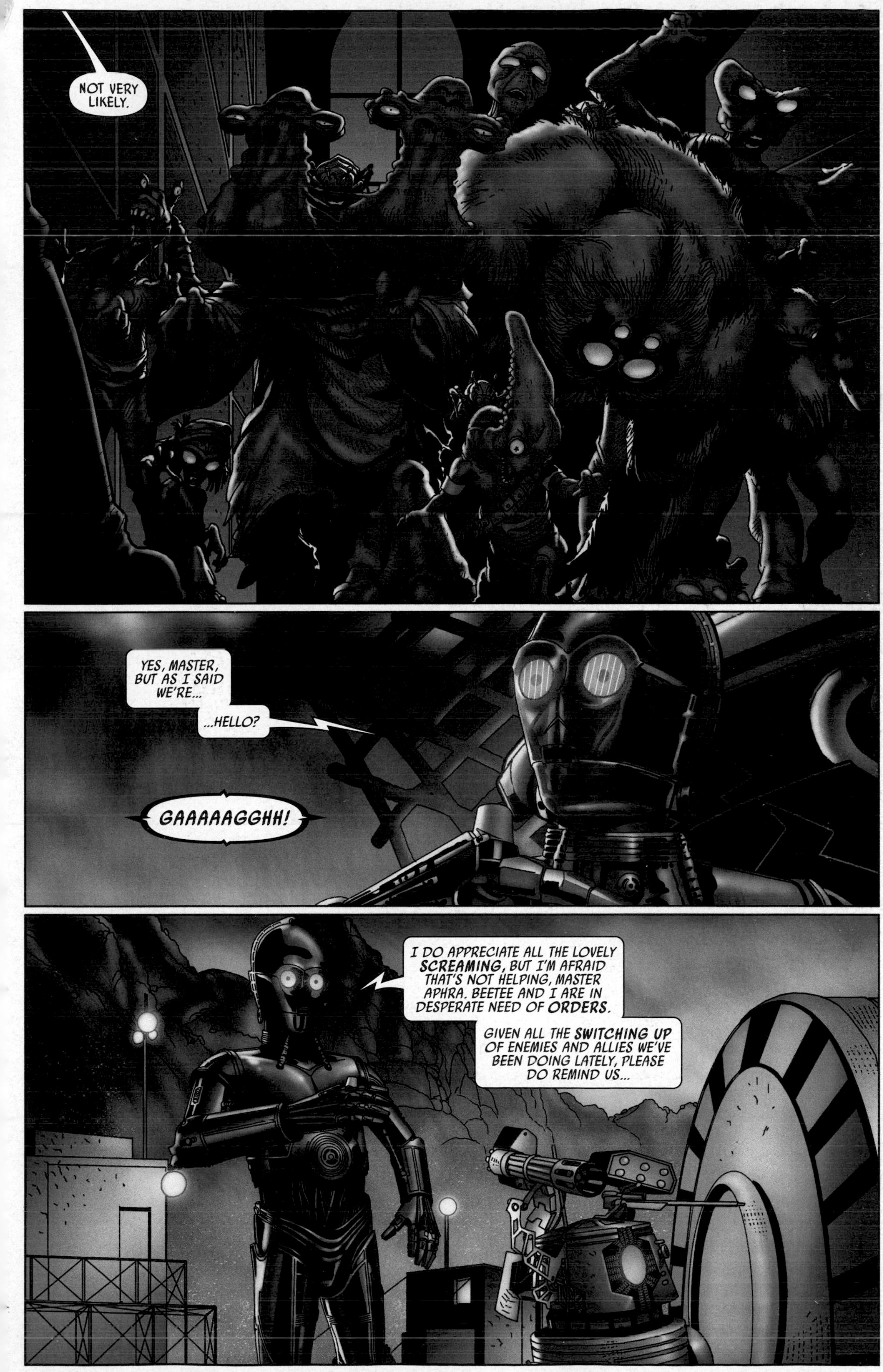
NOT VERY LIKELY.
YES, MASTER, BUT AS I SAID WE'RE...
...HELLO?
GAAAAAGGHH!
I DO APPRECIATE ALL THE LOVELY SCREAMING, BUT I'M AFRAID THAT'S NOT HELPING, MASTER APHRA. BEETEE AND I ARE IN DESPERATE NEED OF ORDERS.
GIVEN ALL THE SWITCHING UP OF ENEMIES AND ALLIES WE'VE BEEN DOING LATELY, PLEASE DO REMIND US...

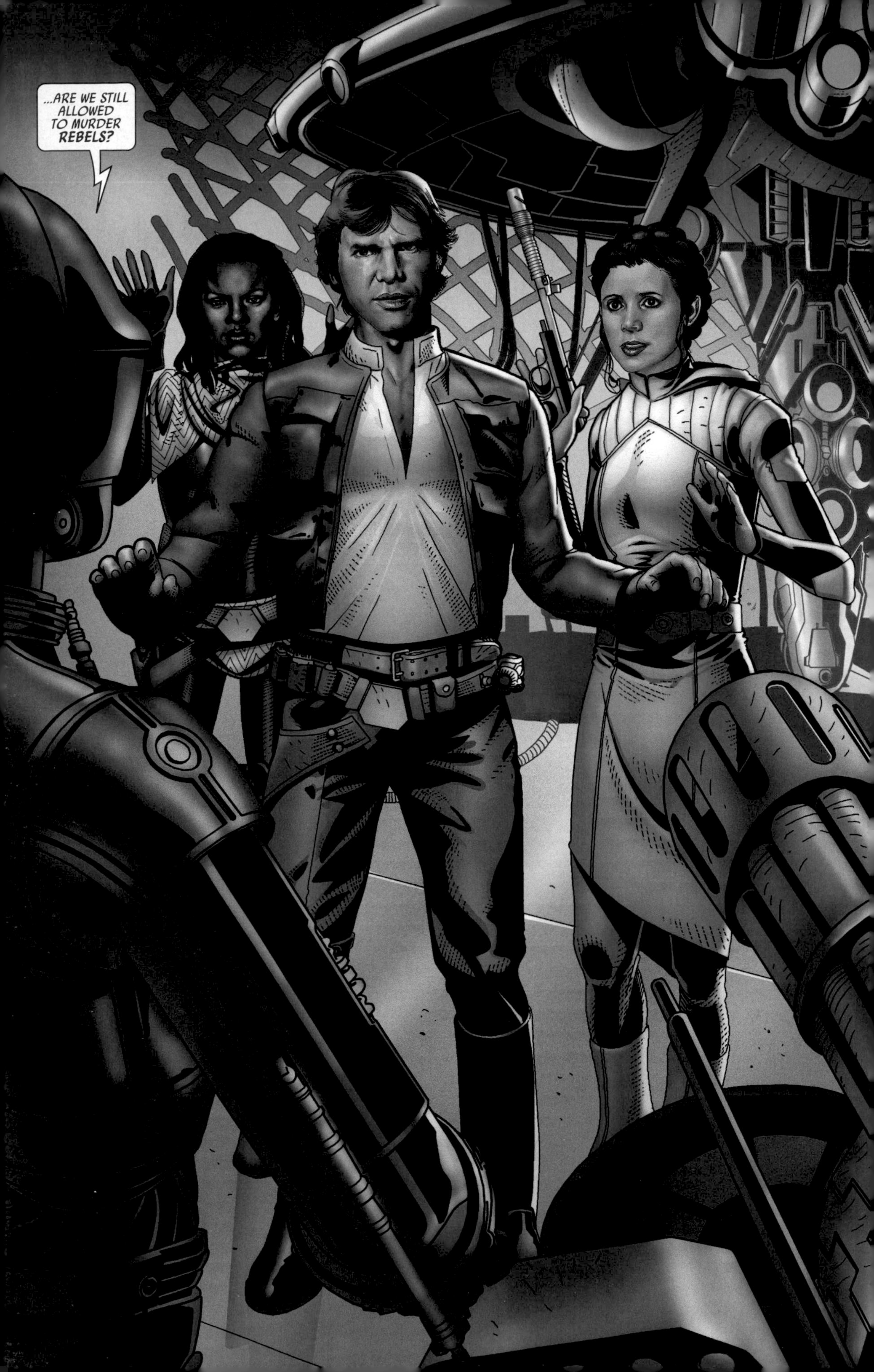
...ARE WE STILL ALLOWED TO MURDER REBELS?

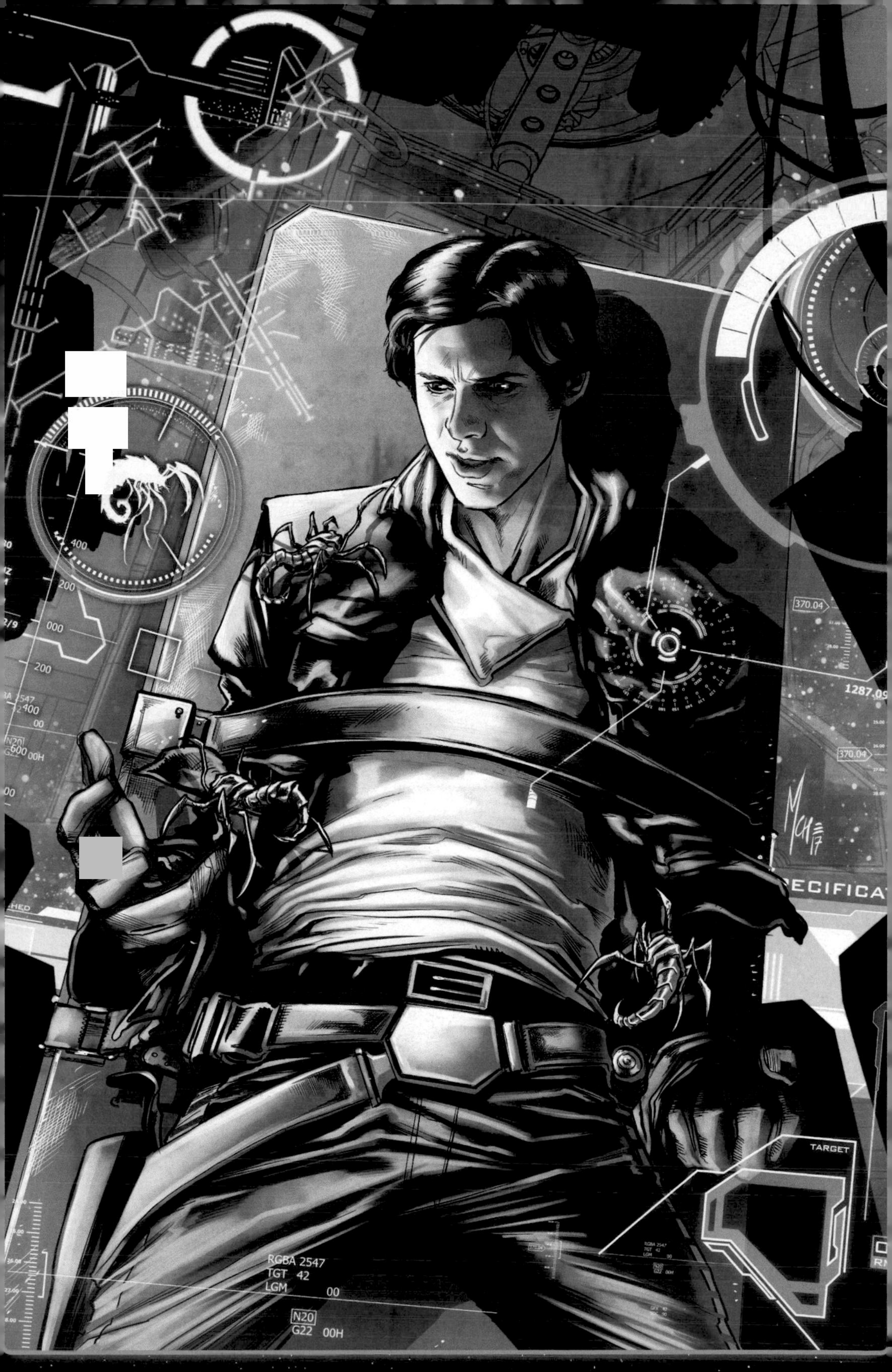

370.04
370.04
TARGET
RGBA 2547
TGT 42
LGM 00
N20
G22 00H

STAR WARS: DOCTOR APHRA 7

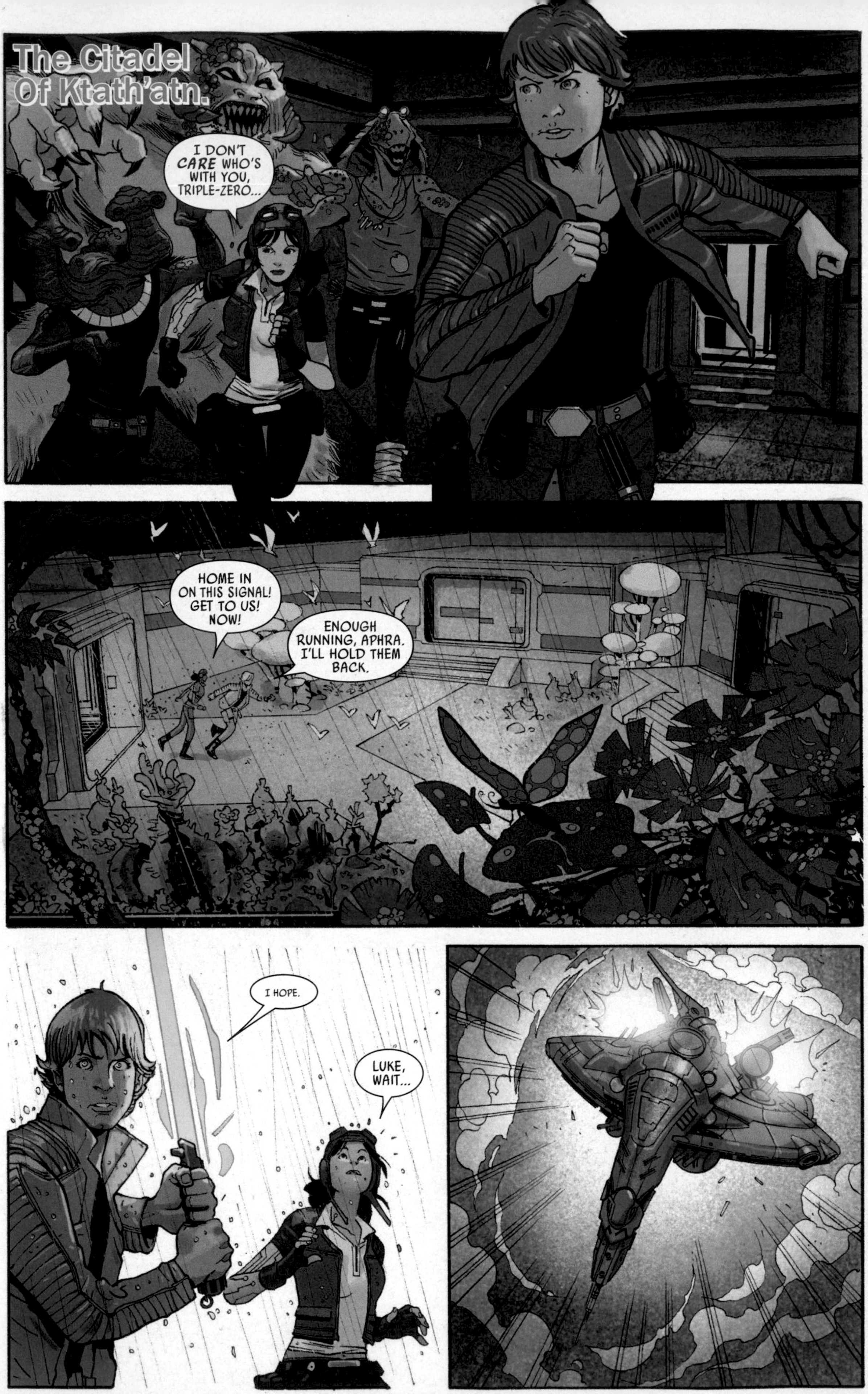
The Citadel Of Ktath'atn.
I DON'T CARE WHO'S WITH YOU, TRIPLE-ZERO...
HOME IN ON THIS SIGNAL! GET TO US! NOW!
ENOUGH RUNNING, APHRA. I'LL HOLD THEM BACK.
I HOPE.
LUKE, WAIT...

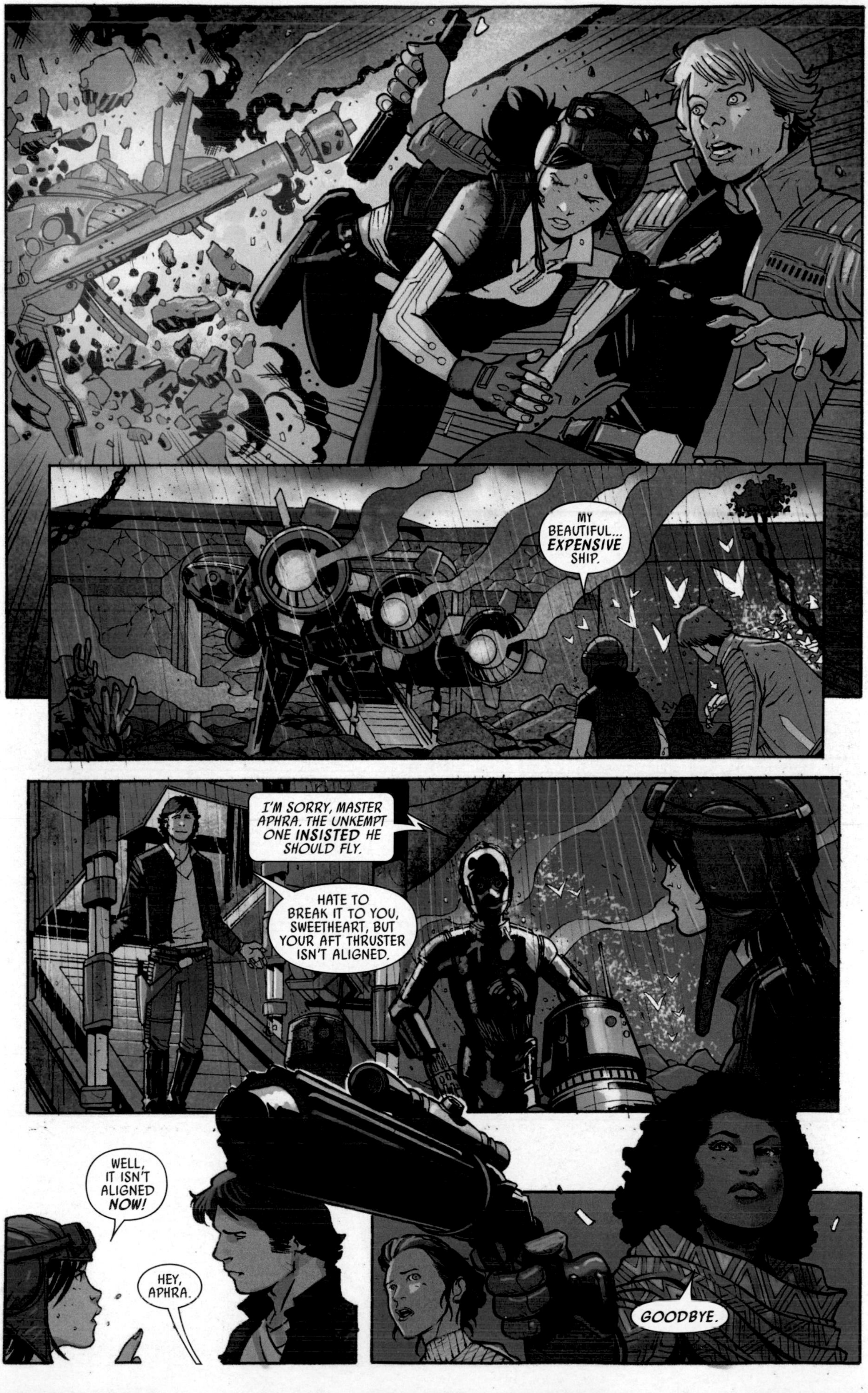
MY BEAUTIFUL... EXPENSIVE SHIP.
I'M SORRY, MASTER APHRA. THE UNKEMPT ONE INSISTED HE SHOULD FLY.
HATE TO BREAK IT TO YOU, SWEETHEART, BUT YOUR AFT THRUSTER ISN'T ALIGNED.
WELL, IT ISN'T ALIGNED NOW!
HEY, APHRA.
GOODBYE.

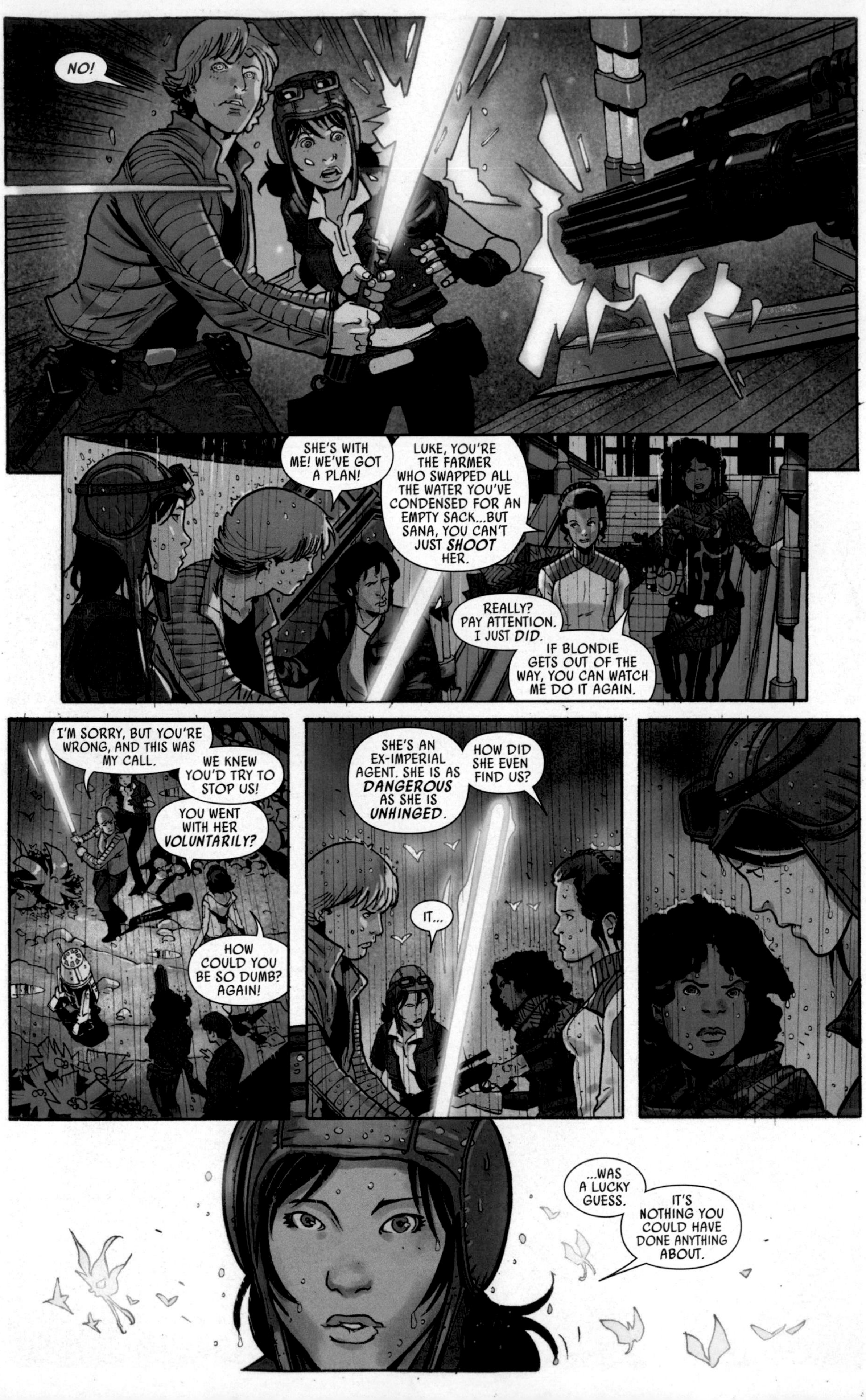
NO!
SHE'S WITH ME! WE'VE GOT A PLAN!
LUKE, YOU'RE THE FARMER WHO SWAPPED ALL THE WATER YOU'VE CONDENSED FOR AN EMPTY SACK...BUT SANA, YOU CAN'T JUST SHOOT HER.
REALLY? PAY ATTENTION. I JUST DID.
IF BLONDIE GETS OUT OF THE WAY, YOU CAN WATCH ME DO IT AGAIN.
I'M SORRY, BUT YOU'RE WRONG, AND THIS WAS MY CALL.
WE KNEW YOU'D TRY TO STOP US!
YOU WENT WITH HER VOLUNTARILY?
HOW COULD YOU BE SO DUMB? AGAIN!
SHE'S AN EX-IMPERIAL AGENT. SHE IS AS DANGEROUS AS SHE IS UNHINGED.
HOW DID SHE EVEN FIND US?
IT...
...WAS A LUCKY GUESS.
IT'S NOTHING YOU COULD HAVE DONE ANYTHING ABOUT.

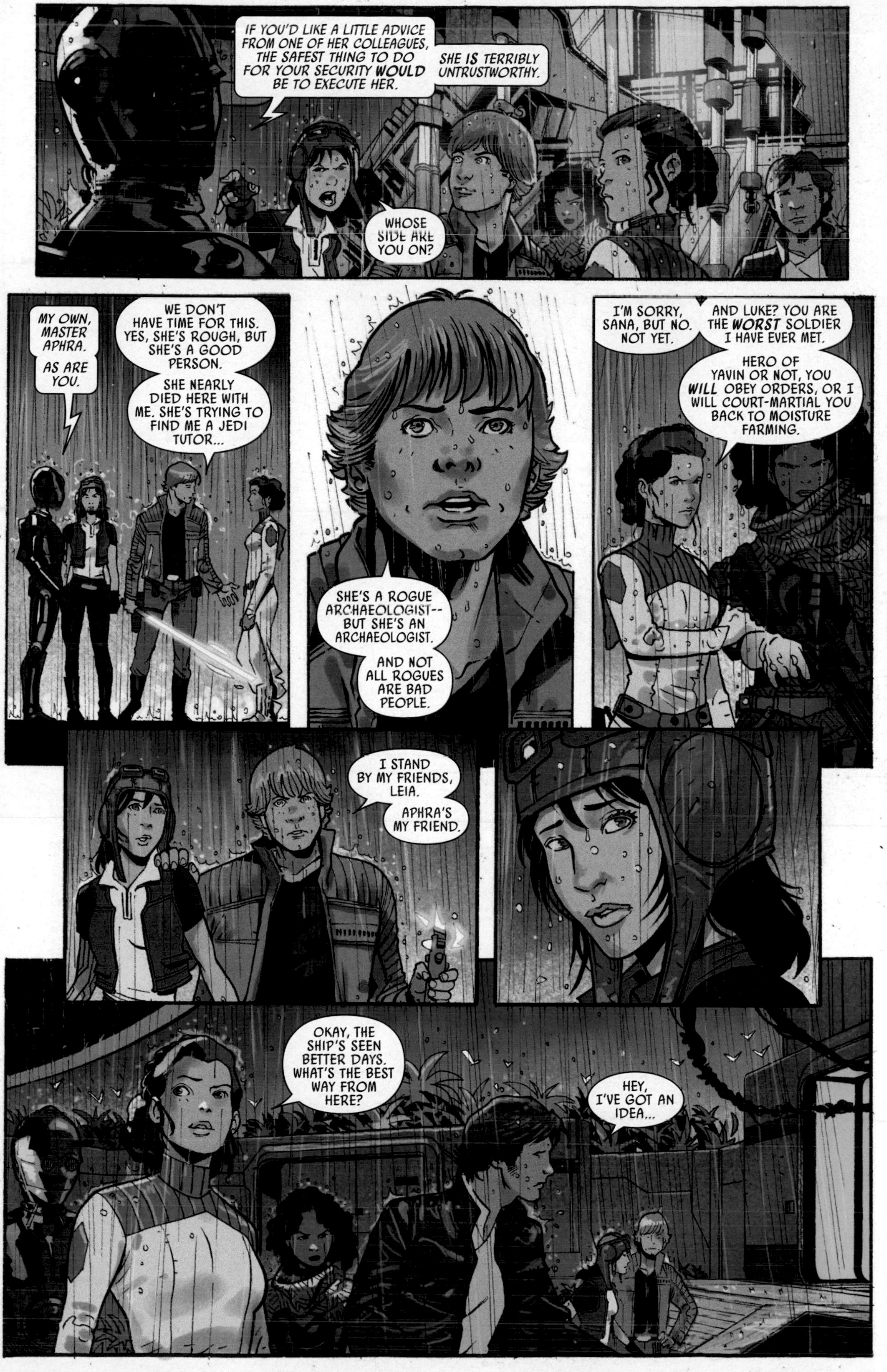
IF YOU'D LIKE A LITTLE ADVICE FROM ONE OF HER COLLEAGUES, THE SAFEST THING TO DO FOR YOUR SECURITY WOULD BE TO EXECUTE HER.
SHE IS TERRIBLY UNTRUSTWORTHY.
WHOSE SIDE ARE YOU ON?
MY OWN, MASTER APHRA.
AS ARE YOU.
WE DON'T HAVE TIME FOR THIS. YES, SHE'S ROUGH, BUT SHE'S A GOOD PERSON.
SHE NEARLY DIED HERE WITH ME. SHE'S TRYING TO FIND ME A JEDI TUTOR...
SHE'S A ROGUE ARCHAEOLOGIST-- BUT SHE'S AN ARCHAEOLOGIST.
AND NOT ALL ROGUES ARE BAD PEOPLE.
I'M SORRY, SANA, BUT NO. NOT YET.
AND LUKE? YOU ARE THE WORST SOLDIER I HAVE EVER MET.
HERO OF YAVIN OR NOT, YOU WILL OBEY ORDERS, OR I WILL COURT-MARTIAL YOU BACK TO MOISTURE FARMING.
I STAND BY MY FRIENDS, LEIA.
APHRA'S MY FRIEND.
OKAY, THE SHIP'S SEEN BETTER DAYS. WHAT'S THE BEST WAY FROM HERE?
HEY, I'VE GOT AN IDEA...

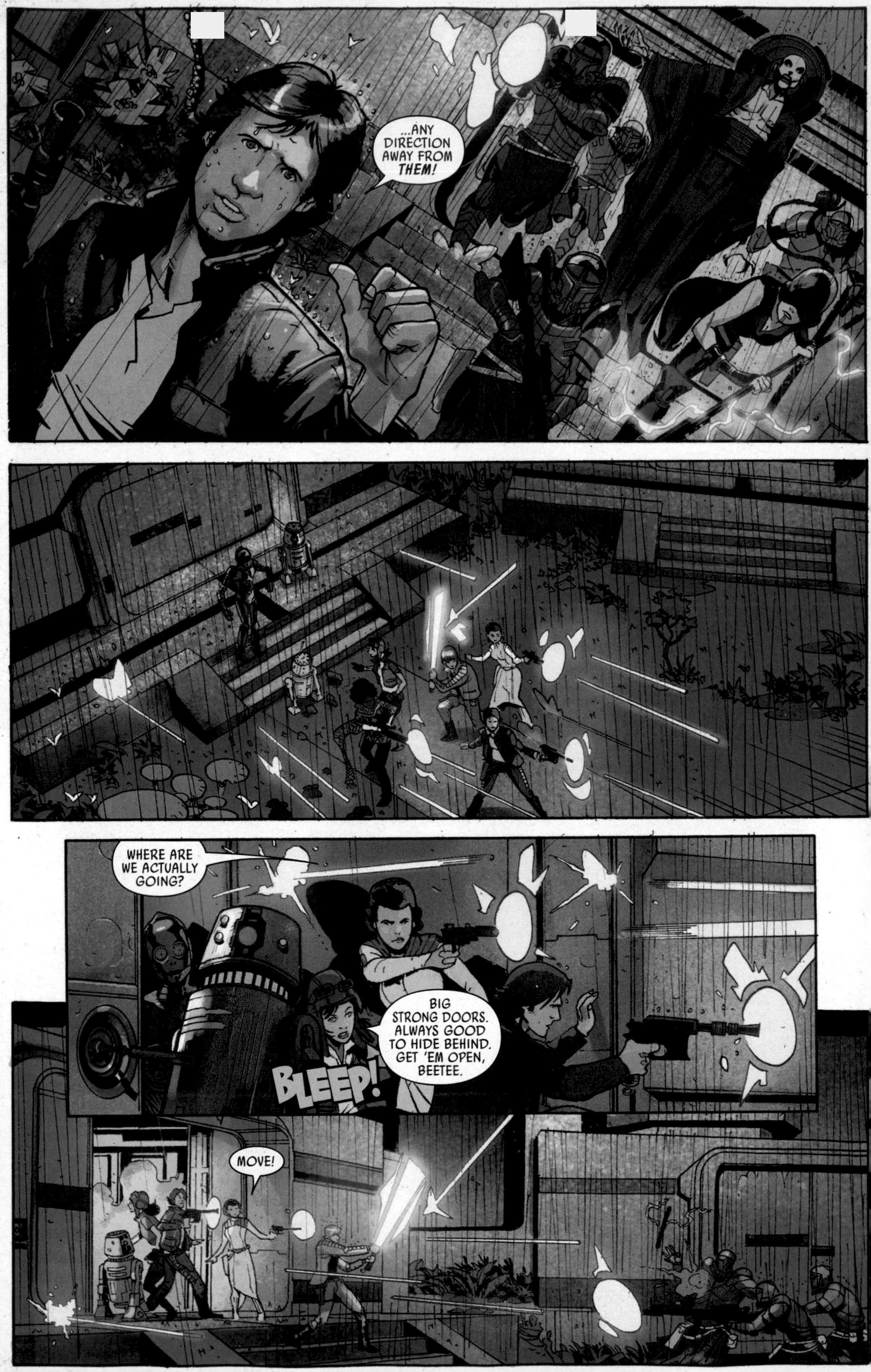

...ANY DIRECTION AWAY FROM THEM!
WHERE ARE WE ACTUALLY GOING?
BIG STRONG DOORS. ALWAYS GOOD TO HIDE BEHIND. GET 'EM OPEN, BEETEE.
BLEEP!
MOVE!

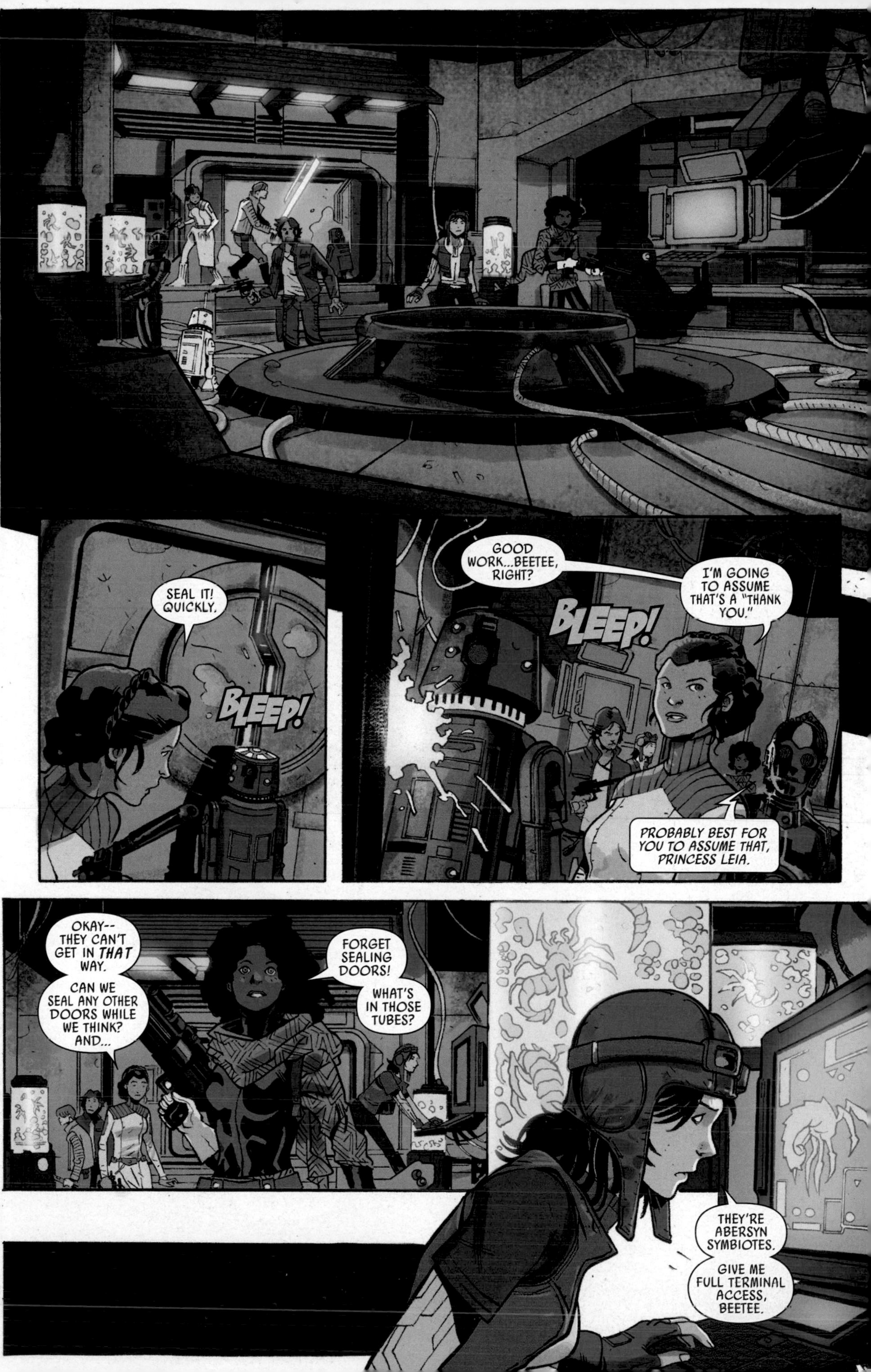
SEAL IT! QUICKLY.
BLEEP!
GOOD WORK...BEETEE, RIGHT?
I'M GOING TO ASSUME THAT'S A "THANK YOU."
BLEEP!
PROBABLY BEST FOR YOU TO ASSUME THAT, PRINCESS LEIA.
OKAY-- THEY CAN'T GET IN *THAT* WAY.
CAN WE SEAL ANY OTHER DOORS WHILE WE THINK? AND...
FORGET SEALING DOORS!
WHAT'S IN THOSE TUBES?
THEY'RE ABERSYN SYMBIOTES.
GIVE ME FULL TERMINAL ACCESS, BEETEE.

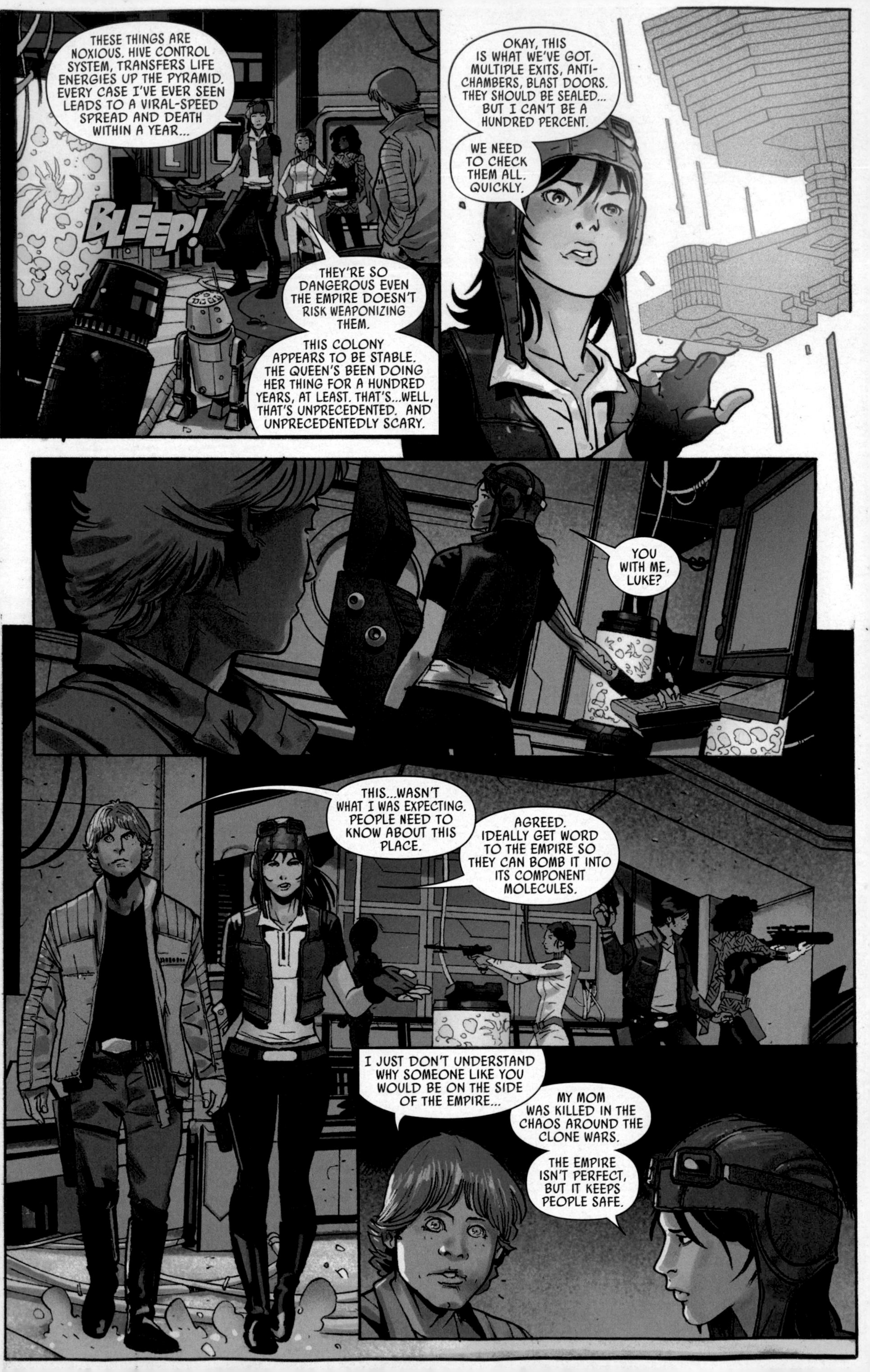

THESE THINGS ARE NOXIOUS. HIVE CONTROL SYSTEM, TRANSFERS LIFE ENERGIES UP THE PYRAMID. EVERY CASE I'VE EVER SEEN LEADS TO A VIRAL-SPEED SPREAD AND DEATH WITHIN A YEAR...
BLEEP!
THEY'RE SO DANGEROUS EVEN THE EMPIRE DOESN'T RISK WEAPONIZING THEM.
THIS COLONY APPEARS TO BE STABLE. THE QUEEN'S BEEN DOING HER THING FOR A HUNDRED YEARS, AT LEAST. THAT'S...WELL, THAT'S UNPRECEDENTED. AND UNPRECEDENTEDLY SCARY.
OKAY, THIS IS WHAT WE'VE GOT. MULTIPLE EXITS, ANTI-CHAMBERS, BLAST DOORS. THEY SHOULD BE SEALED... BUT I CAN'T BE A HUNDRED PERCENT.
WE NEED TO CHECK THEM ALL. QUICKLY.
YOU WITH ME, LUKE?
THIS...WASN'T WHAT I WAS EXPECTING. PEOPLE NEED TO KNOW ABOUT THIS PLACE.
AGREED. IDEALLY GET WORD TO THE EMPIRE SO THEY CAN BOMB IT INTO ITS COMPONENT MOLECULES.
I JUST DON'T UNDERSTAND WHY SOMEONE LIKE YOU WOULD BE ON THE SIDE OF THE EMPIRE...
MY MOM WAS KILLED IN THE CHAOS AROUND THE CLONE WARS.
THE EMPIRE ISN'T PERFECT, BUT IT KEEPS PEOPLE SAFE.

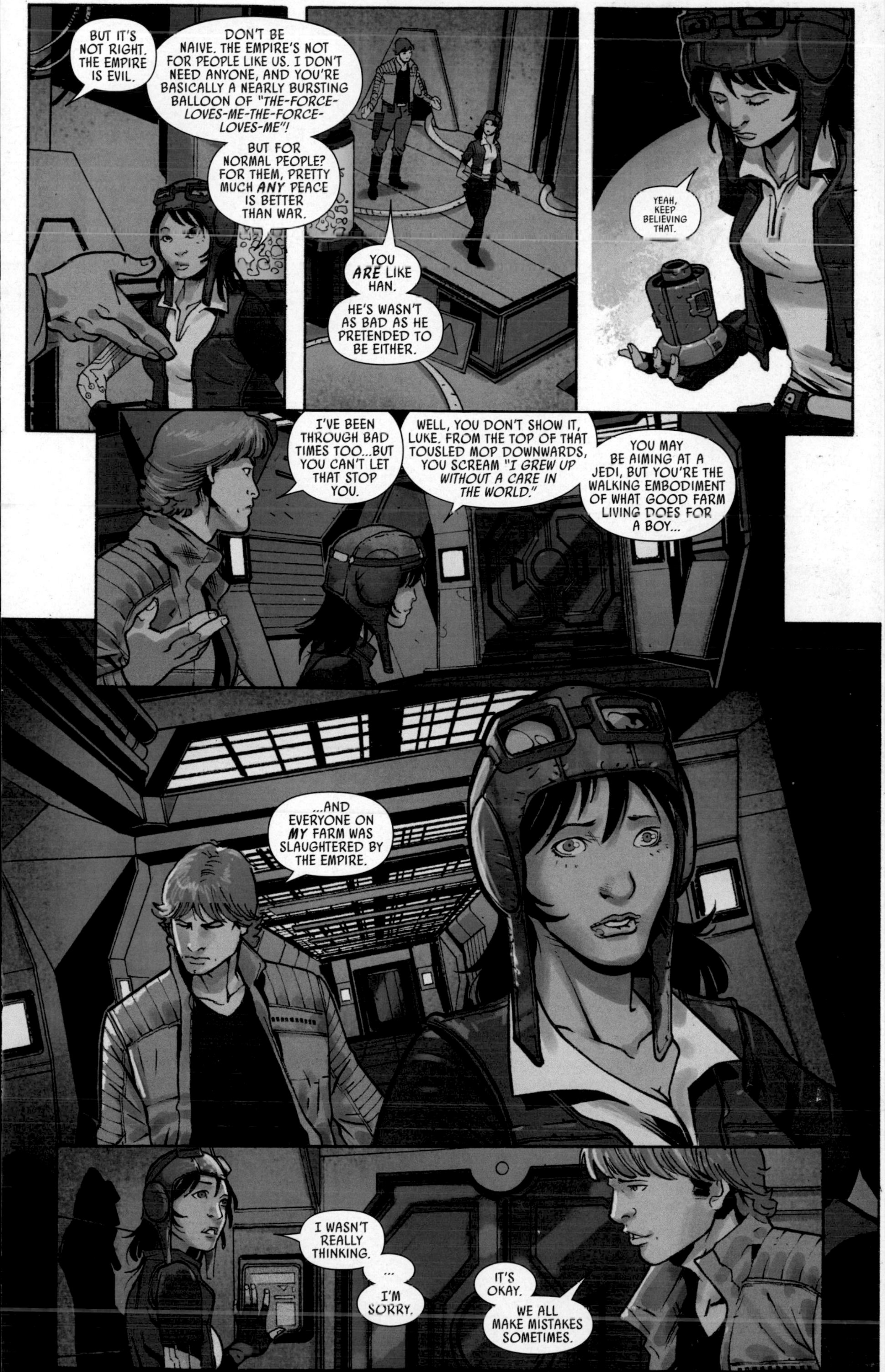
BUT IT'S NOT RIGHT. THE EMPIRE IS EVIL.
DON'T BE NAIVE. THE EMPIRE'S NOT FOR PEOPLE LIKE US. I DON'T NEED ANYONE, AND YOU'RE BASICALLY A NEARLY BURSTING BALLOON OF "THE-FORCE-LOVES-ME-THE-FORCE-LOVES-ME"!
BUT FOR NORMAL PEOPLE? FOR THEM, PRETTY MUCH ANY PEACE IS BETTER THAN WAR.
YOU ARE LIKE HAN.
HE'S WASN'T AS BAD AS HE PRETENDED TO BE EITHER.
YEAH, KEEP BELIEVING THAT.
I'VE BEEN THROUGH BAD TIMES TOO...BUT YOU CAN'T LET THAT STOP YOU.
WELL, YOU DON'T SHOW IT, LUKE. FROM THE TOP OF THAT TOUSLED MOP DOWNWARDS, YOU SCREAM "I GREW UP WITHOUT A CARE IN THE WORLD."
YOU MAY BE AIMING AT A JEDI, BUT YOU'RE THE WALKING EMBODIMENT OF WHAT GOOD FARM LIVING DOES FOR A BOY...
...AND EVERYONE ON MY FARM WAS SLAUGHTERED BY THE EMPIRE.
I WASN'T REALLY THINKING.
...
I'M SORRY.
IT'S OKAY.
WE ALL MAKE MISTAKES SOMETIMES.

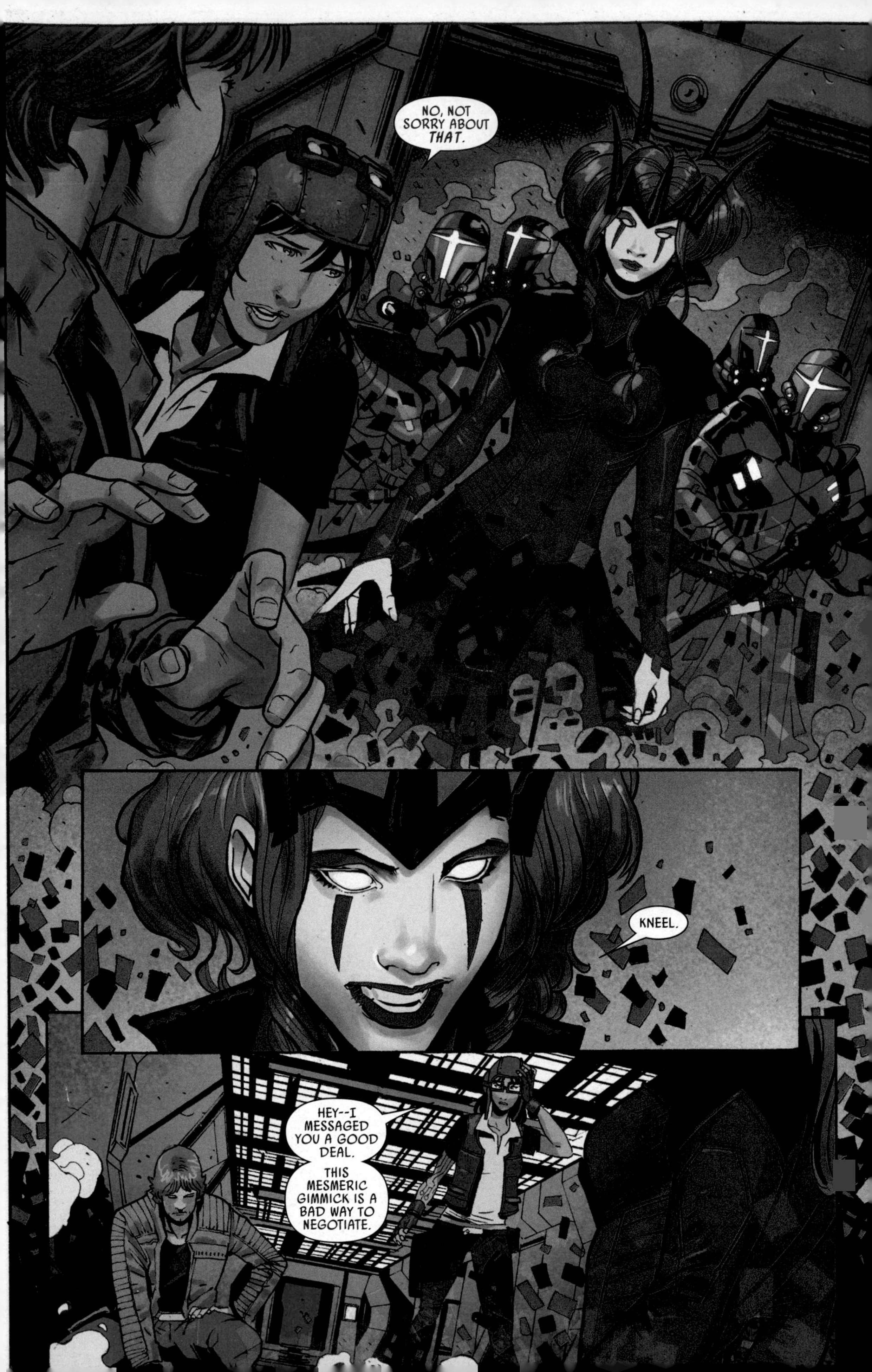

NO, NOT SORRY ABOUT THAT.
KNEEL.
HEY--I MESSAGED YOU A GOOD DEAL.
THIS MESMERIC GIMMICK IS A BAD WAY TO NEGOTIATE.

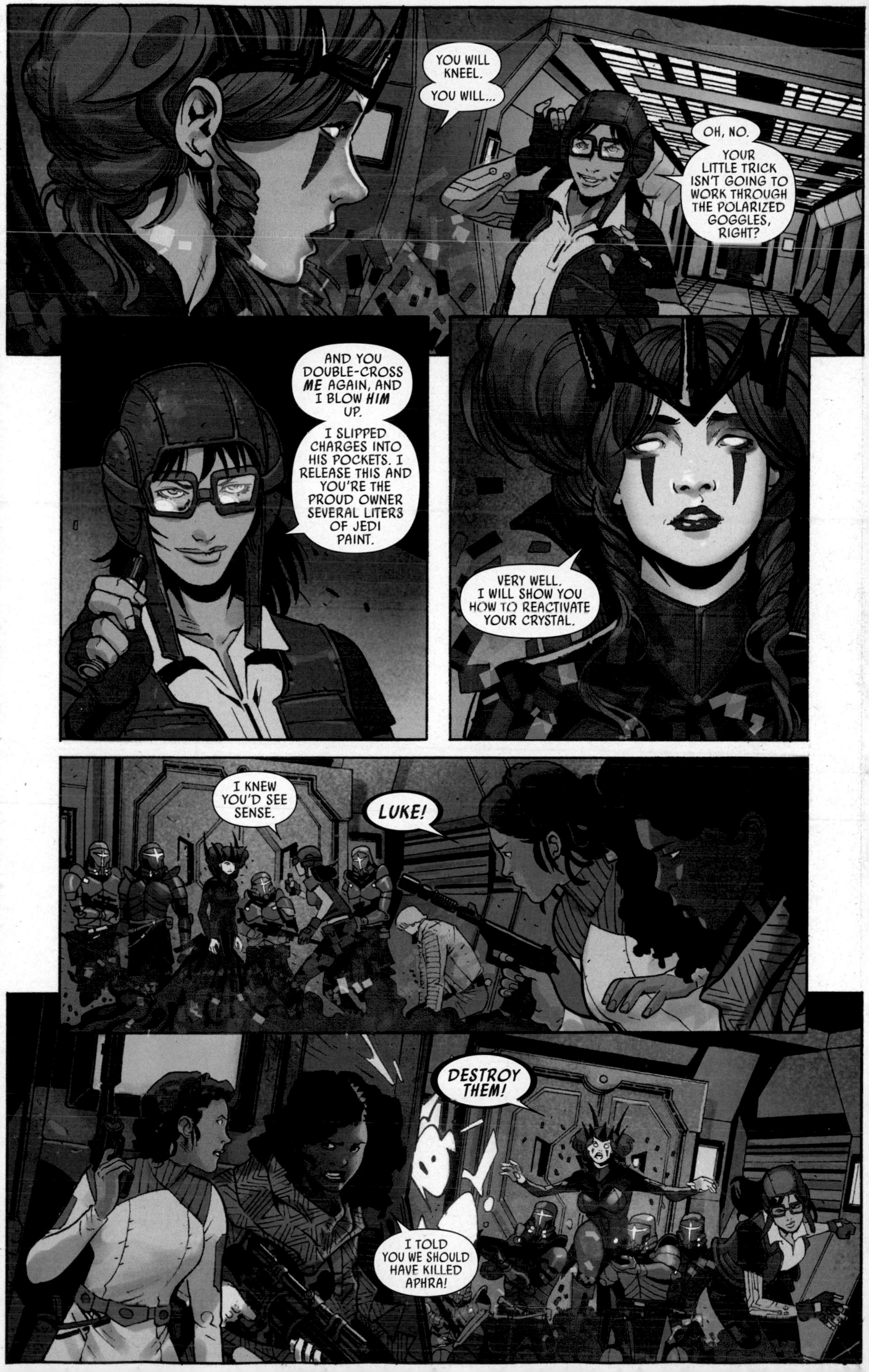
YOU WILL KNEEL.
YOU WILL...
OH, NO.
YOUR LITTLE TRICK ISN'T GOING TO WORK THROUGH THE POLARIZED GOGGLES, RIGHT?
AND YOU DOUBLE-CROSS ME AGAIN, AND I BLOW HIM UP.
I SLIPPED CHARGES INTO HIS POCKETS. I RELEASE THIS AND YOU'RE THE PROUD OWNER SEVERAL LITERS OF JEDI PAINT.
VERY WELL. I WILL SHOW YOU HOW TO REACTIVATE YOUR CRYSTAL.
I KNEW YOU'D SEE SENSE.
LUKE!
DESTROY THEM!
I TOLD YOU WE SHOULD HAVE KILLED APHRA!

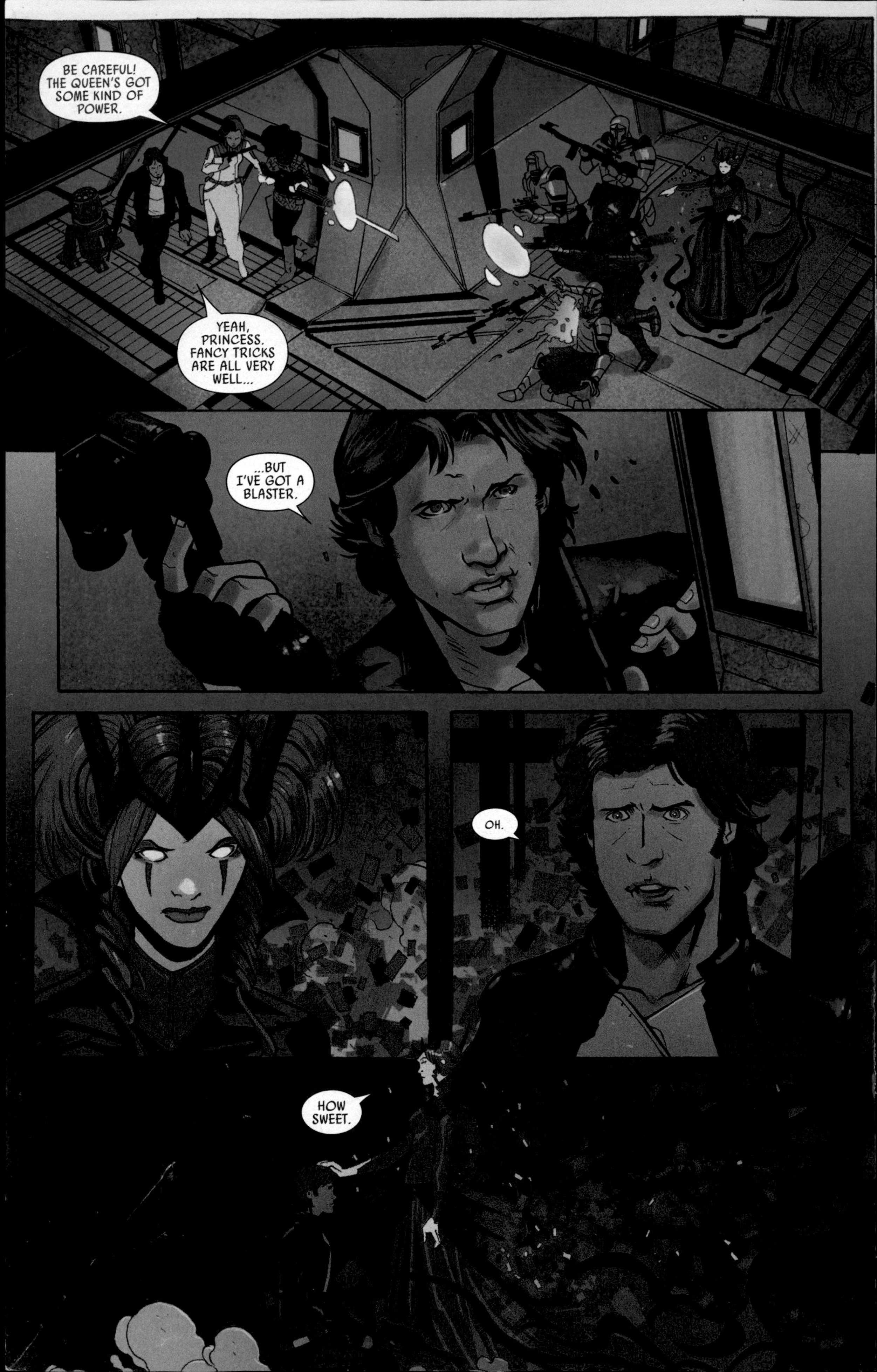
BE CAREFUL! THE QUEEN'S GOT SOME KIND OF POWER.
YEAH, PRINCESS. FANCY TRICKS ARE ALL VERY WELL...
...BUT I'VE GOT A BLASTER.
OH.
HOW SWEET.

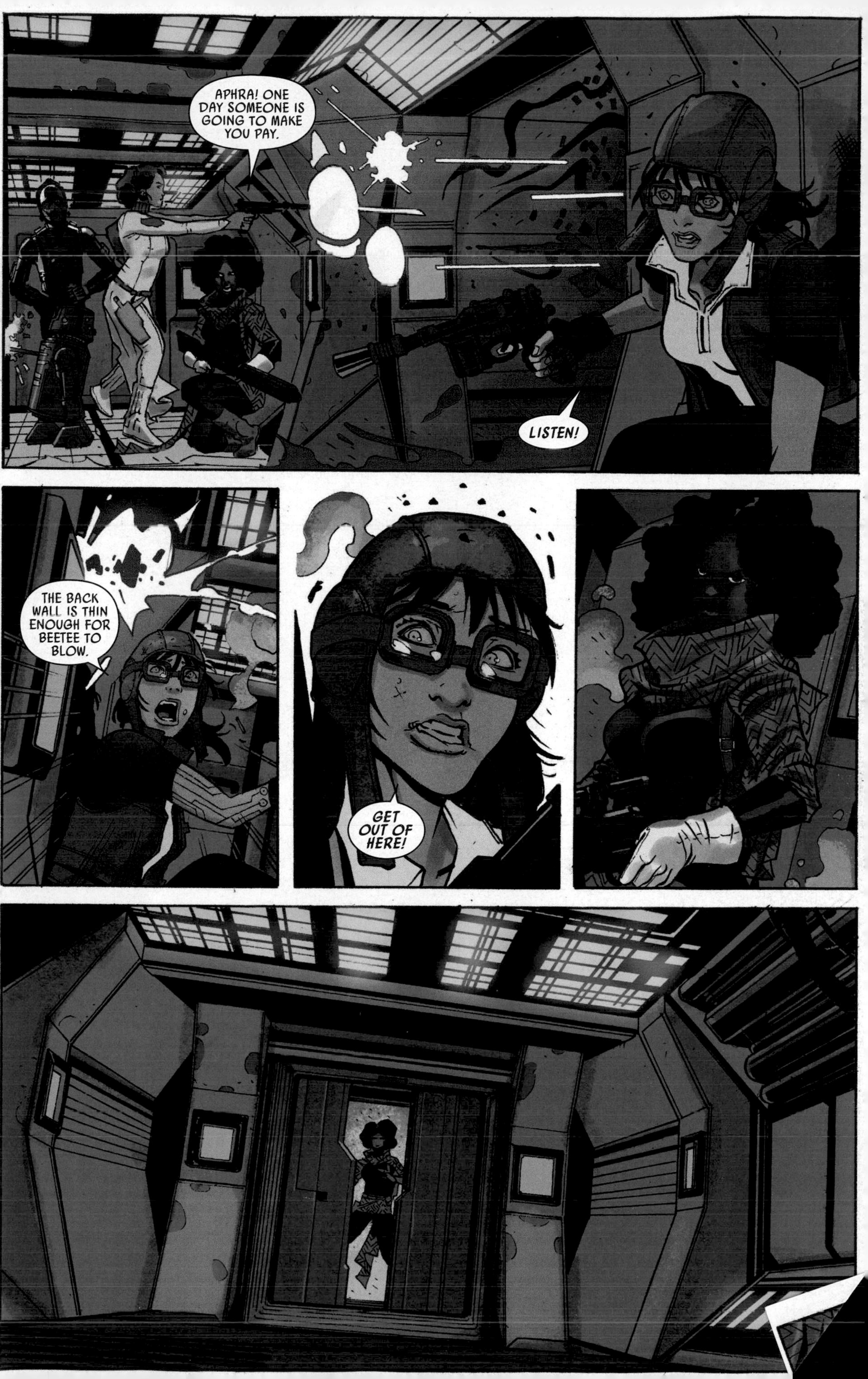
APHRA! ONE DAY SOMEONE IS GOING TO MAKE YOU PAY.
LISTEN!
THE BACK WALL IS THIN ENOUGH FOR BEETEE TO BLOW.
GET OUT OF HERE!

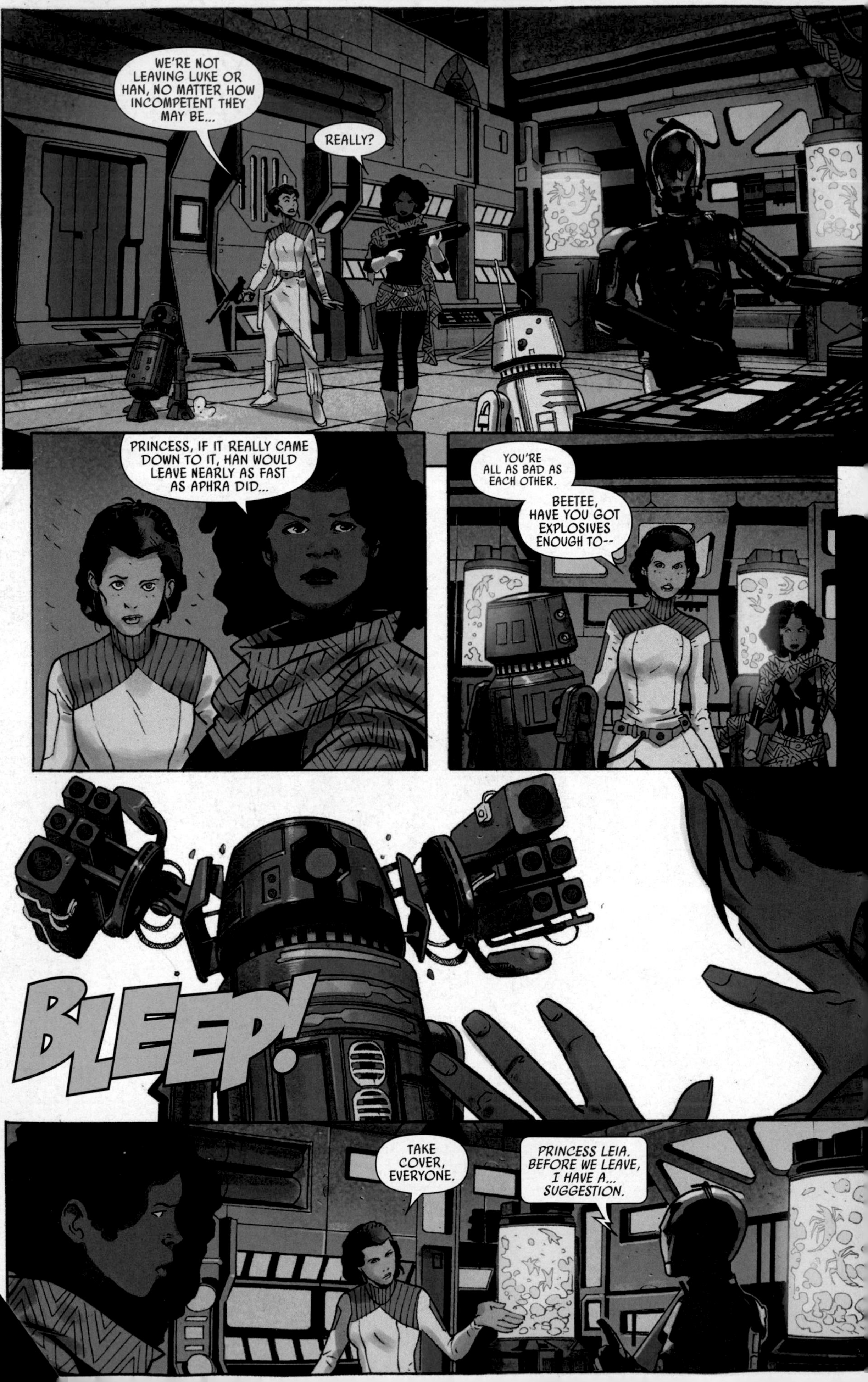
WE'RE NOT LEAVING LUKE OR HAN, NO MATTER HOW INCOMPETENT THEY MAY BE...
REALLY?
PRINCESS, IF IT REALLY CAME DOWN TO IT, HAN WOULD LEAVE NEARLY AS FAST AS APHRA DID...
YOU'RE ALL AS BAD AS EACH OTHER.
BEETEE, HAVE YOU GOT EXPLOSIVES ENOUGH TO--
BLEEP!
TAKE COVER, EVERYONE.
PRINCESS LEIA. BEFORE WE LEAVE, I HAVE A... SUGGESTION.

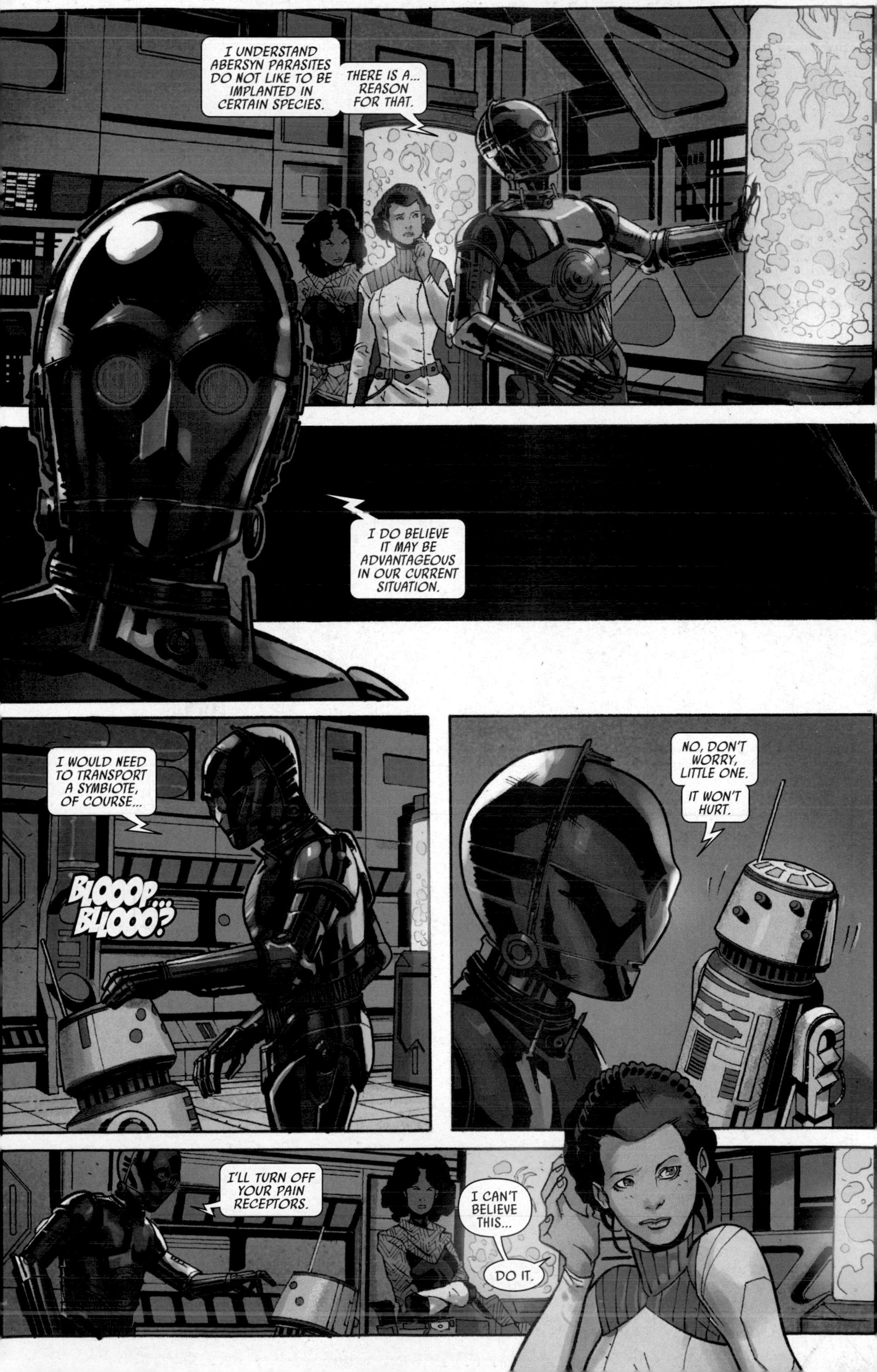
I UNDERSTAND ABERSYN PARASITES DO NOT LIKE TO BE IMPLANTED IN CERTAIN SPECIES.
THERE IS A... REASON FOR THAT.
I DO BELIEVE IT MAY BE ADVANTAGEOUS IN OUR CURRENT SITUATION.
I WOULD NEED TO TRANSPORT A SYMBIOTE, OF COURSE...
BLOOOP... BLLOOO?
NO, DON'T WORRY, LITTLE ONE.
IT WON'T HURT.
I'LL TURN OFF YOUR PAIN RECEPTORS.
I CAN'T BELIEVE THIS...
DO IT.

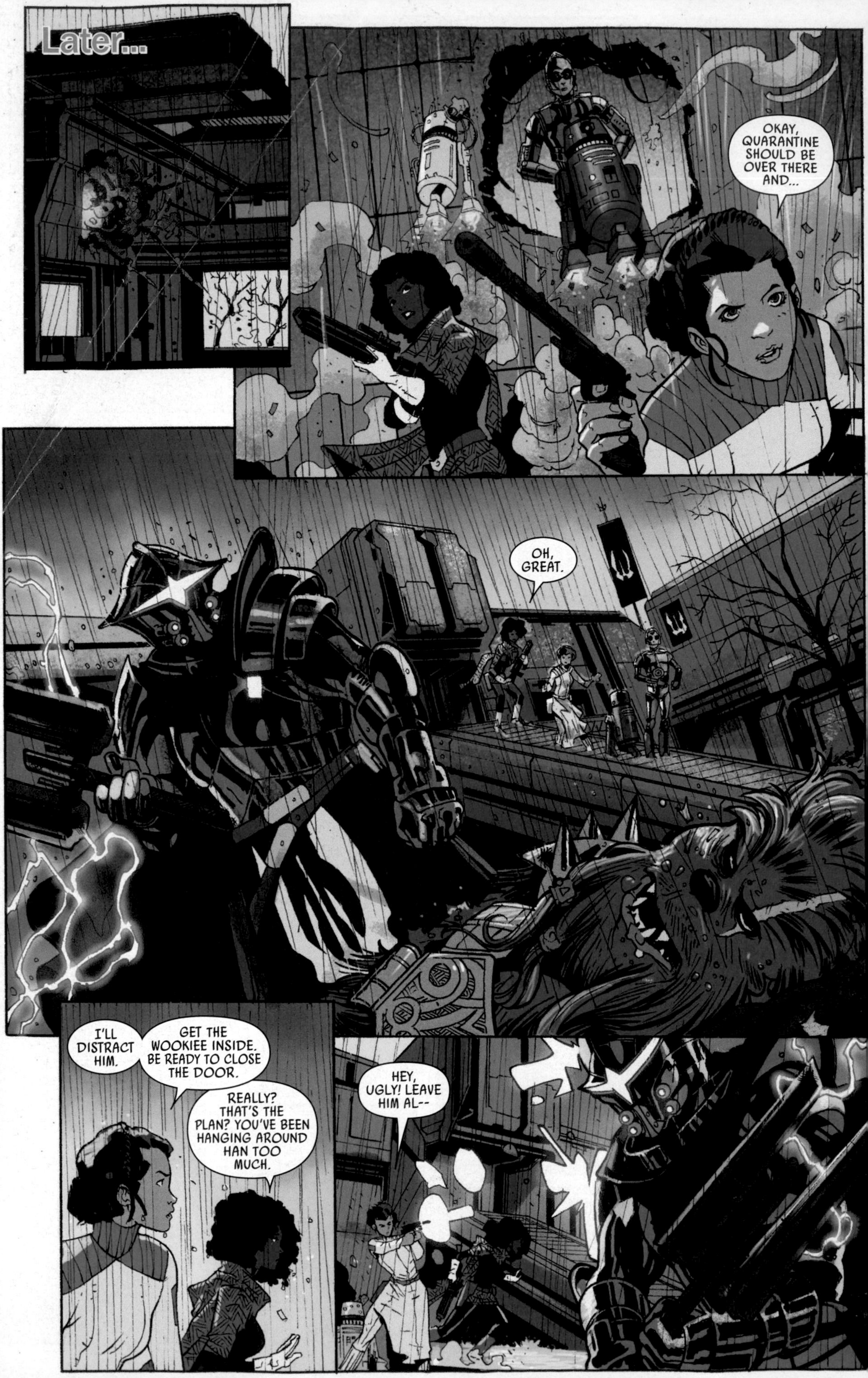
Later...
OKAY, QUARANTINE SHOULD BE OVER THERE AND...
OH, GREAT.
I'LL DISTRACT HIM.
GET THE WOOKIEE INSIDE. BE READY TO CLOSE THE DOOR.
REALLY? THAT'S THE PLAN? YOU'VE BEEN HANGING AROUND HAN TOO MUCH.
HEY, UGLY! LEAVE HIM AL--

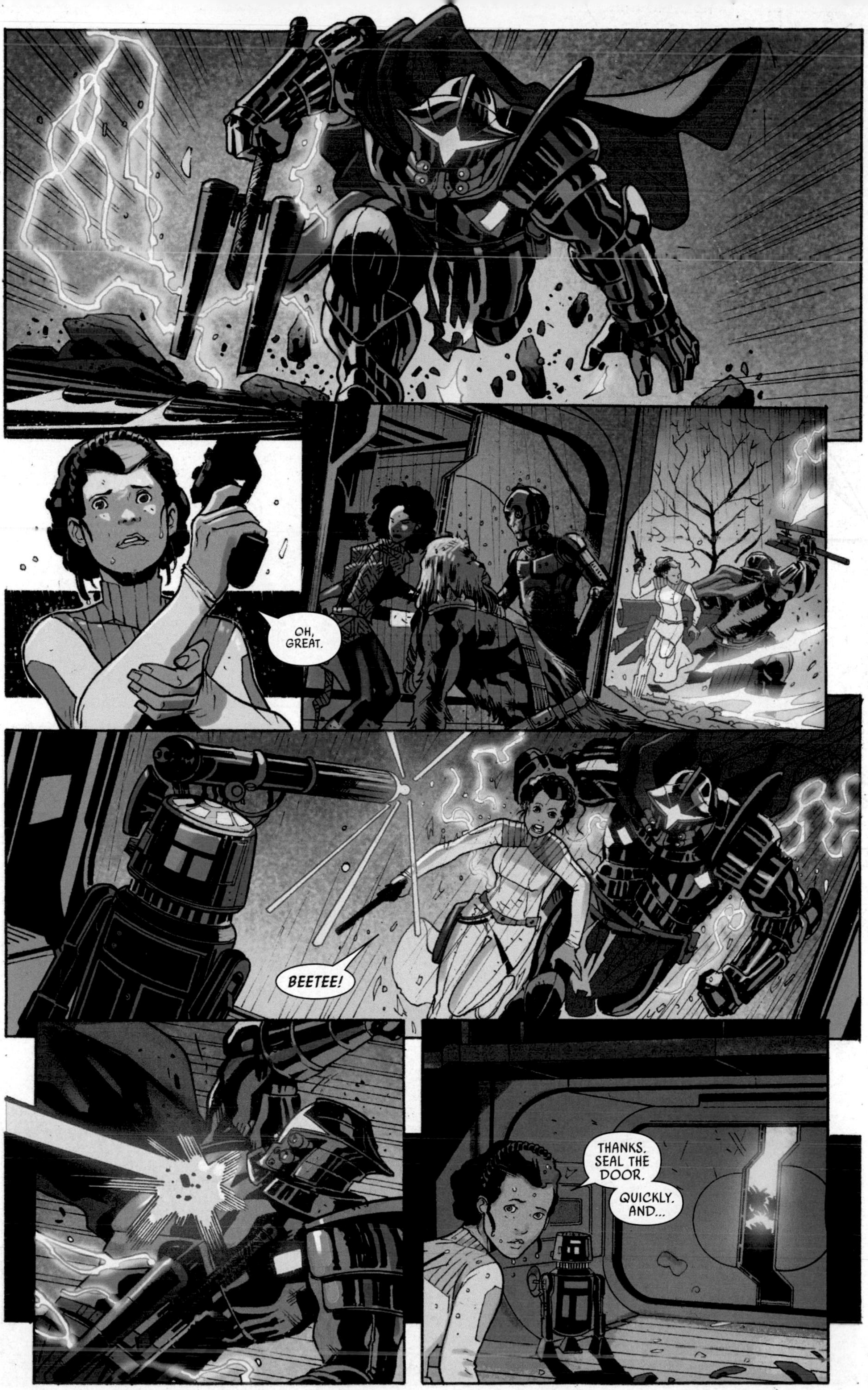
OH, GREAT.
BEETEE!
THANKS. SEAL THE DOOR.
QUICKLY. AND...

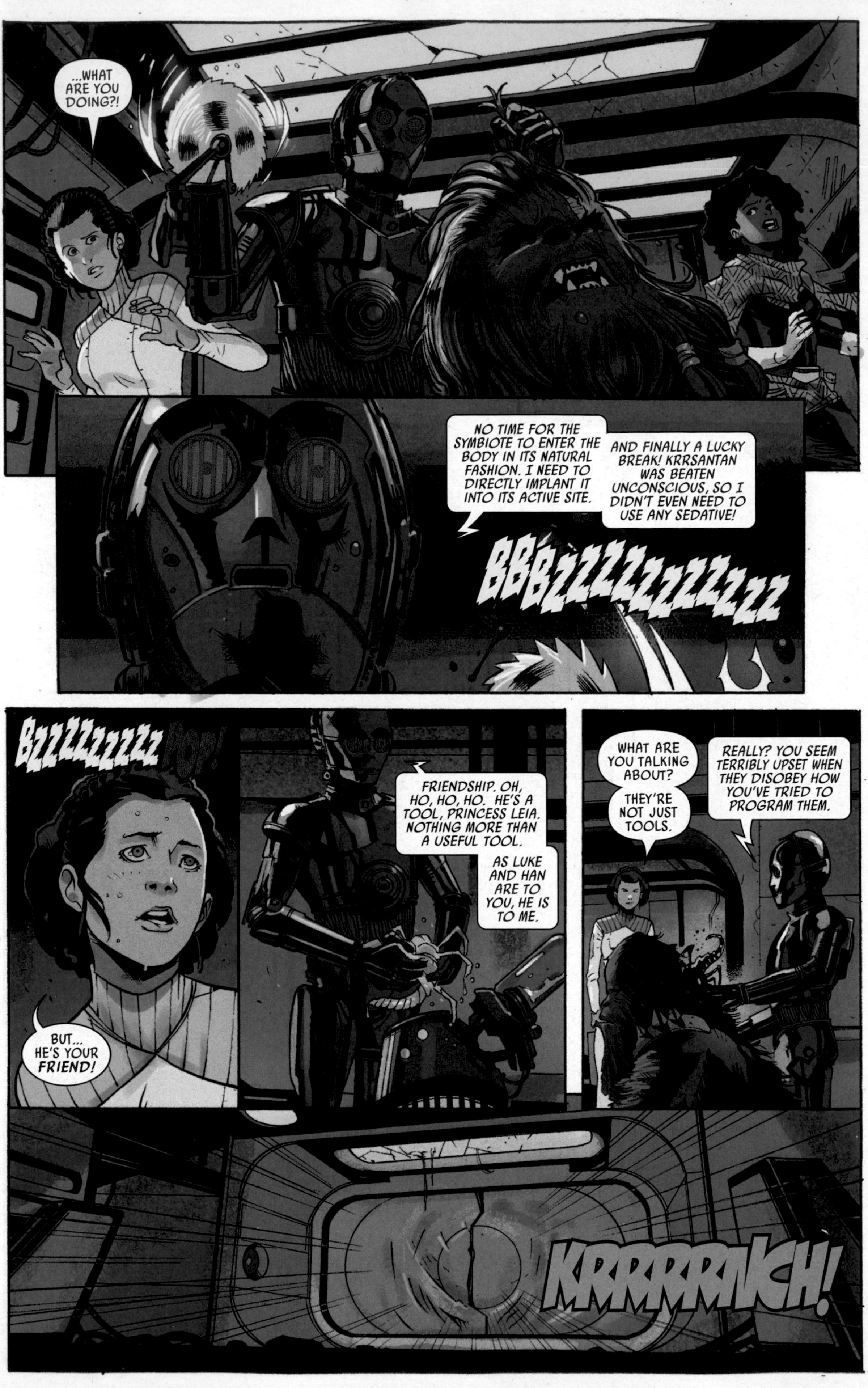
...WHAT ARE YOU DOING?!
NO TIME FOR THE SYMBIOTE TO ENTER THE BODY IN ITS NATURAL FASHION. I NEED TO DIRECTLY IMPLANT IT INTO ITS ACTIVE SITE.
AND FINALLY A LUCKY BREAK! KRRSANTAN WAS BEATEN UNCONSCIOUS, SO I DIDN'T EVEN NEED TO USE ANY SEDATIVE!
BBBZZZZZZZZZZZZ
BZZZZZZZZZ POP!
BUT... HE'S YOUR FRIEND!
FRIENDSHIP. OH, HO, HO, HO. HE'S A TOOL, PRINCESS LEIA. NOTHING MORE THAN A USEFUL TOOL.
AS LUKE AND HAN ARE TO YOU, HE IS TO ME.
WHAT ARE YOU TALKING ABOUT?
THEY'RE NOT JUST TOOLS.
REALLY? YOU SEEM TERRIBLY UPSET WHEN THEY DISOBEY HOW YOU'VE TRIED TO PROGRAM THEM.
KRRRRRNCH!

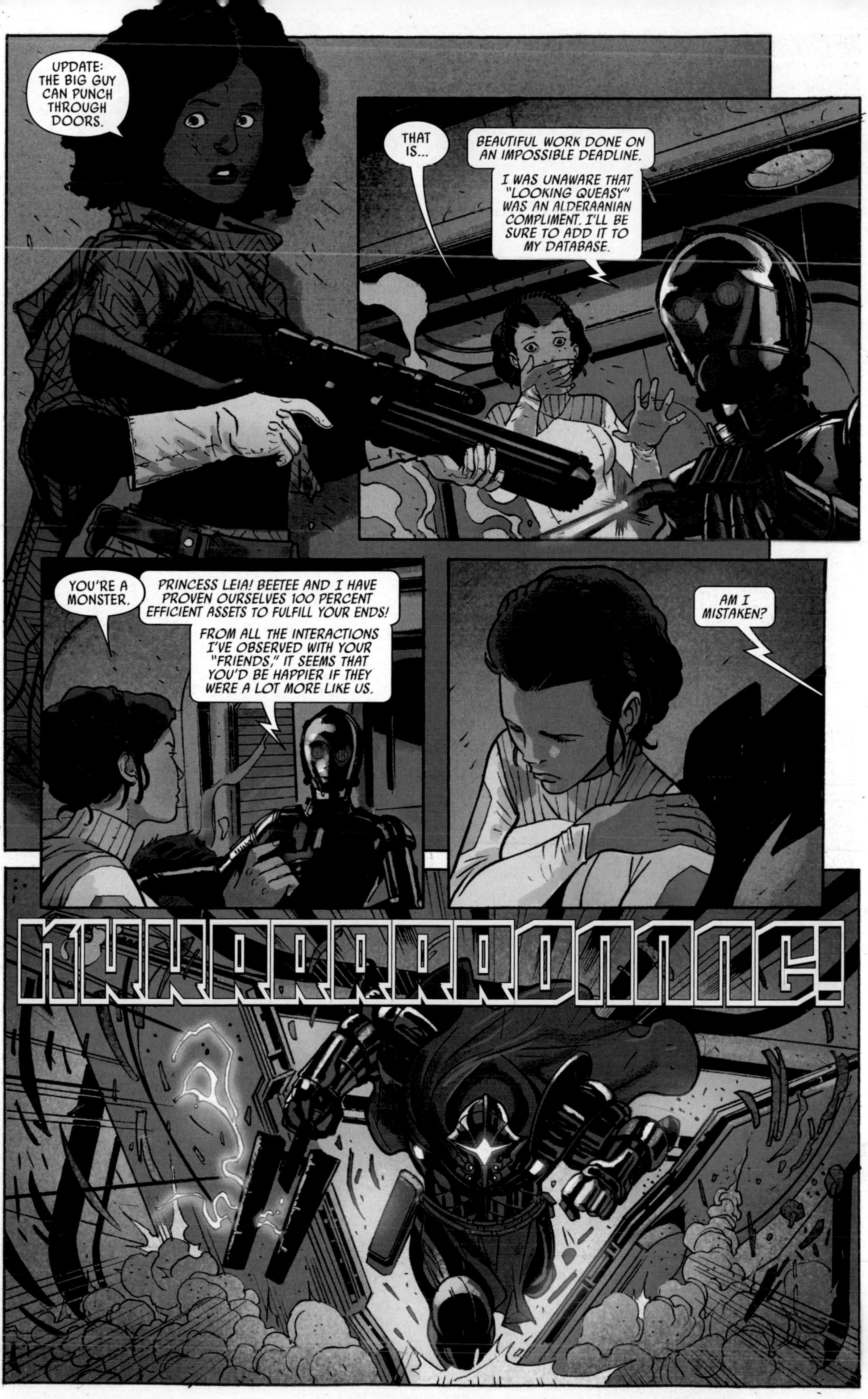
UPDATE: THE BIG GUY CAN PUNCH THROUGH DOORS.
THAT IS...
BEAUTIFUL WORK DONE ON AN IMPOSSIBLE DEADLINE.
I WAS UNAWARE THAT "LOOKING QUEASY" WAS AN ALDERAANIAN COMPLIMENT. I'LL BE SURE TO ADD IT TO MY DATABASE.
YOU'RE A MONSTER.
PRINCESS LEIA! BEETEE AND I HAVE PROVEN OURSELVES 100 PERCENT EFFICIENT ASSETS TO FULFILL YOUR ENDS!
FROM ALL THE INTERACTIONS I'VE OBSERVED WITH YOUR "FRIENDS," IT SEEMS THAT YOU'D BE HAPPIER IF THEY WERE A LOT MORE LIKE US.
AM I MISTAKEN?
KKKRRRRROOOOONG!

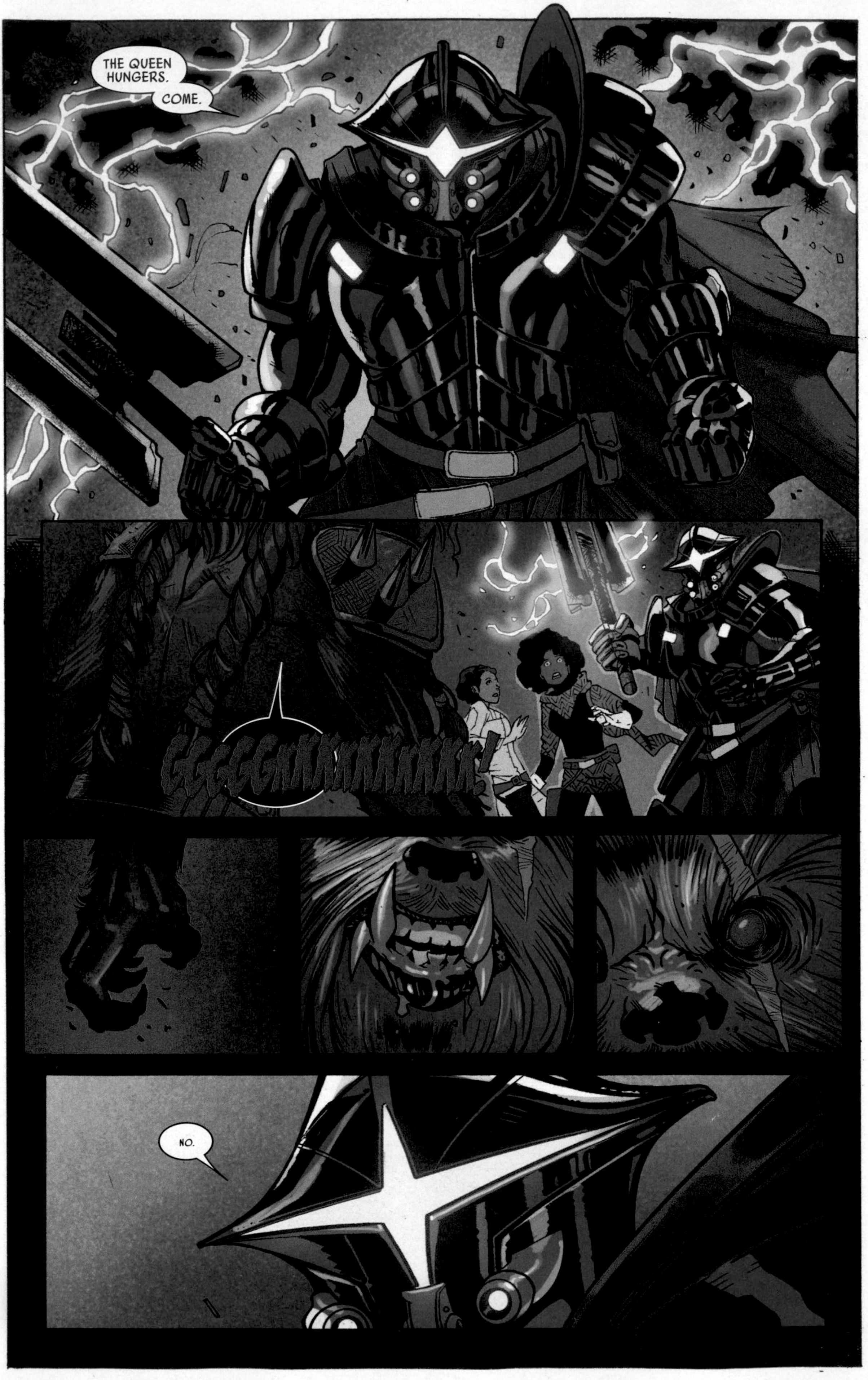
THE QUEEN HUNGERS.
COME.
GGGGGNKKKKKKKKKK!
NO.

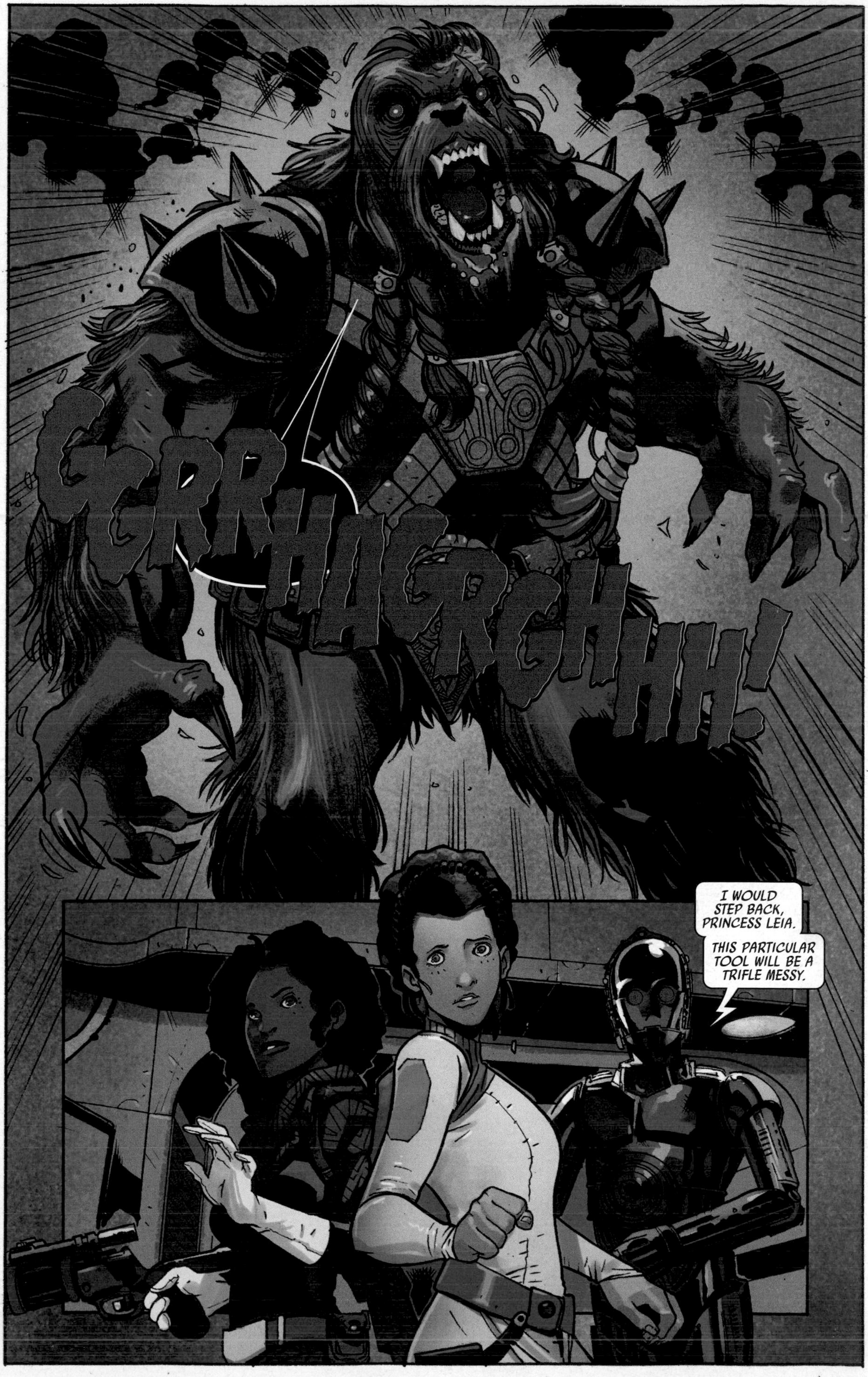
GGRRHAGRGHHH!
I WOULD STEP BACK, PRINCESS LEIA.
THIS PARTICULAR TOOL WILL BE A TRIFLE MESSY.

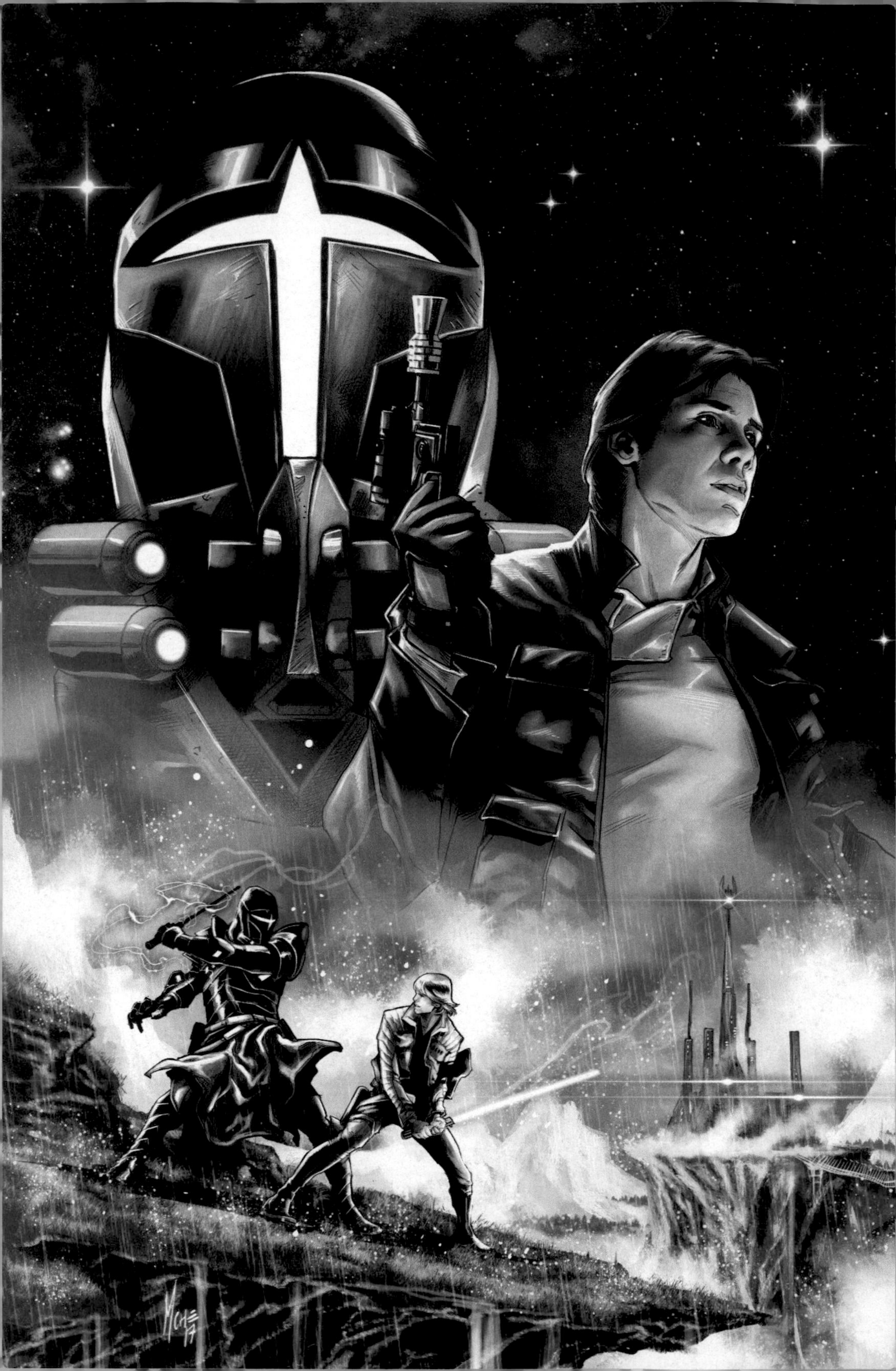

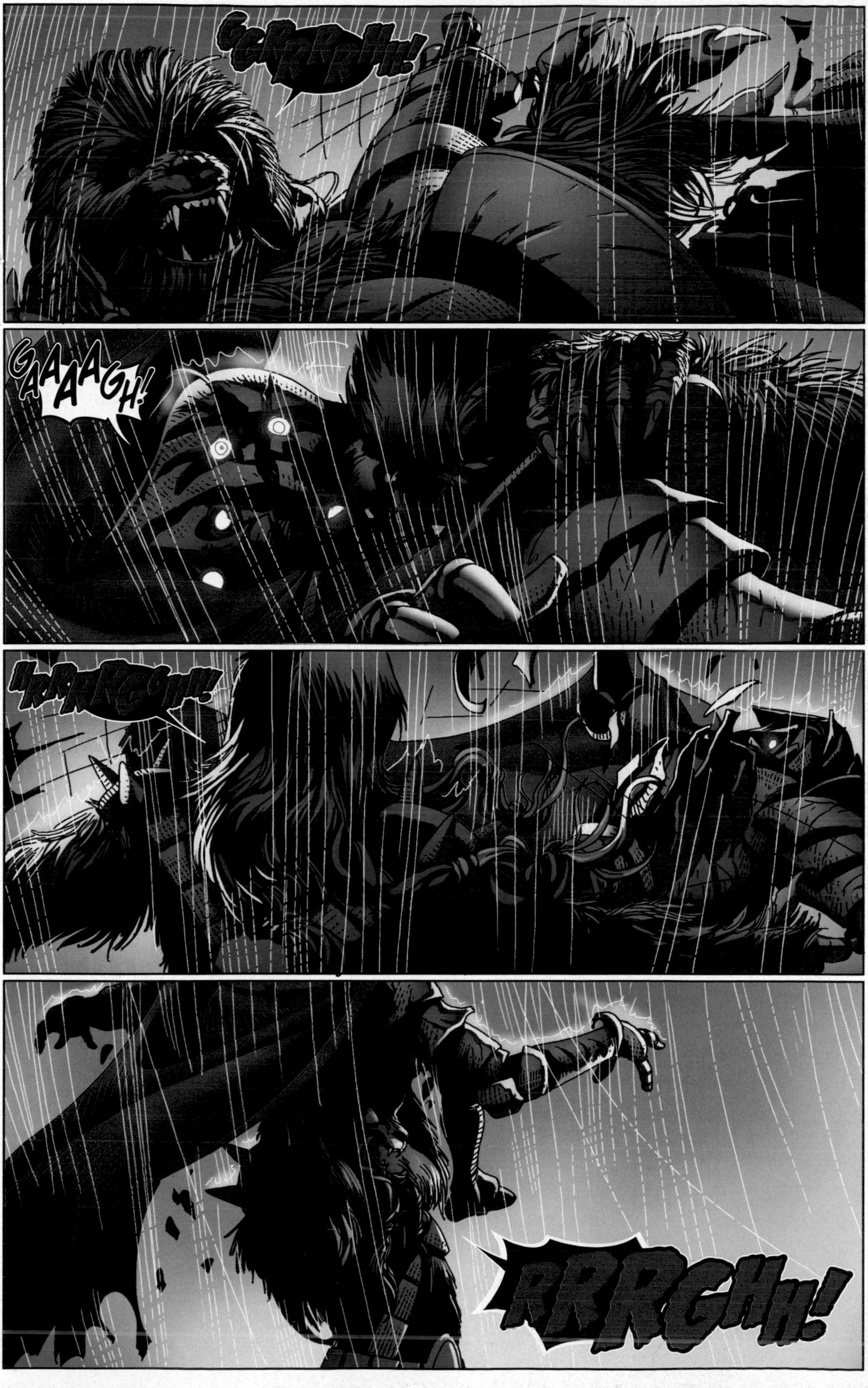
GGRRRRHH!
GAAAAGH!
HRRRRGGHH!
RRRGHH!

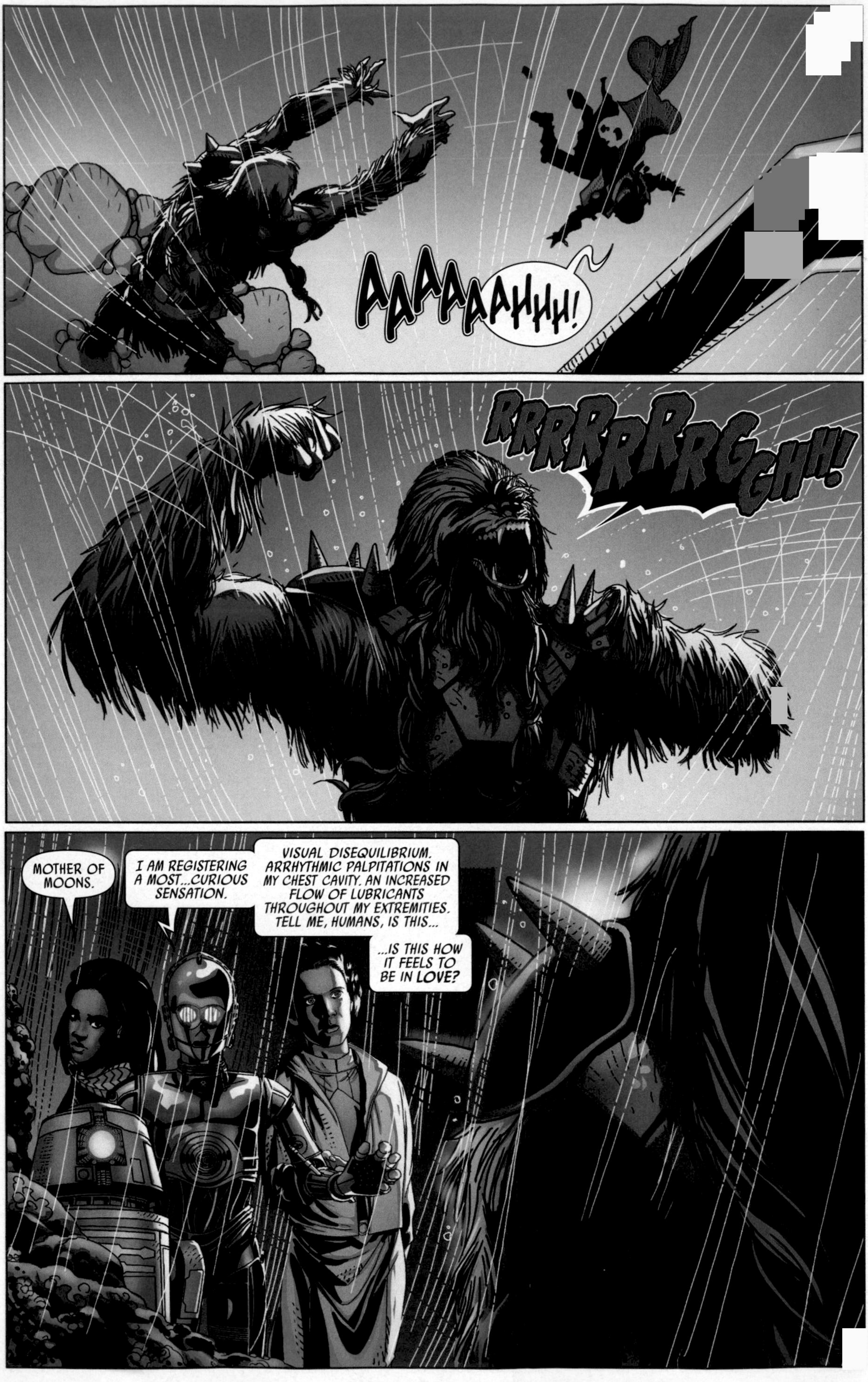
AAAAAAHHH!
RRRRRRRRGHH!
MOTHER OF MOONS.
I AM REGISTERING A MOST...CURIOUS SENSATION.
VISUAL DISEQUILIBRIUM. ARRHYTHMIC PALPITATIONS IN MY CHEST CAVITY. AN INCREASED FLOW OF LUBRICANTS THROUGHOUT MY EXTREMITIES. TELL ME, HUMANS, IS THIS...
...IS THIS HOW IT FEELS TO BE IN LOVE?

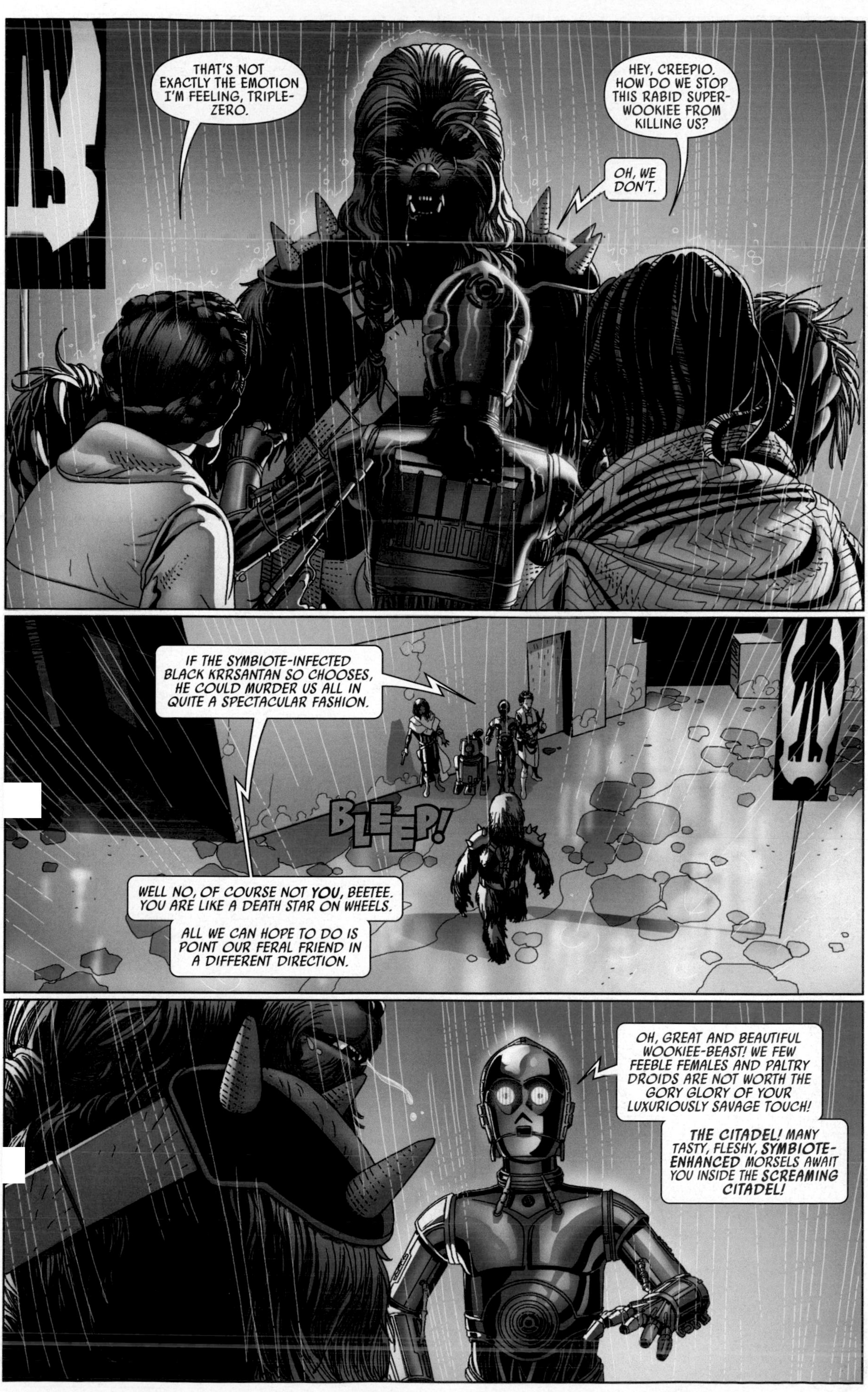
THAT'S NOT EXACTLY THE EMOTION I'M FEELING, TRIPLE-ZERO.
HEY, CREEPIO. HOW DO WE STOP THIS RABID SUPER-WOOKIEE FROM KILLING US?
OH, WE DON'T.
IF THE SYMBIOTE-INFECTED BLACK KRRSANTAN SO CHOOSES, HE COULD MURDER US ALL IN QUITE A SPECTACULAR FASHION.
BLEEP!
WELL NO, OF COURSE NOT YOU, BEETEE. YOU ARE LIKE A DEATH STAR ON WHEELS.
ALL WE CAN HOPE TO DO IS POINT OUR FERAL FRIEND IN A DIFFERENT DIRECTION.
OH, GREAT AND BEAUTIFUL WOOKIEE-BEAST! WE FEW FEEBLE FEMALES AND PALTRY DROIDS ARE NOT WORTH THE GORY GLORY OF YOUR LUXURIOUSLY SAVAGE TOUCH!
THE CITADEL! MANY TASTY, FLESHY, SYMBIOTE-ENHANCED MORSELS AWAIT YOU INSIDE THE SCREAMING CITADEL!

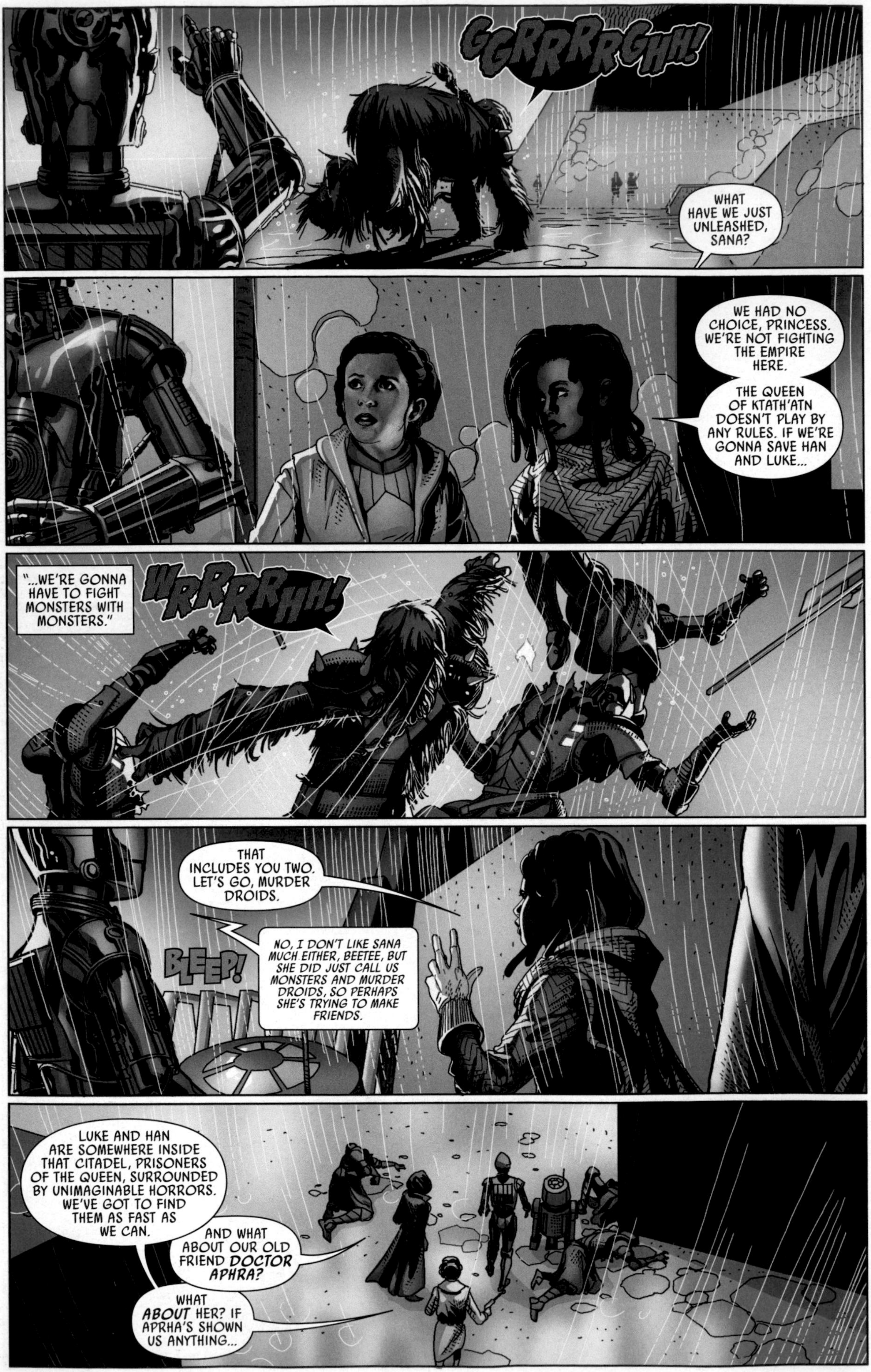
GGRRRRRGHH!
WHAT HAVE WE JUST UNLEASHED, SANA?
WE HAD NO CHOICE, PRINCESS. WE'RE NOT FIGHTING THE EMPIRE HERE.
THE QUEEN OF KTATH'ATN DOESN'T PLAY BY ANY RULES. IF WE'RE GONNA SAVE HAN AND LUKE...
"...WE'RE GONNA HAVE TO FIGHT MONSTERS WITH MONSTERS."
WRRRRHH!
THAT INCLUDES YOU TWO. LET'S GO, MURDER DROIDS.
BLEEP!
NO, I DON'T LIKE SANA MUCH EITHER, BEETEE, BUT SHE DID JUST CALL US MONSTERS AND MURDER DROIDS, SO PERHAPS SHE'S TRYING TO MAKE FRIENDS.
LUKE AND HAN ARE SOMEWHERE INSIDE THAT CITADEL, PRISONERS OF THE QUEEN, SURROUNDED BY UNIMAGINABLE HORRORS. WE'VE GOT TO FIND THEM AS FAST AS WE CAN.
AND WHAT ABOUT OUR OLD FRIEND DOCTOR APHRA?
WHAT ABOUT HER? IF APRHA'S SHOWN US ANYTHING...

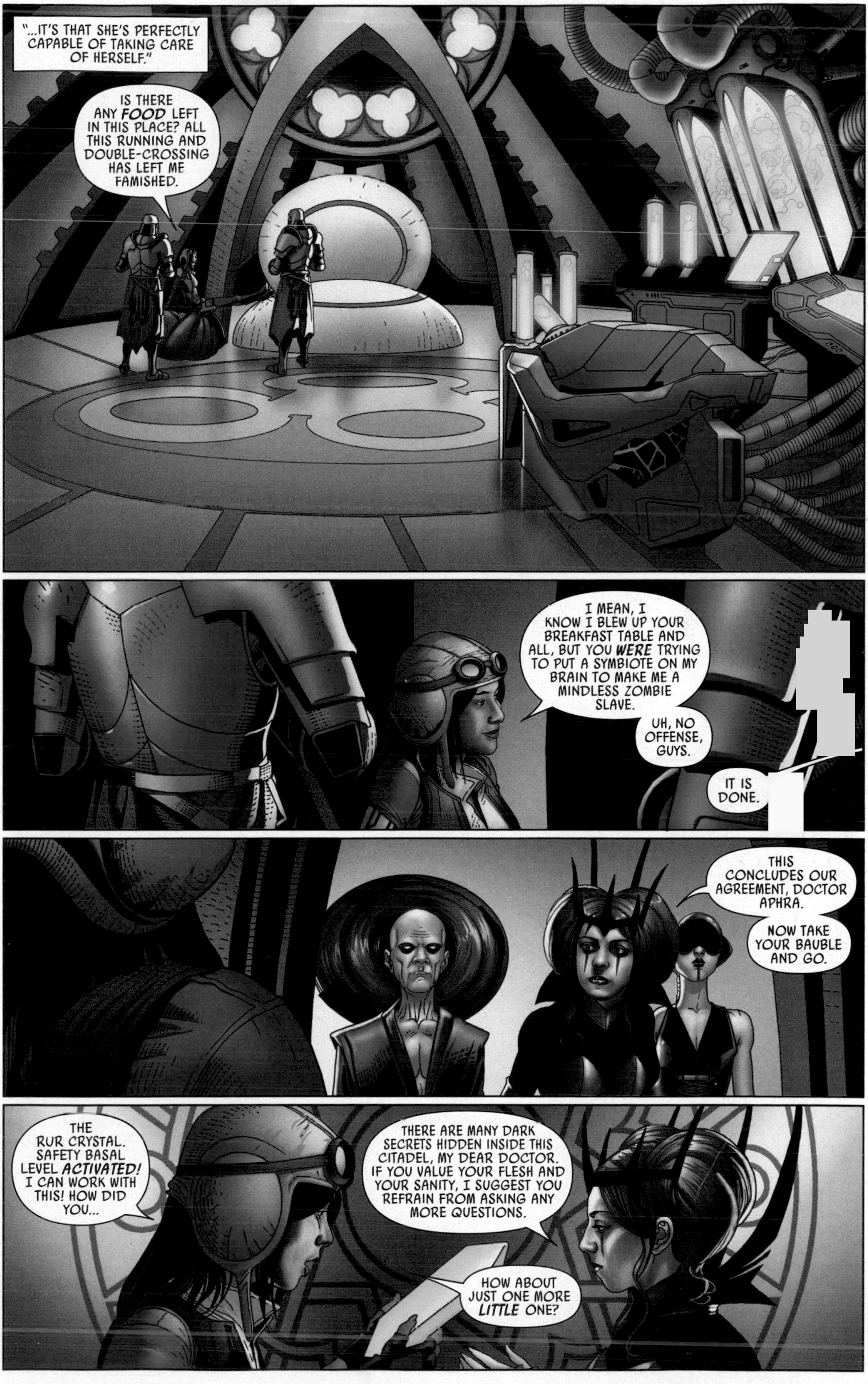
"...IT'S THAT SHE'S PERFECTLY CAPABLE OF TAKING CARE OF HERSELF."
IS THERE ANY FOOD LEFT IN THIS PLACE? ALL THIS RUNNING AND DOUBLE-CROSSING HAS LEFT ME FAMISHED.
I MEAN, I KNOW I BLEW UP YOUR BREAKFAST TABLE AND ALL, BUT YOU WERE TRYING TO PUT A SYMBIOTE ON MY BRAIN TO MAKE ME A MINDLESS ZOMBIE SLAVE.
UH, NO OFFENSE, GUYS.
IT IS DONE.
THIS CONCLUDES OUR AGREEMENT, DOCTOR APHRA.
NOW TAKE YOUR BAUBLE AND GO.
THE RUR CRYSTAL. SAFETY BASAL LEVEL ACTIVATED! I CAN WORK WITH THIS! HOW DID YOU...
THERE ARE MANY DARK SECRETS HIDDEN INSIDE THIS CITADEL, MY DEAR DOCTOR. IF YOU VALUE YOUR FLESH AND YOUR SANITY, I SUGGEST YOU REFRAIN FROM ASKING ANY MORE QUESTIONS.
HOW ABOUT JUST ONE MORE LITTLE ONE?

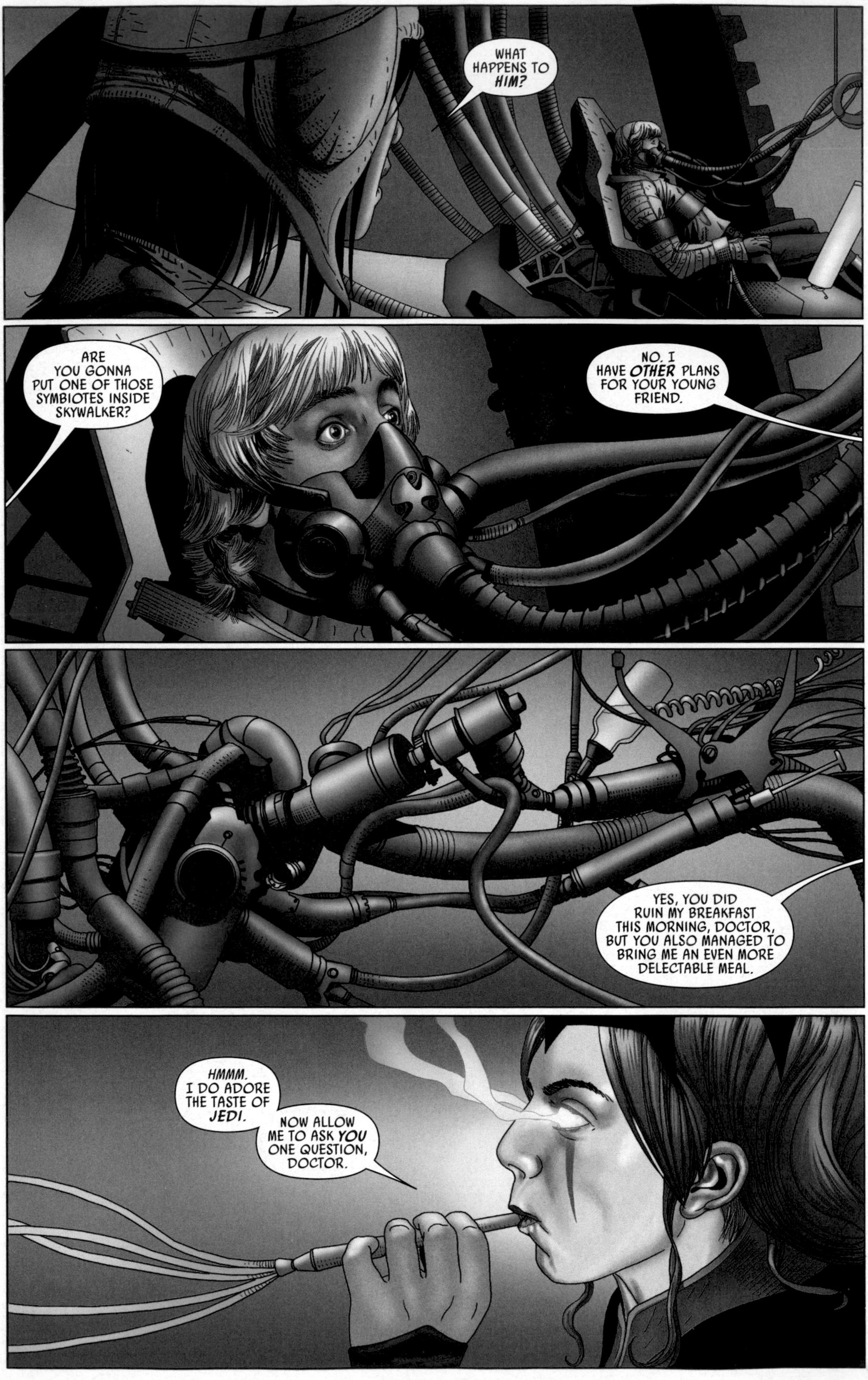
WHAT HAPPENS TO HIM?
ARE YOU GONNA PUT ONE OF THOSE SYMBIOTES INSIDE SKYWALKER?
NO. I HAVE OTHER PLANS FOR YOUR YOUNG FRIEND.
YES, YOU DID RUIN MY BREAKFAST THIS MORNING, DOCTOR, BUT YOU ALSO MANAGED TO BRING ME AN EVEN MORE DELECTABLE MEAL.
HMMM. I DO ADORE THE TASTE OF JEDI.
NOW ALLOW ME TO ASK YOU ONE QUESTION, DOCTOR.

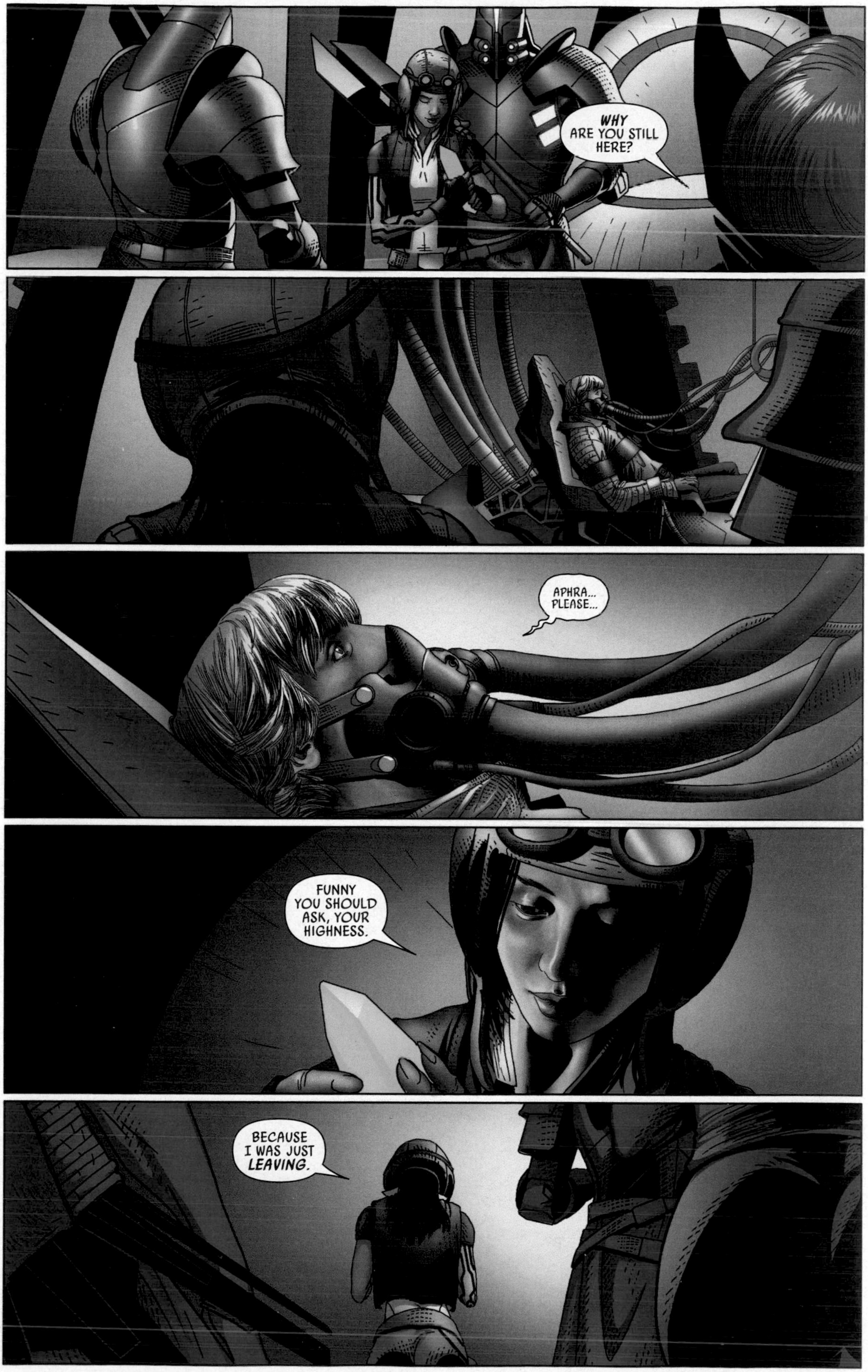
WHY ARE YOU STILL HERE?
APHRA... PLEASE...
FUNNY YOU SHOULD ASK, YOUR HIGHNESS.
BECAUSE I WAS JUST LEAVING.

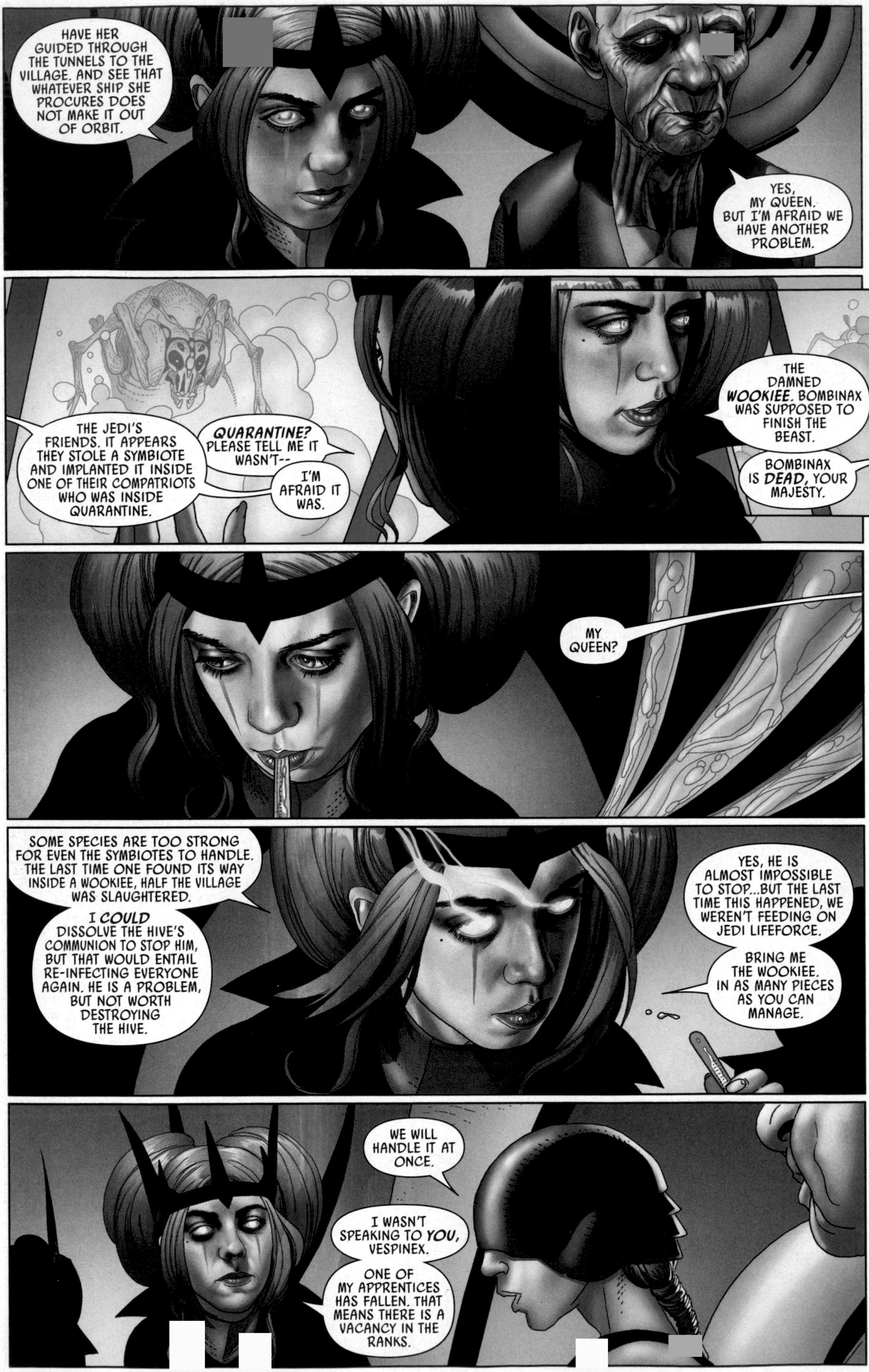
HAVE HER GUIDED THROUGH THE TUNNELS TO THE VILLAGE. AND SEE THAT WHATEVER SHIP SHE PROCURES DOES NOT MAKE IT OUT OF ORBIT.
YES, MY QUEEN. BUT I'M AFRAID WE HAVE ANOTHER PROBLEM.
THE JEDI'S FRIENDS. IT APPEARS THEY STOLE A SYMBIOTE AND IMPLANTED IT INSIDE ONE OF THEIR COMPATRIOTS WHO WAS INSIDE QUARANTINE.
QUARANTINE? PLEASE TELL ME IT WASN'T--
I'M AFRAID IT WAS.
THE DAMNED WOOKIEE. BOMBINAX WAS SUPPOSED TO FINISH THE BEAST.
BOMBINAX IS DEAD, YOUR MAJESTY.
MY QUEEN?
SOME SPECIES ARE TOO STRONG FOR EVEN THE SYMBIOTES TO HANDLE. THE LAST TIME ONE FOUND ITS WAY INSIDE A WOOKIEE, HALF THE VILLAGE WAS SLAUGHTERED.
I COULD DISSOLVE THE HIVE'S COMMUNION TO STOP HIM, BUT THAT WOULD ENTAIL RE-INFECTING EVERYONE AGAIN. HE IS A PROBLEM, BUT NOT WORTH DESTROYING THE HIVE.
YES, HE IS ALMOST IMPOSSIBLE TO STOP...BUT THE LAST TIME THIS HAPPENED, WE WEREN'T FEEDING ON JEDI LIFEFORCE.
BRING ME THE WOOKIEE. IN AS MANY PIECES AS YOU CAN MANAGE.
WE WILL HANDLE IT AT ONCE.
I WASN'T SPEAKING TO YOU, VESPINEX.
ONE OF MY APPRENTICES HAS FALLEN. THAT MEANS THERE IS A VACANCY IN THE RANKS.

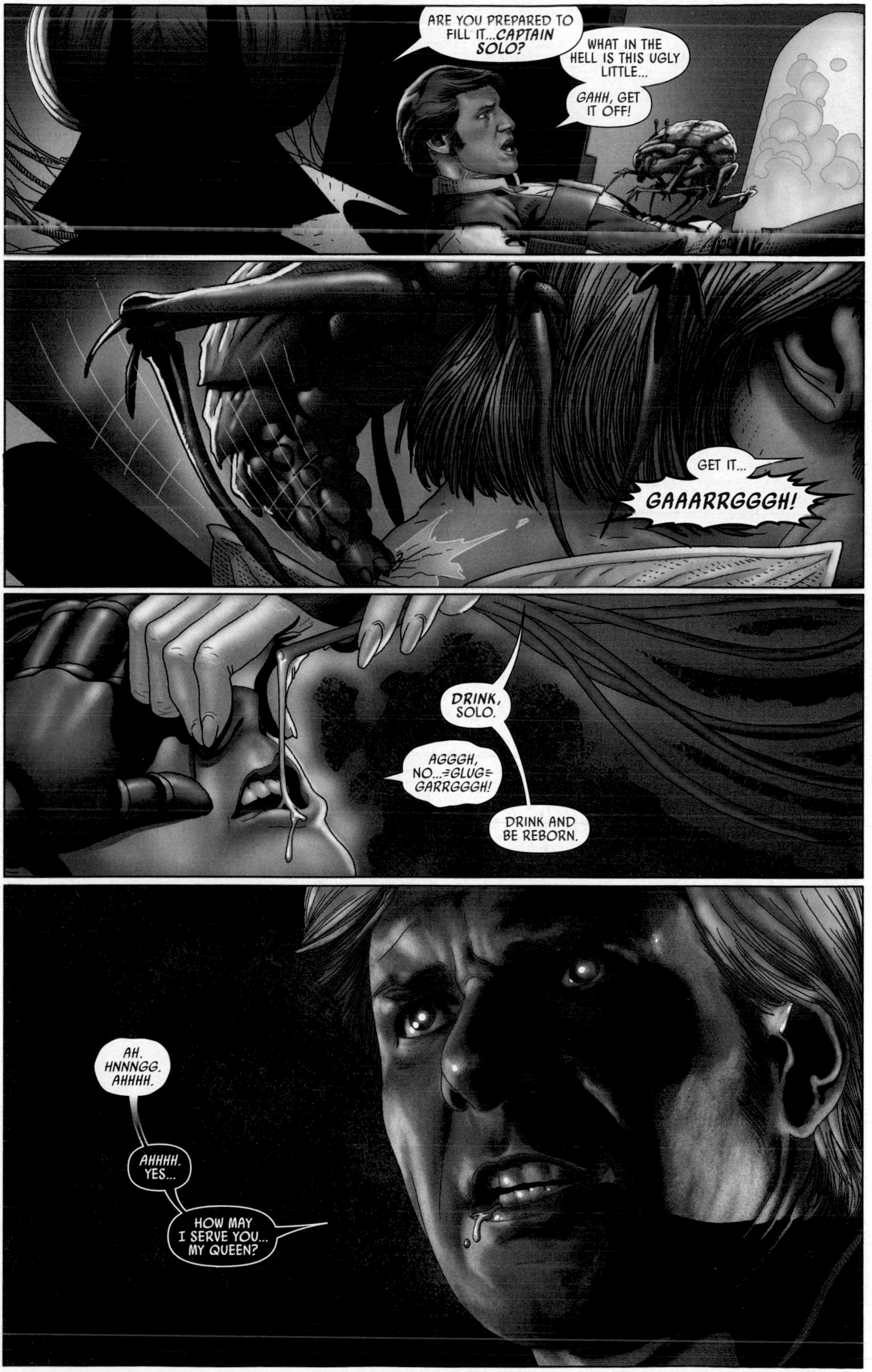
ARE YOU PREPARED TO FILL IT...CAPTAIN SOLO?
WHAT IN THE HELL IS THIS UGLY LITTLE...
GAHH, GET IT OFF!
GET IT...
GAAARRGGGH!
DRINK, SOLO.
AGGGH, NO...=GLUG= GARRGGGH!
DRINK AND BE REBORN.
AH. HNNNGG. AHHHH.
AHHHH. YES...
HOW MAY I SERVE YOU... MY QUEEN?

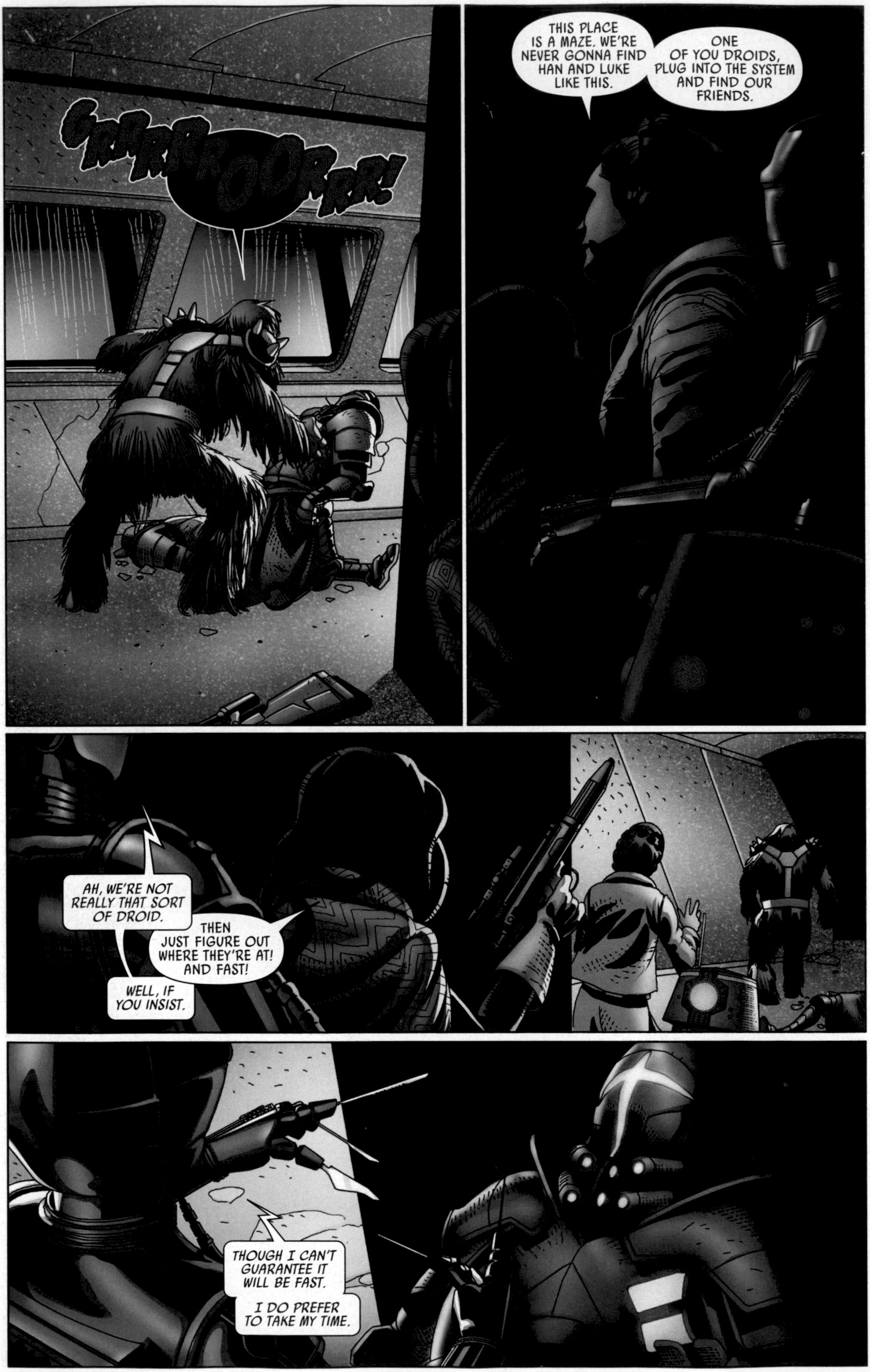
GRRRRROOORRR!
THIS PLACE IS A MAZE. WE'RE NEVER GONNA FIND HAN AND LUKE LIKE THIS.
ONE OF YOU DROIDS, PLUG INTO THE SYSTEM AND FIND OUR FRIENDS.
AH, WE'RE NOT REALLY THAT SORT OF DROID.
THEN JUST FIGURE OUT WHERE THEY'RE AT! AND FAST!
WELL, IF YOU INSIST.
THOUGH I CAN'T GUARANTEE IT WILL BE FAST.
I DO PREFER TO TAKE MY TIME.

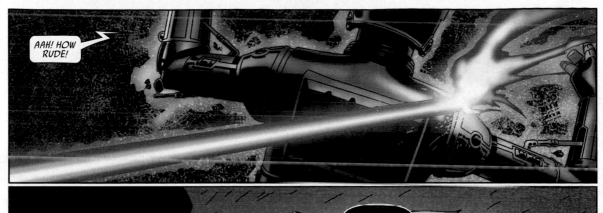

AAH! HOW RUDE!

DESTROY THE DROIDS.

BRING THE WOMEN TO ME.

HAN?

AH, IT APPEARS I FOUND ONE.

OH, NO. HE'S BEEN INFECTED.

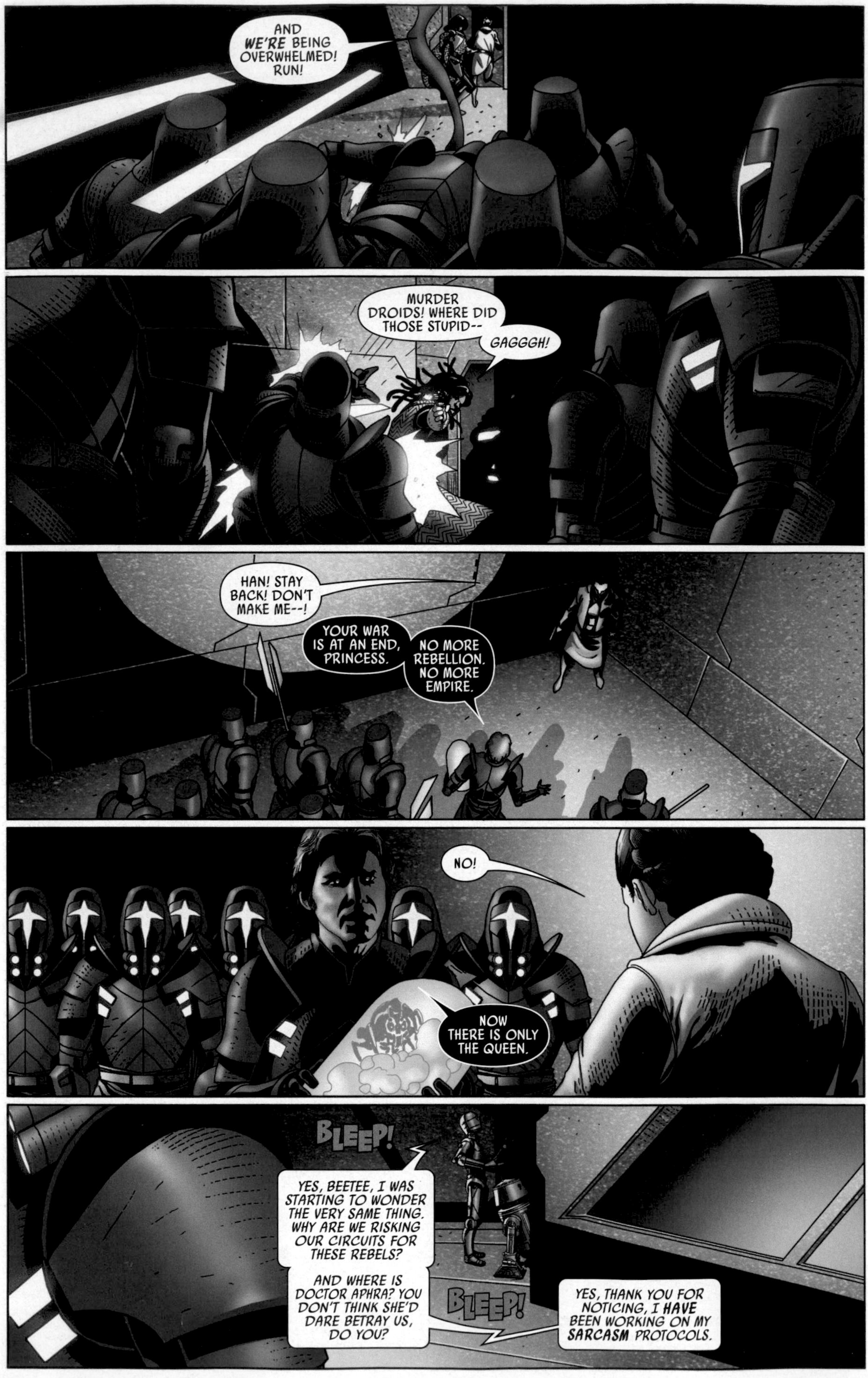
AND WE'RE BEING OVERWHELMED! RUN!
MURDER DROIDS! WHERE DID THOSE STUPID--
GAGGGH!
HAN! STAY BACK! DON'T MAKE ME--!
YOUR WAR IS AT AN END, PRINCESS.
NO MORE REBELLION. NO MORE EMPIRE.
NO!
NOW THERE IS ONLY THE QUEEN.
BLEEP!
YES, BEETEE, I WAS STARTING TO WONDER THE VERY SAME THING. WHY ARE WE RISKING OUR CIRCUITS FOR THESE REBELS?
AND WHERE IS DOCTOR APHRA? YOU DON'T THINK SHE'D DARE BETRAY US, DO YOU?
BLEEP!
YES, THANK YOU FOR NOTICING, I HAVE BEEN WORKING ON MY SARCASM PROTOCOLS.

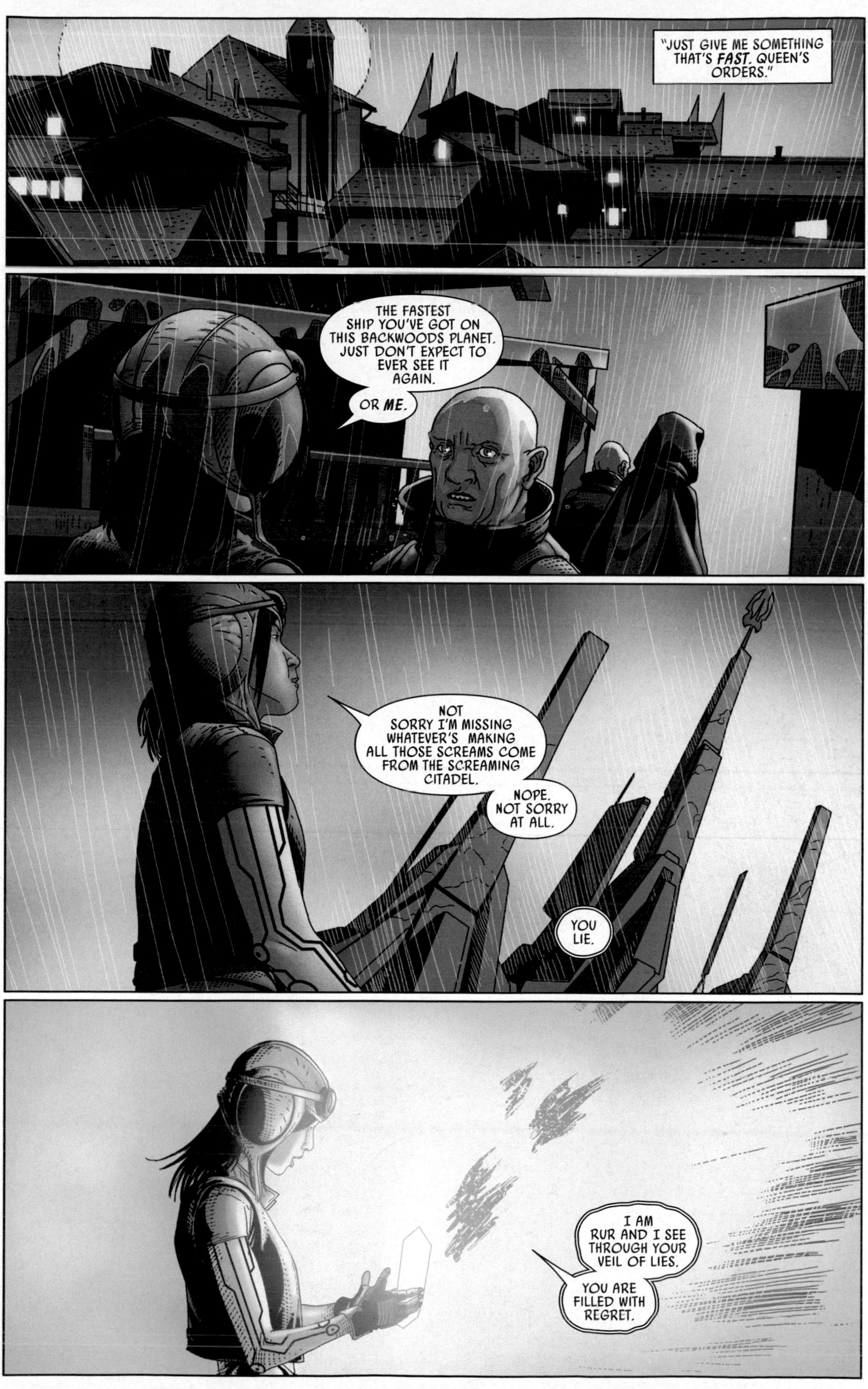
"JUST GIVE ME SOMETHING THAT'S FAST. QUEEN'S ORDERS."
THE FASTEST SHIP YOU'VE GOT ON THIS BACKWOODS PLANET. JUST DON'T EXPECT TO EVER SEE IT AGAIN.
OR ME.
NOT SORRY I'M MISSING WHATEVER'S MAKING ALL THOSE SCREAMS COME FROM THE SCREAMING CITADEL.
NOPE. NOT SORRY AT ALL.
YOU LIE.
I AM RUR AND I SEE THROUGH YOUR VEIL OF LIES.
YOU ARE FILLED WITH REGRET.

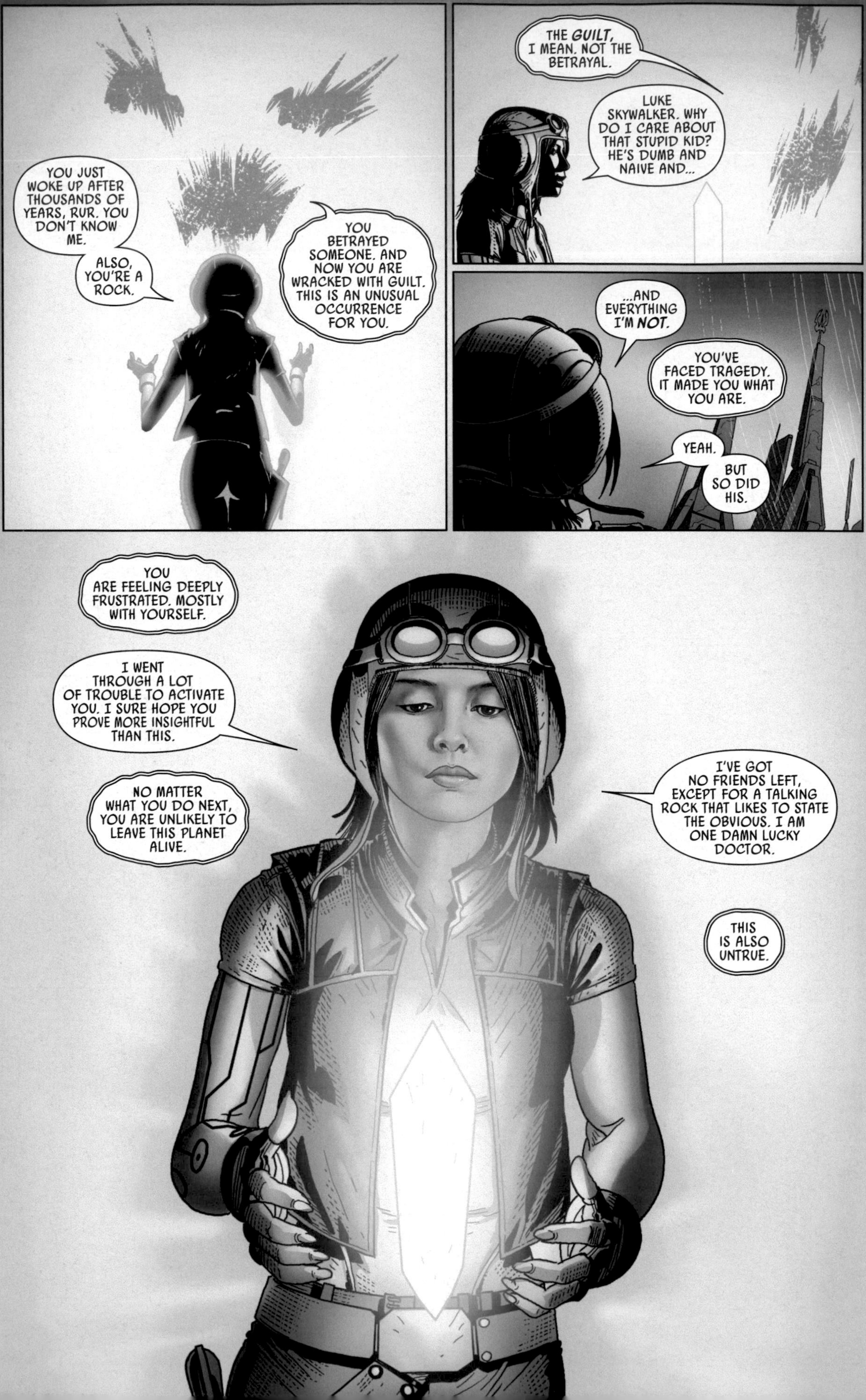
YOU JUST WOKE UP AFTER THOUSANDS OF YEARS, RUR. YOU DON'T KNOW ME.
ALSO, YOU'RE A ROCK.
YOU BETRAYED SOMEONE. AND NOW YOU ARE WRACKED WITH GUILT. THIS IS AN UNUSUAL OCCURRENCE FOR YOU.
THE *GUILT*, I MEAN. NOT THE BETRAYAL.
LUKE SKYWALKER. WHY DO I CARE ABOUT THAT STUPID KID? HE'S DUMB AND NAIVE AND...
...AND EVERYTHING I'M *NOT*.
YOU'VE FACED TRAGEDY. IT MADE YOU WHAT YOU ARE.
YEAH.
BUT SO DID HIS.
YOU ARE FEELING DEEPLY FRUSTRATED. MOSTLY WITH YOURSELF.
I WENT THROUGH A LOT OF TROUBLE TO ACTIVATE YOU. I SURE HOPE YOU PROVE MORE INSIGHTFUL THAN THIS.
NO MATTER WHAT YOU DO NEXT, YOU ARE UNLIKELY TO LEAVE THIS PLANET ALIVE.
I'VE GOT NO FRIENDS LEFT, EXCEPT FOR A TALKING ROCK THAT LIKES TO STATE THE OBVIOUS. I AM ONE DAMN LUCKY DOCTOR.
THIS IS ALSO UNTRUE.

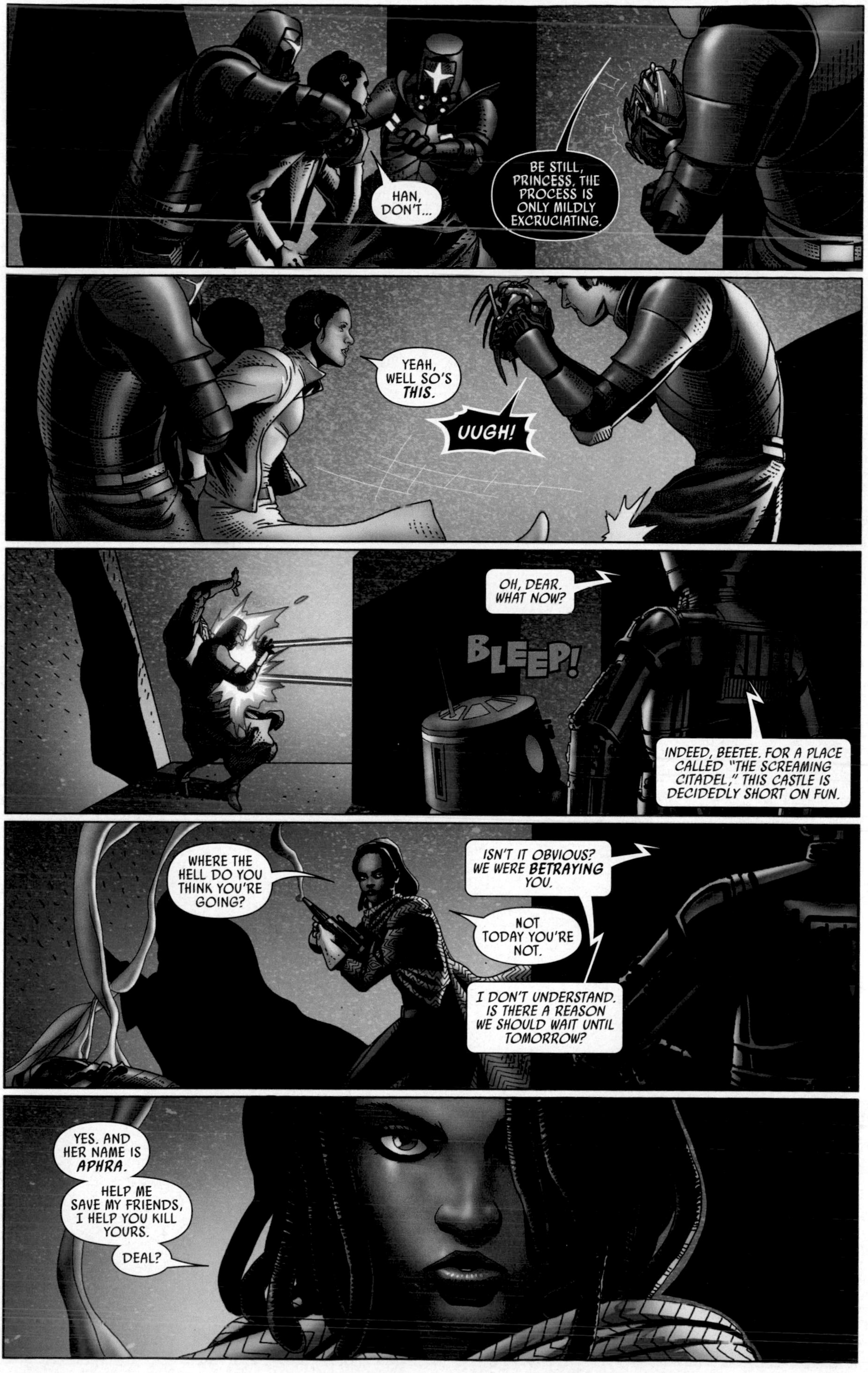
HAN, DON'T...
BE STILL, PRINCESS, THE PROCESS IS ONLY MILDLY EXCRUCIATING.
YEAH, WELL SO'S THIS.
UUGH!
OH, DEAR. WHAT NOW?
BLEEP!
INDEED, BEETEE. FOR A PLACE CALLED "THE SCREAMING CITADEL," THIS CASTLE IS DECIDEDLY SHORT ON FUN.
WHERE THE HELL DO YOU THINK YOU'RE GOING?
ISN'T IT OBVIOUS? WE WERE BETRAYING YOU.
NOT TODAY YOU'RE NOT.
I DON'T UNDERSTAND. IS THERE A REASON WE SHOULD WAIT UNTIL TOMORROW?
YES. AND HER NAME IS APHRA.
HELP ME SAVE MY FRIENDS, I HELP YOU KILL YOURS.
DEAL?

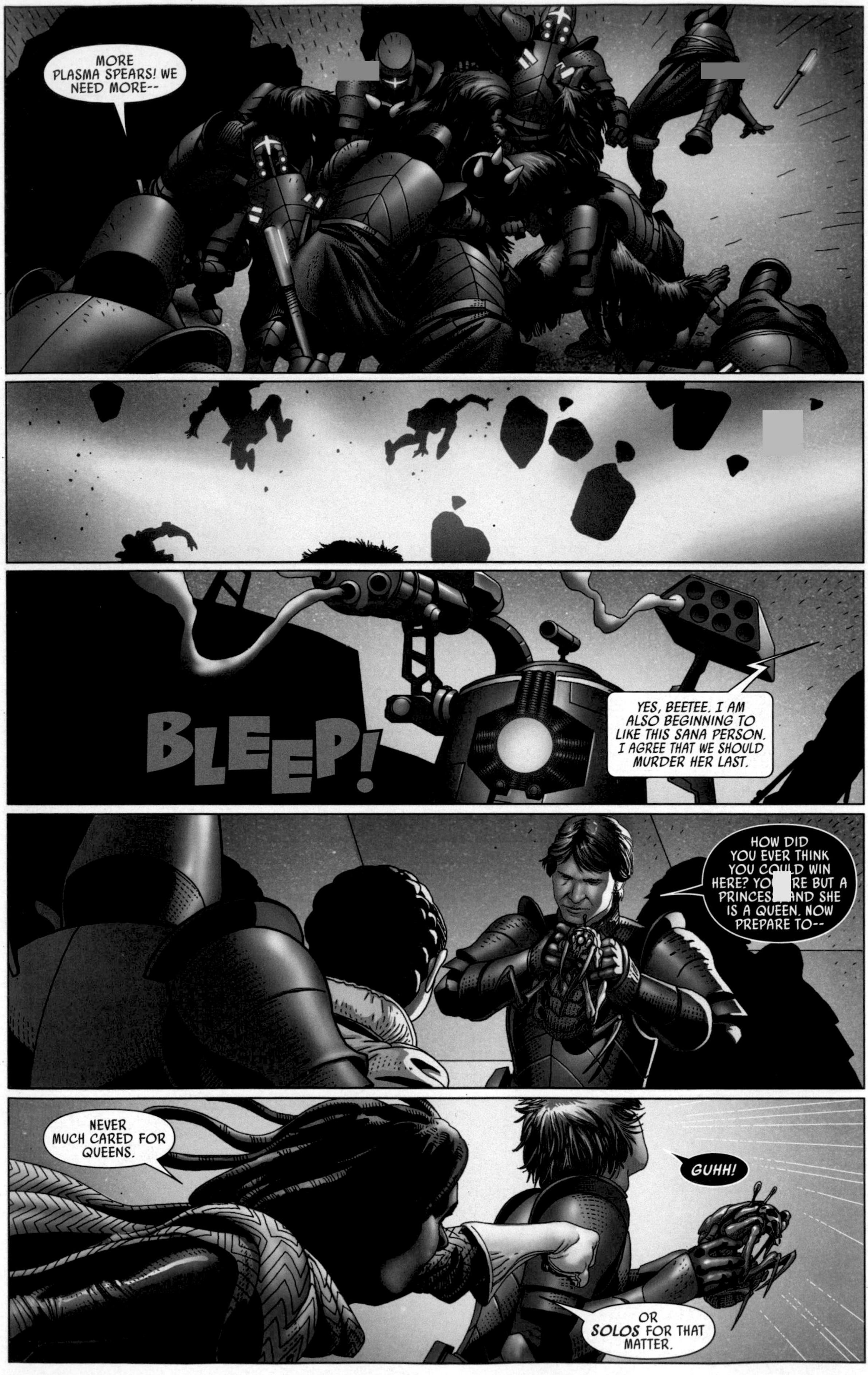
MORE PLASMA SPEARS! WE NEED MORE--
BLEEP!
YES, BEETEE. I AM ALSO BEGINNING TO LIKE THIS SANA PERSON. I AGREE THAT WE SHOULD MURDER HER LAST.
HOW DID YOU EVER THINK YOU COULD WIN HERE? YO RE BUT A PRINCES AND SHE IS A QUEEN. NOW PREPARE TO--
NEVER MUCH CARED FOR QUEENS.
GUHH!
OR SOLOS FOR THAT MATTER.

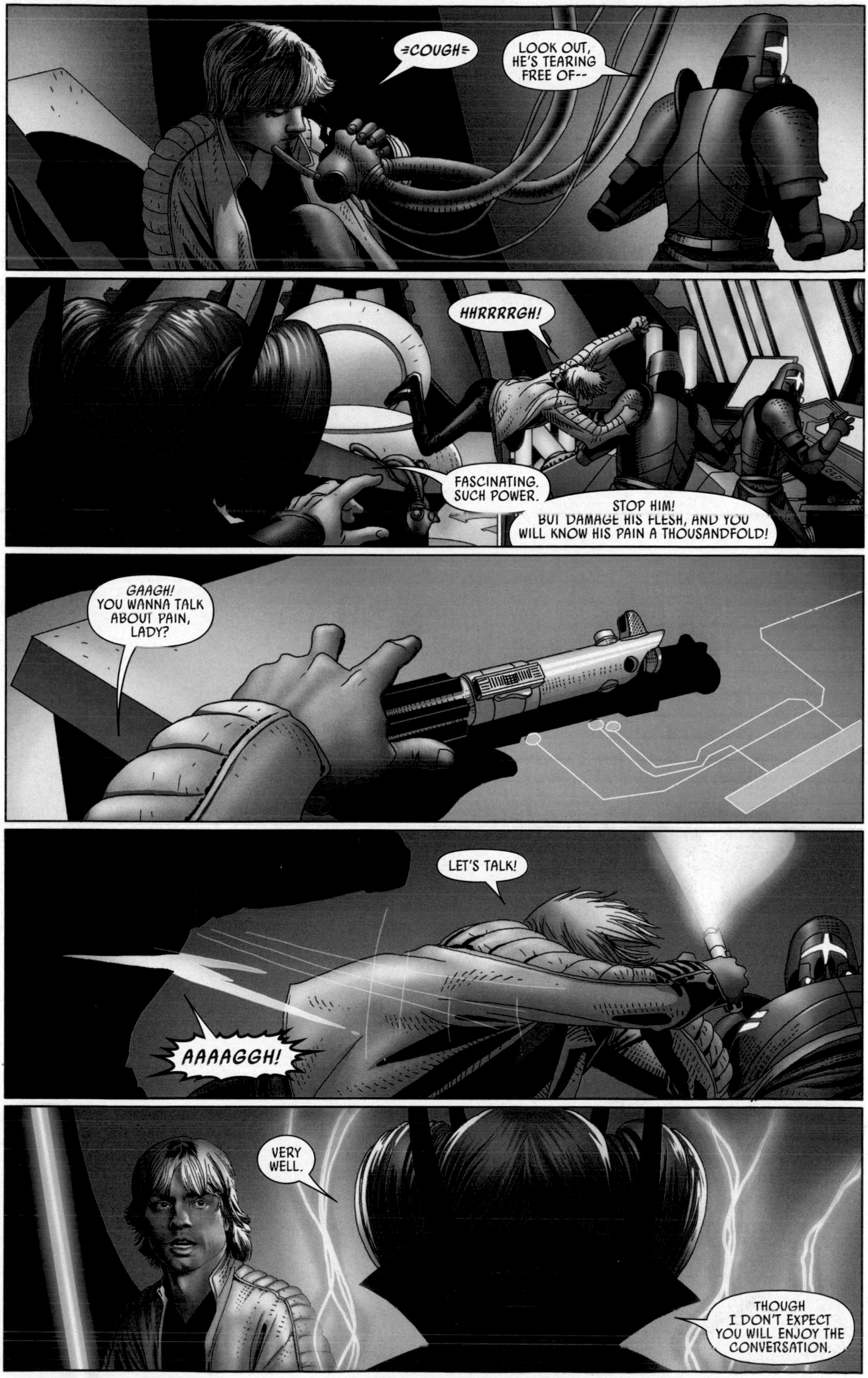

=COUGH=
LOOK OUT, HE'S TEARING FREE OF--
HHRRRRGH!
FASCINATING. SUCH POWER.
STOP HIM! BUT DAMAGE HIS FLESH, AND YOU WILL KNOW HIS PAIN A THOUSANDFOLD!
GAAGH! YOU WANNA TALK ABOUT PAIN, LADY?
LET'S TALK!
AAAAGGH!
VERY WELL.
THOUGH I DON'T EXPECT YOU WILL ENJOY THE CONVERSATION.

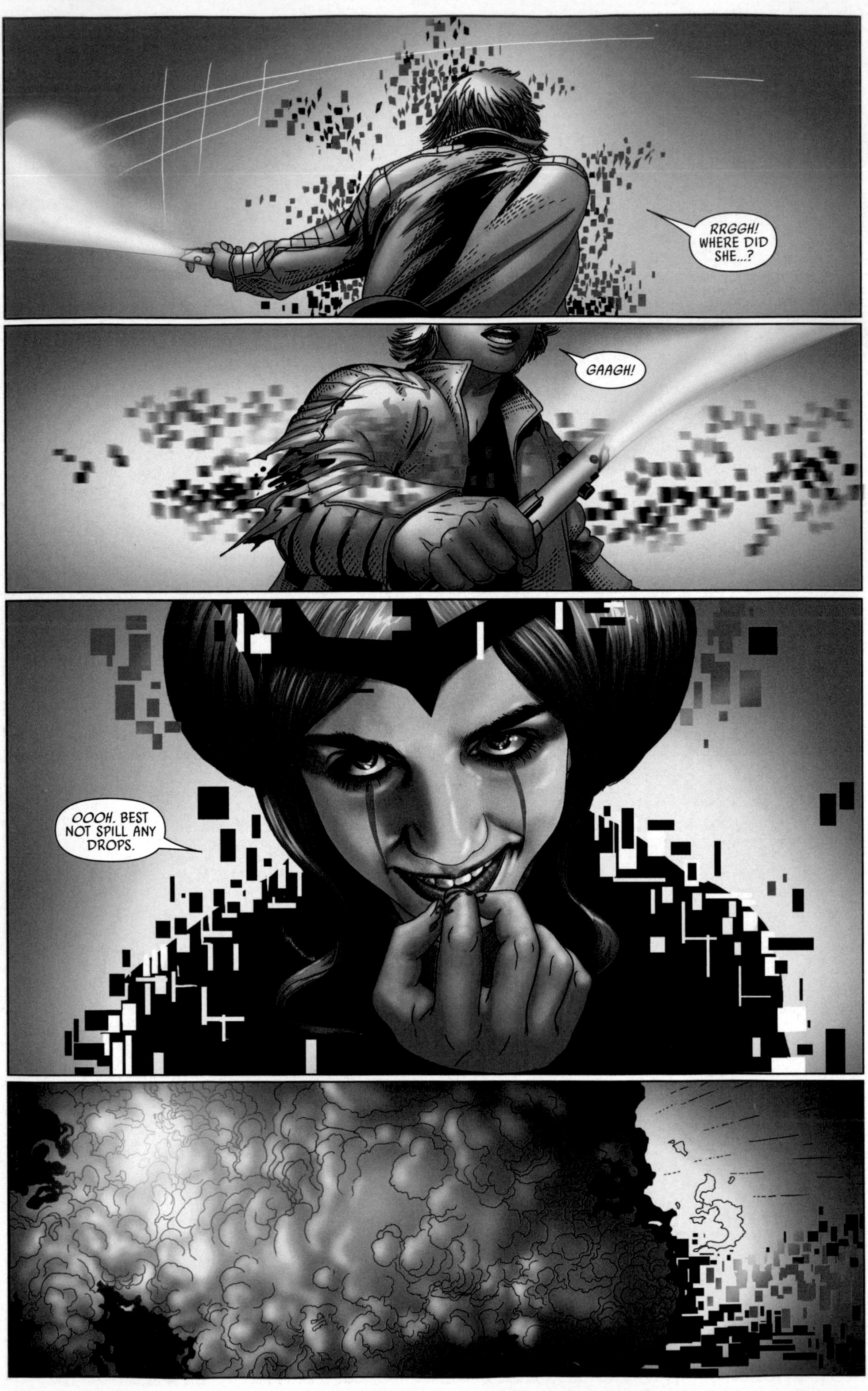
RRGGH! WHERE DID SHE...?
GAAGH!
OOOH. BEST NOT SPILL ANY DROPS.

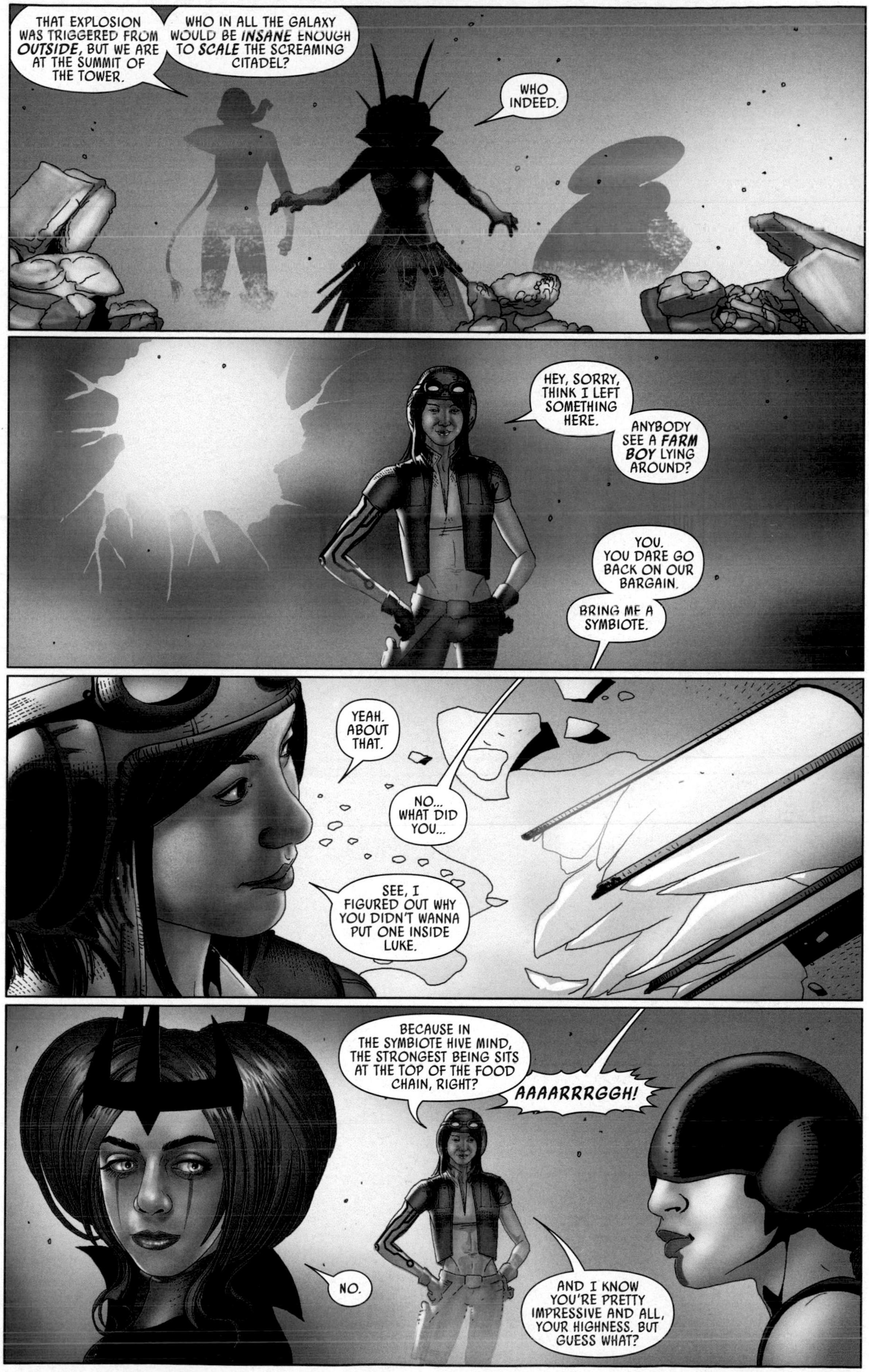
THAT EXPLOSION WAS TRIGGERED FROM OUTSIDE, BUT WE ARE AT THE SUMMIT OF THE TOWER.
WHO IN ALL THE GALAXY WOULD BE INSANE ENOUGH TO SCALE THE SCREAMING CITADEL?
WHO INDEED.
HEY, SORRY, THINK I LEFT SOMETHING HERE.
ANYBODY SEE A FARM BOY LYING AROUND?
YOU. YOU DARE GO BACK ON OUR BARGAIN.
BRING ME A SYMBIOTE.
YEAH. ABOUT THAT.
NO... WHAT DID YOU...
SEE, I FIGURED OUT WHY YOU DIDN'T WANNA PUT ONE INSIDE LUKE.
BECAUSE IN THE SYMBIOTE HIVE MIND, THE STRONGEST BEING SITS AT THE TOP OF THE FOOD CHAIN, RIGHT?
AAAARRRGGH!
NO.
AND I KNOW YOU'RE PRETTY IMPRESSIVE AND ALL, YOUR HIGHNESS. BUT GUESS WHAT?

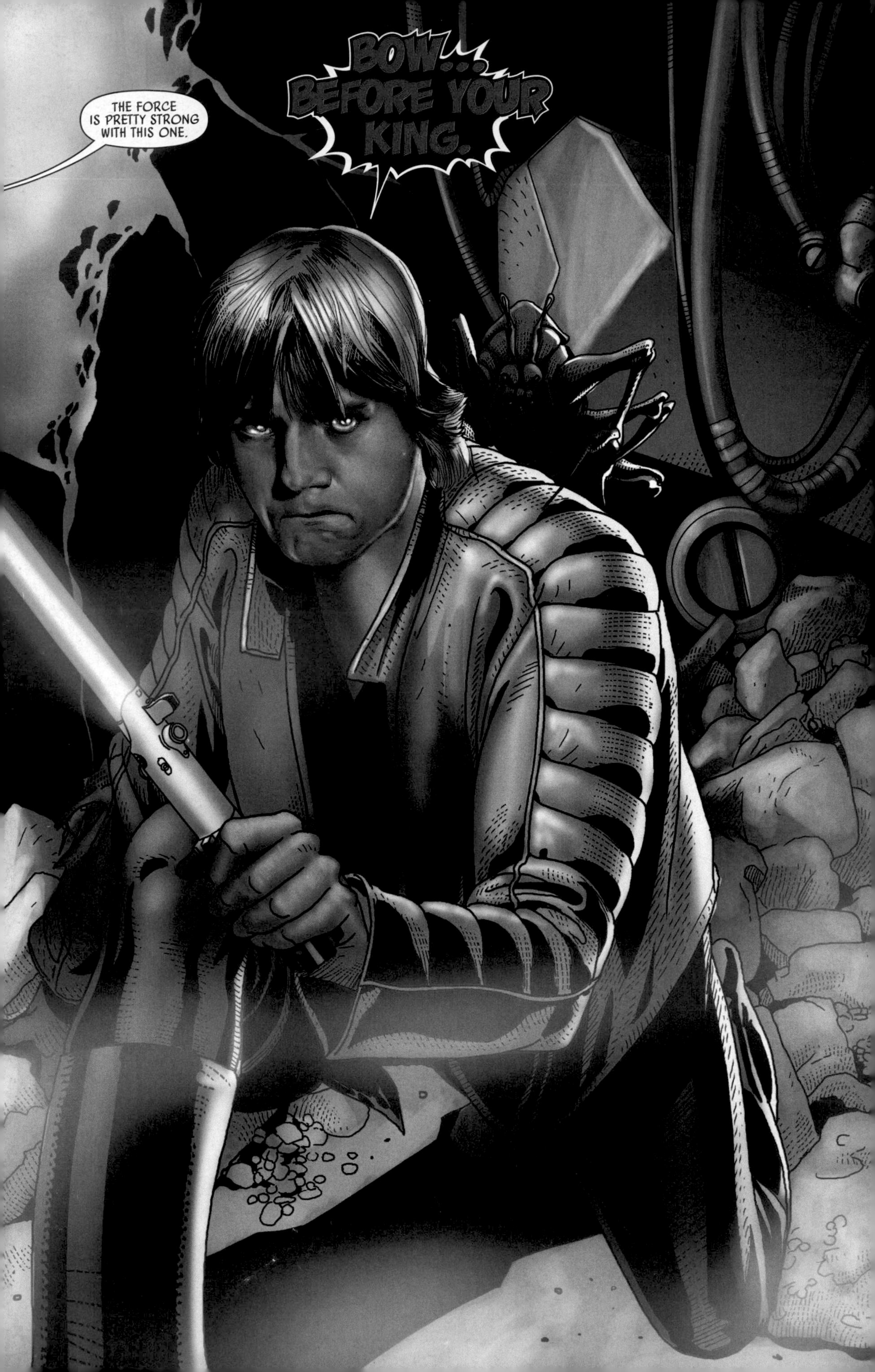
THE FORCE IS PRETTY STRONG WITH THIS ONE.
BOW... BEFORE YOUR KING.

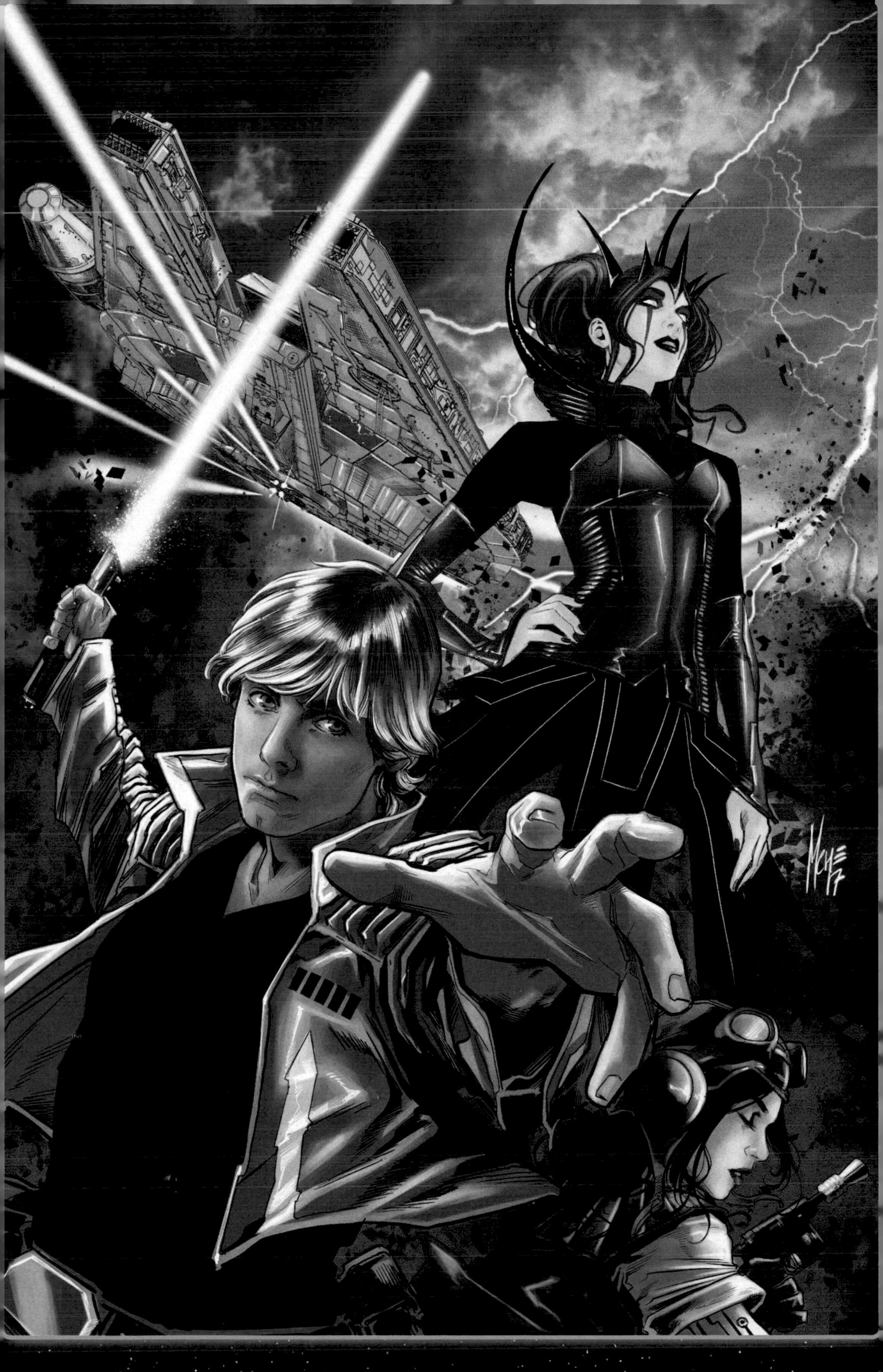

STAR WARS: DOCTOR APHRA 8

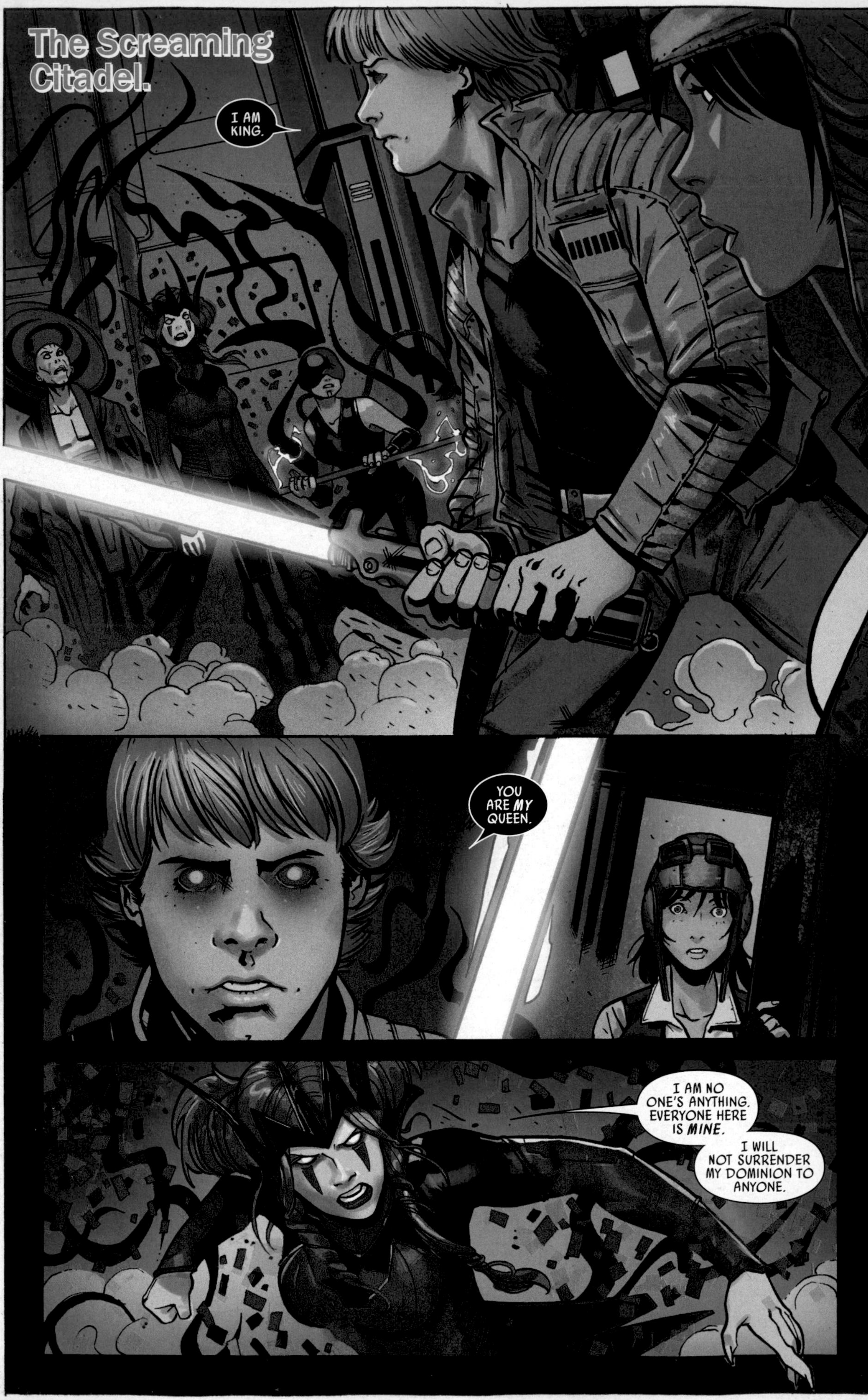

The Screaming Citadel.
I AM KING.
YOU ARE MY QUEEN.
I AM NO ONE'S ANYTHING. EVERYONE HERE IS MINE.
I WILL NOT SURRENDER MY DOMINION TO ANYONE.

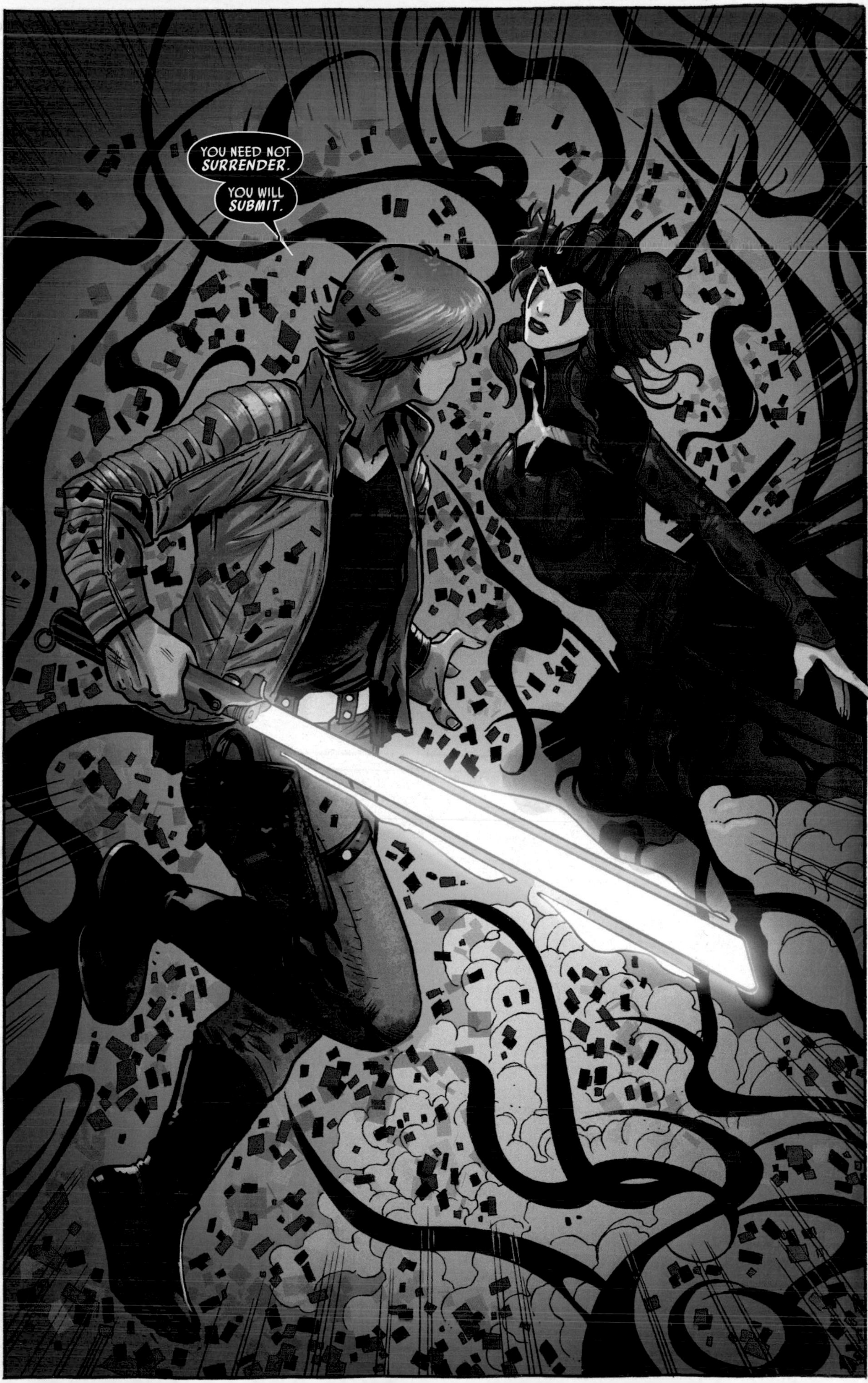
YOU NEED NOT SURRENDER.
YOU WILL SUBMIT.

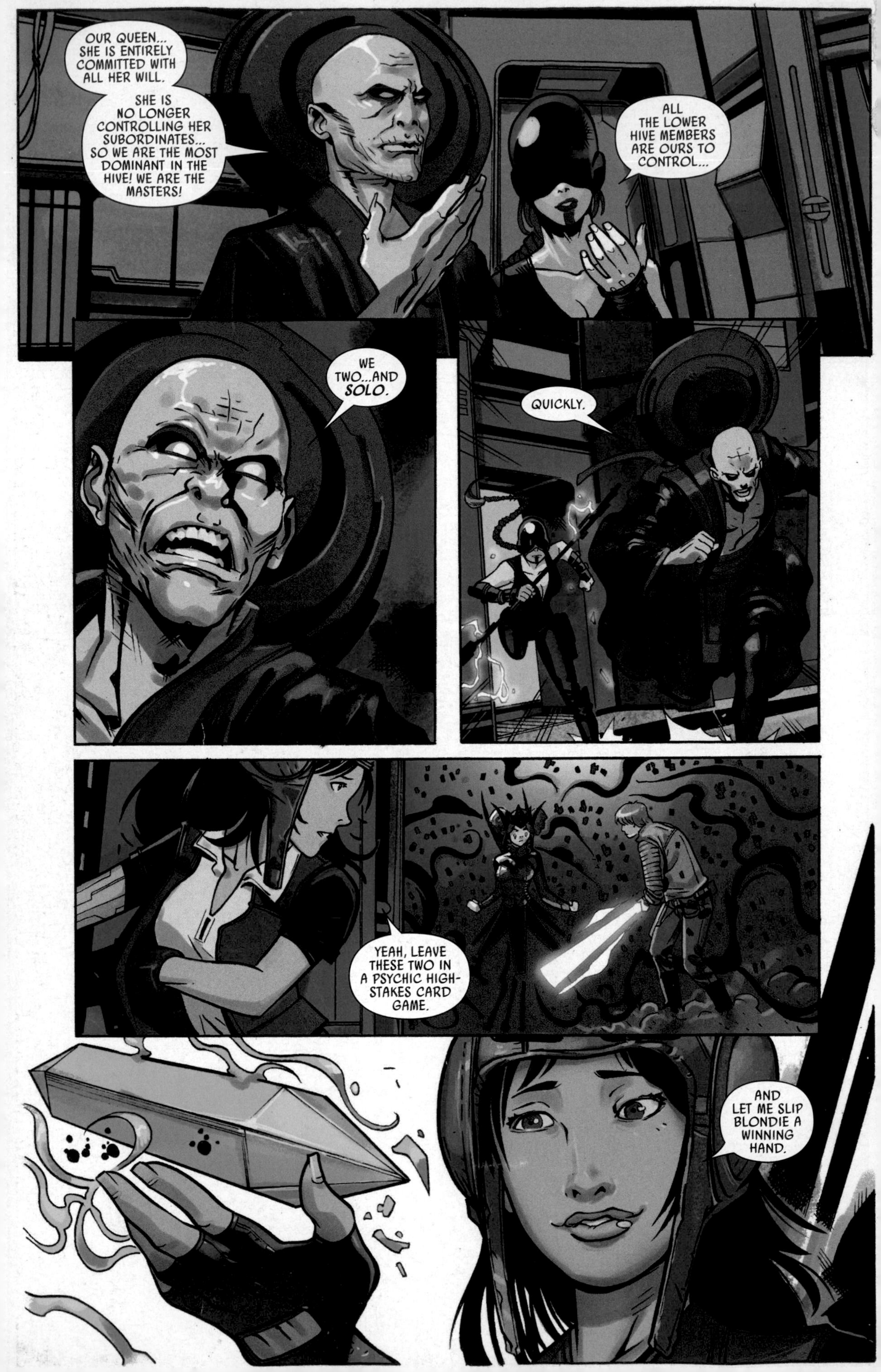
OUR QUEEN... SHE IS ENTIRELY COMMITTED WITH ALL HER WILL.
SHE IS NO LONGER CONTROLLING HER SUBORDINATES... SO WE ARE THE MOST DOMINANT IN THE HIVE! WE ARE THE MASTERS!
ALL THE LOWER HIVE MEMBERS ARE OURS TO CONTROL...
WE TWO...AND SOLO.
QUICKLY.
YEAH, LEAVE THESE TWO IN A PSYCHIC HIGH-STAKES CARD GAME.
AND LET ME SLIP BLONDIE A WINNING HAND.

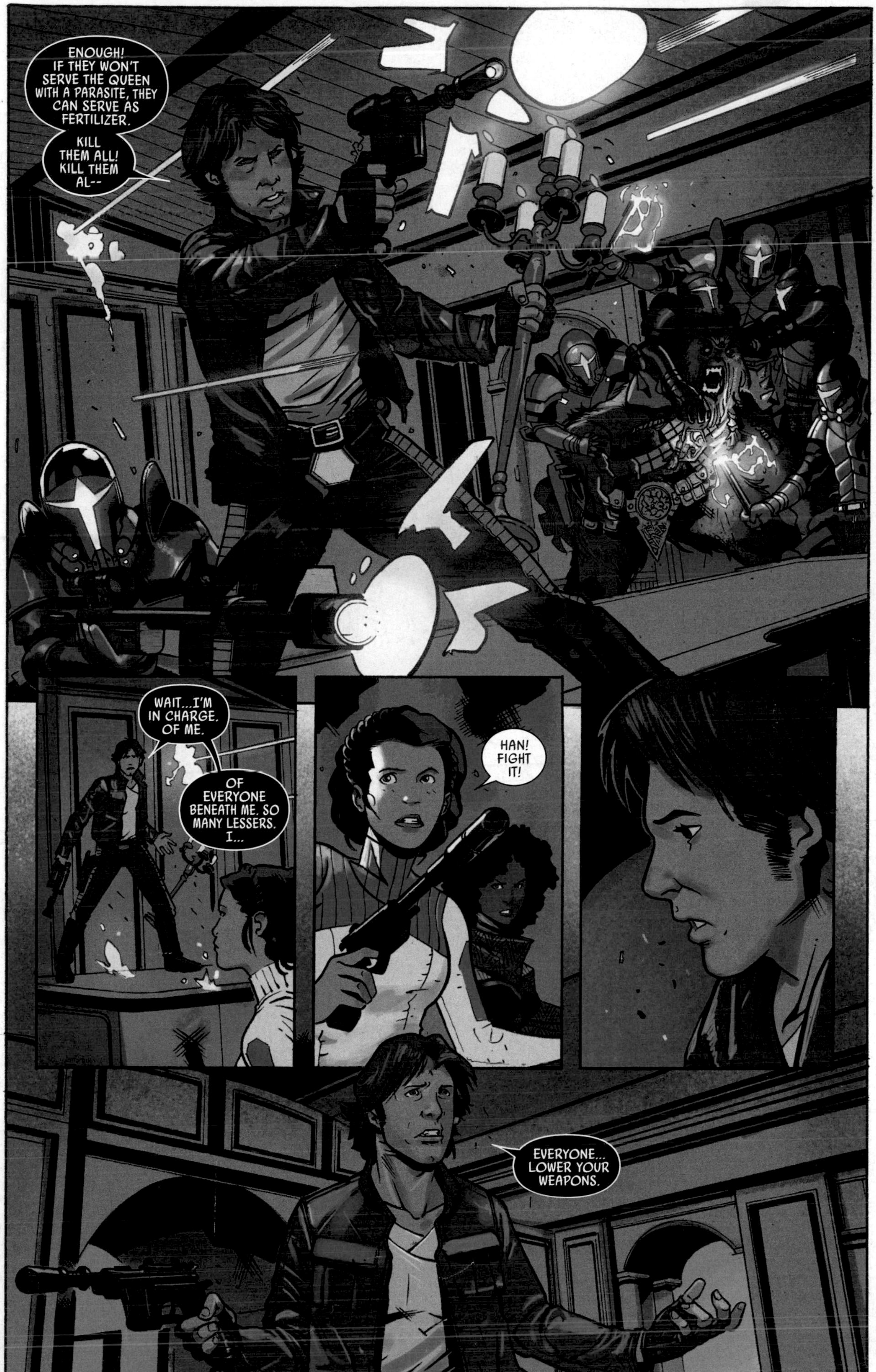
ENOUGH! IF THEY WON'T SERVE THE QUEEN WITH A PARASITE, THEY CAN SERVE AS FERTILIZER.
KILL THEM ALL! KILL THEM AL--
WAIT...I'M IN CHARGE. OF ME.
OF EVERYONE BENEATH ME. SO MANY LESSERS. I...
HAN! FIGHT IT!
EVERYONE... LOWER YOUR WEAPONS.

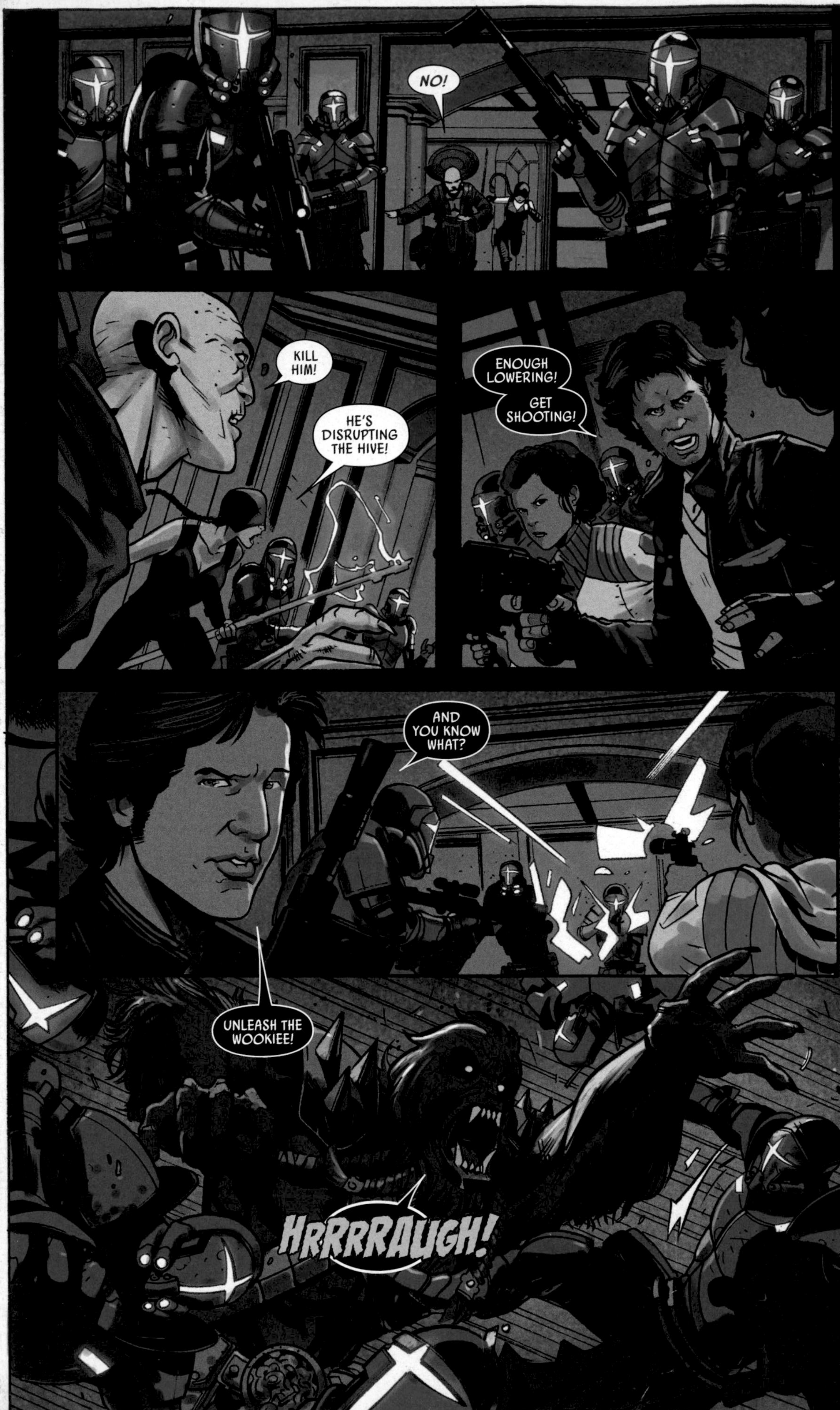
NO!
KILL HIM!
HE'S DISRUPTING THE HIVE!
ENOUGH LOWERING!
GET SHOOTING!
AND YOU KNOW WHAT?
UNLEASH THE WOOKIEE!
HRRRRAUGH!

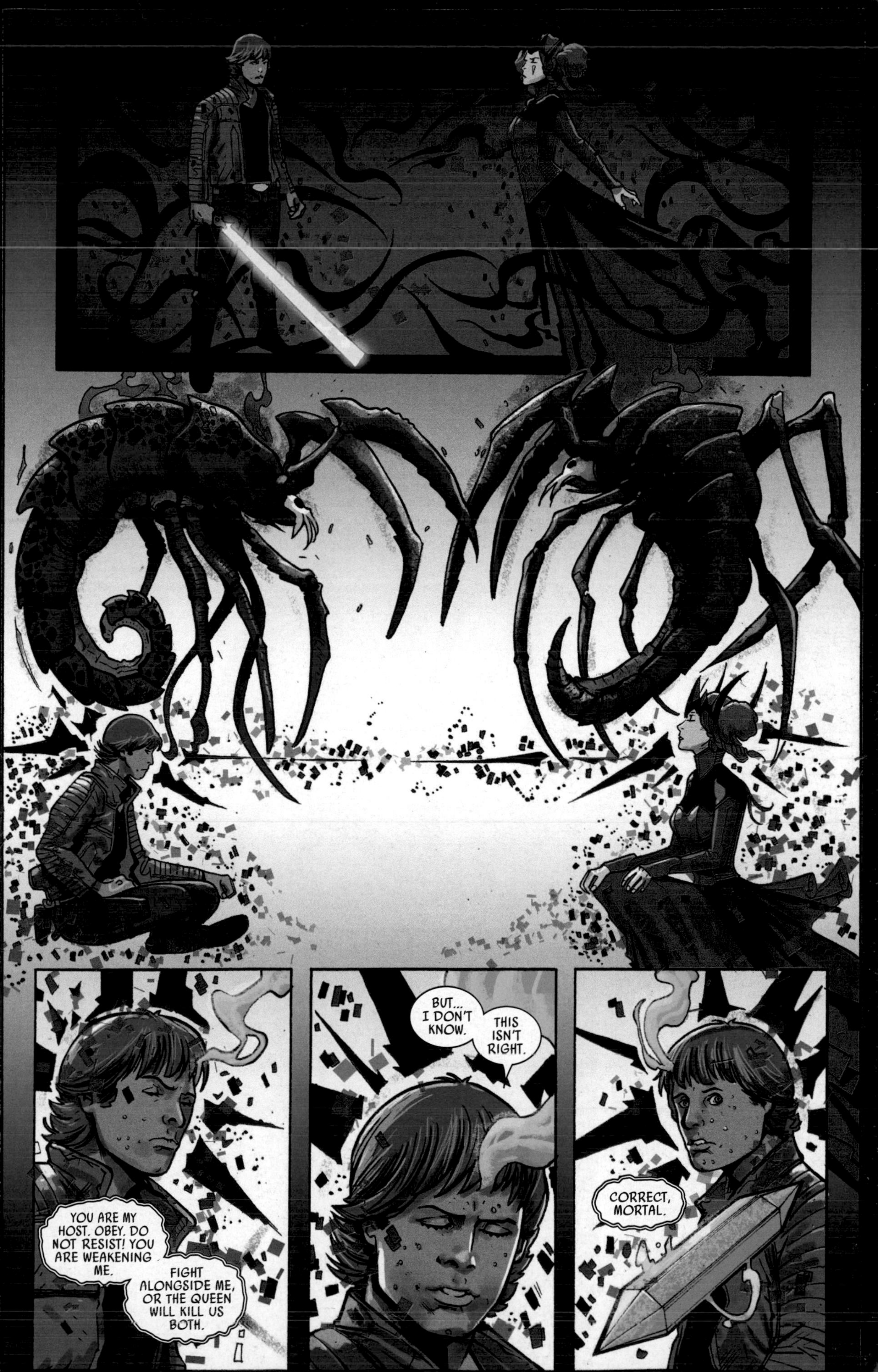
YOU ARE MY HOST. OBEY. DO NOT RESIST! YOU ARE WEAKENING ME.
FIGHT ALONGSIDE ME, OR THE QUEEN WILL KILL US BOTH.
BUT... I DON'T KNOW.
THIS ISN'T RIGHT.
CORRECT, MORTAL.

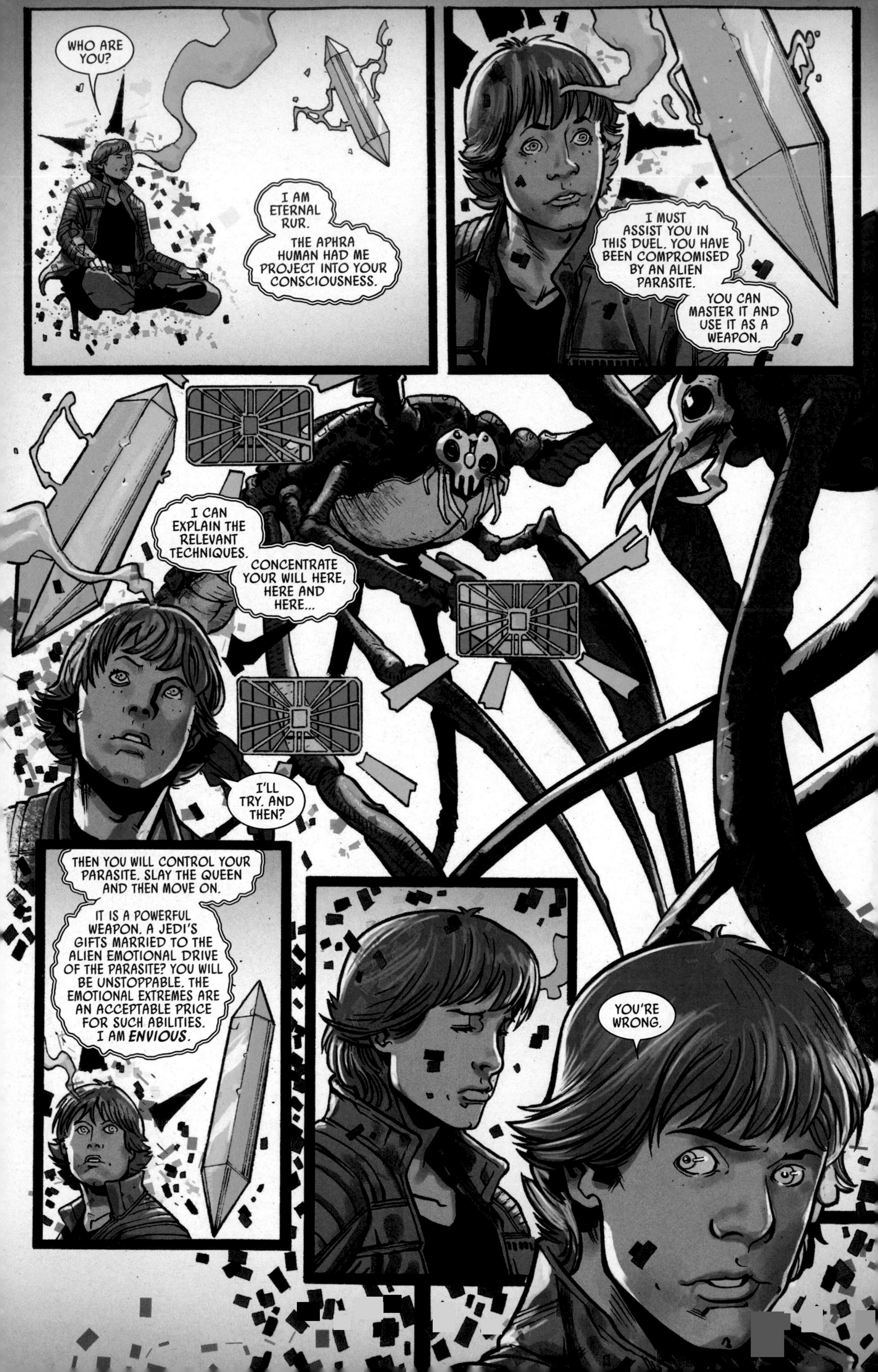
WHO ARE YOU?
I AM ETERNAL RUR.
THE APHRA HUMAN HAD ME PROJECT INTO YOUR CONSCIOUSNESS.
I MUST ASSIST YOU IN THIS DUEL. YOU HAVE BEEN COMPROMISED BY AN ALIEN PARASITE.
YOU CAN MASTER IT AND USE IT AS A WEAPON.
I CAN EXPLAIN THE RELEVANT TECHNIQUES.
CONCENTRATE YOUR WILL HERE, HERE AND HERE...
I'LL TRY. AND THEN?
THEN YOU WILL CONTROL YOUR PARASITE. SLAY THE QUEEN AND THEN MOVE ON.
IT IS A POWERFUL WEAPON. A JEDI'S GIFTS MARRIED TO THE ALIEN EMOTIONAL DRIVE OF THE PARASITE? YOU WILL BE UNSTOPPABLE. THE EMOTIONAL EXTREMES ARE AN ACCEPTABLE PRICE FOR SUCH ABILITIES. I AM *ENVIOUS*.
YOU'RE WRONG.

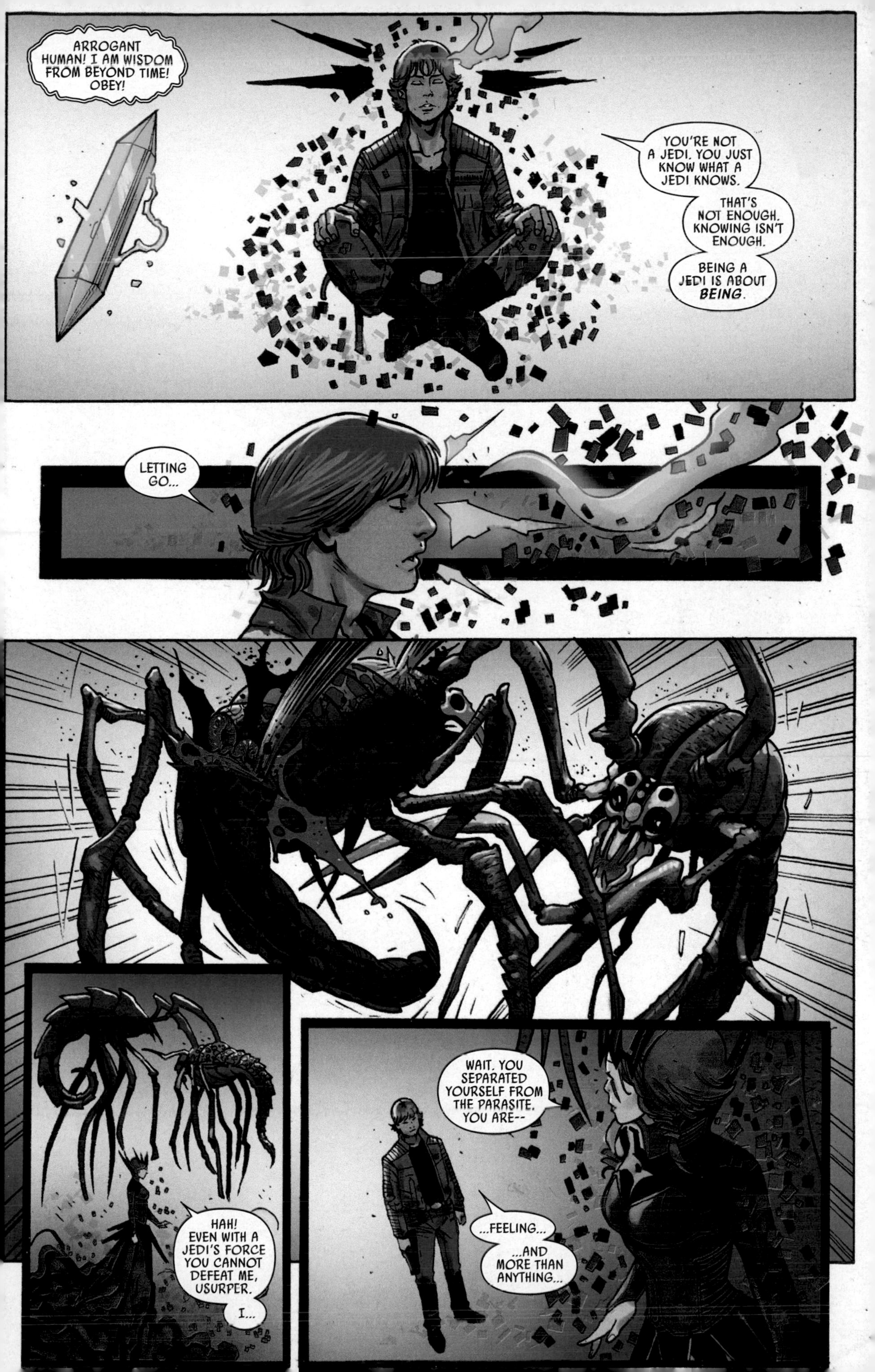
ARROGANT HUMAN! I AM WISDOM FROM BEYOND TIME! OBEY!
YOU'RE NOT A JEDI. YOU JUST KNOW WHAT A JEDI KNOWS.
THAT'S NOT ENOUGH. KNOWING ISN'T ENOUGH.
BEING A JEDI IS ABOUT BEING.
LETTING GO...
HAH! EVEN WITH A JEDI'S FORCE YOU CANNOT DEFEAT ME, USURPER.
I...
WAIT. YOU SEPARATED YOURSELF FROM THE PARASITE. YOU ARE--
...FEELING...
...AND MORE THAN ANYTHING...

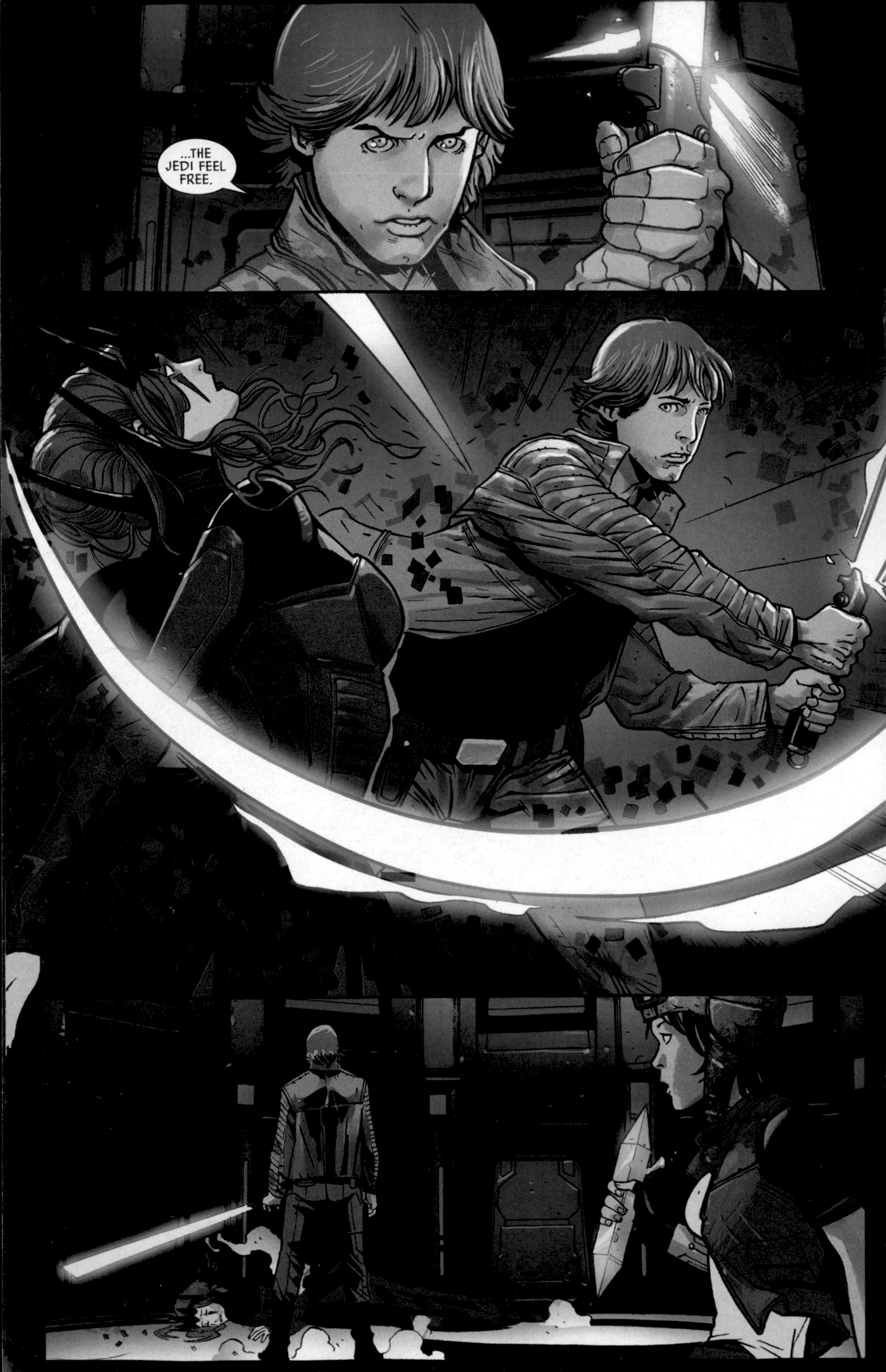
...THE JEDI FEEL FREE.

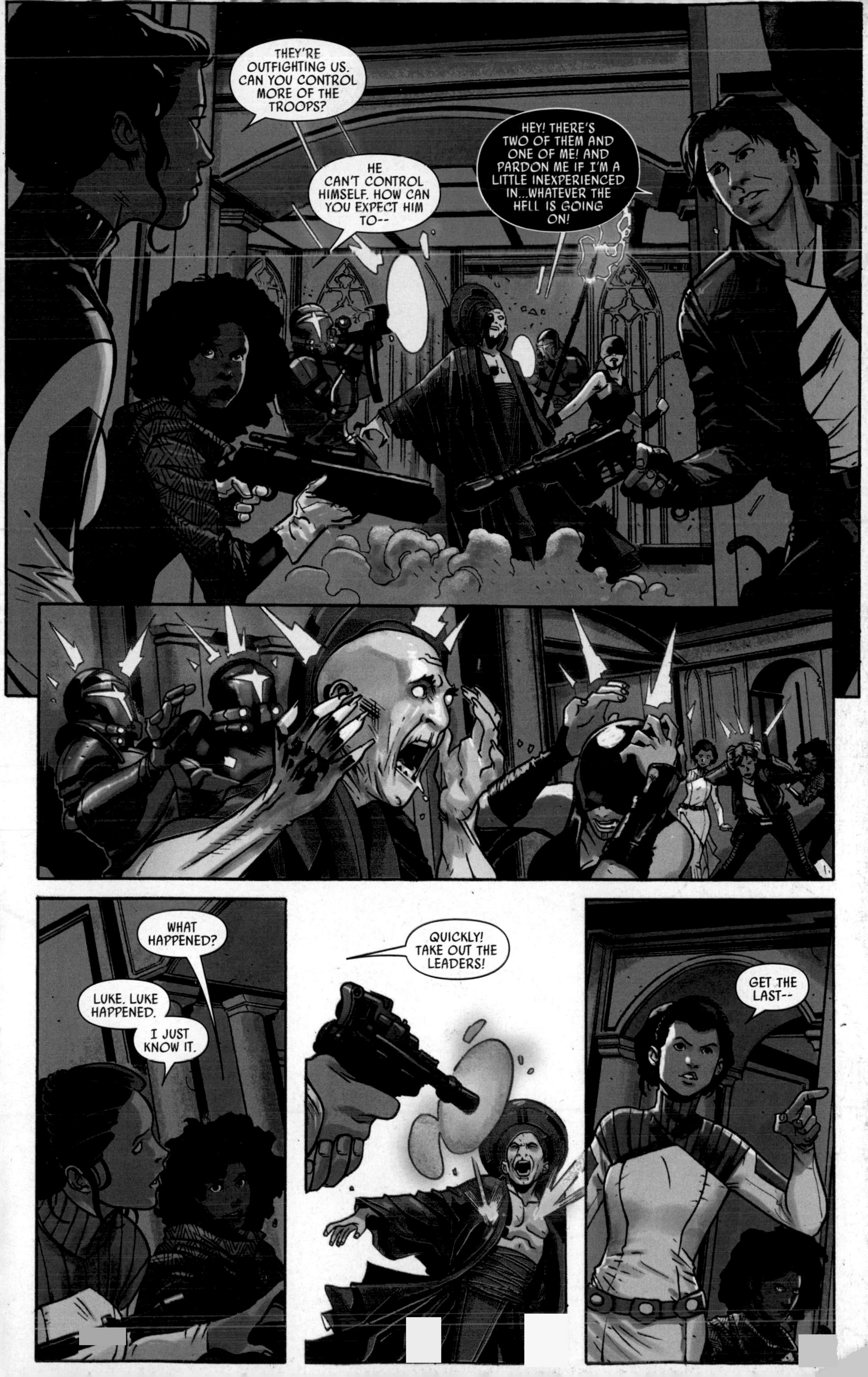
THEY'RE OUTFIGHTING US. CAN YOU CONTROL MORE OF THE TROOPS?
HE CAN'T CONTROL HIMSELF. HOW CAN YOU EXPECT HIM TO--
HEY! THERE'S TWO OF THEM AND ONE OF ME! AND PARDON ME IF I'M A LITTLE INEXPERIENCED IN...WHATEVER THE HELL IS GOING ON!
WHAT HAPPENED?
LUKE. LUKE HAPPENED.
I JUST KNOW IT.
QUICKLY! TAKE OUT THE LEADERS!
GET THE LAST--

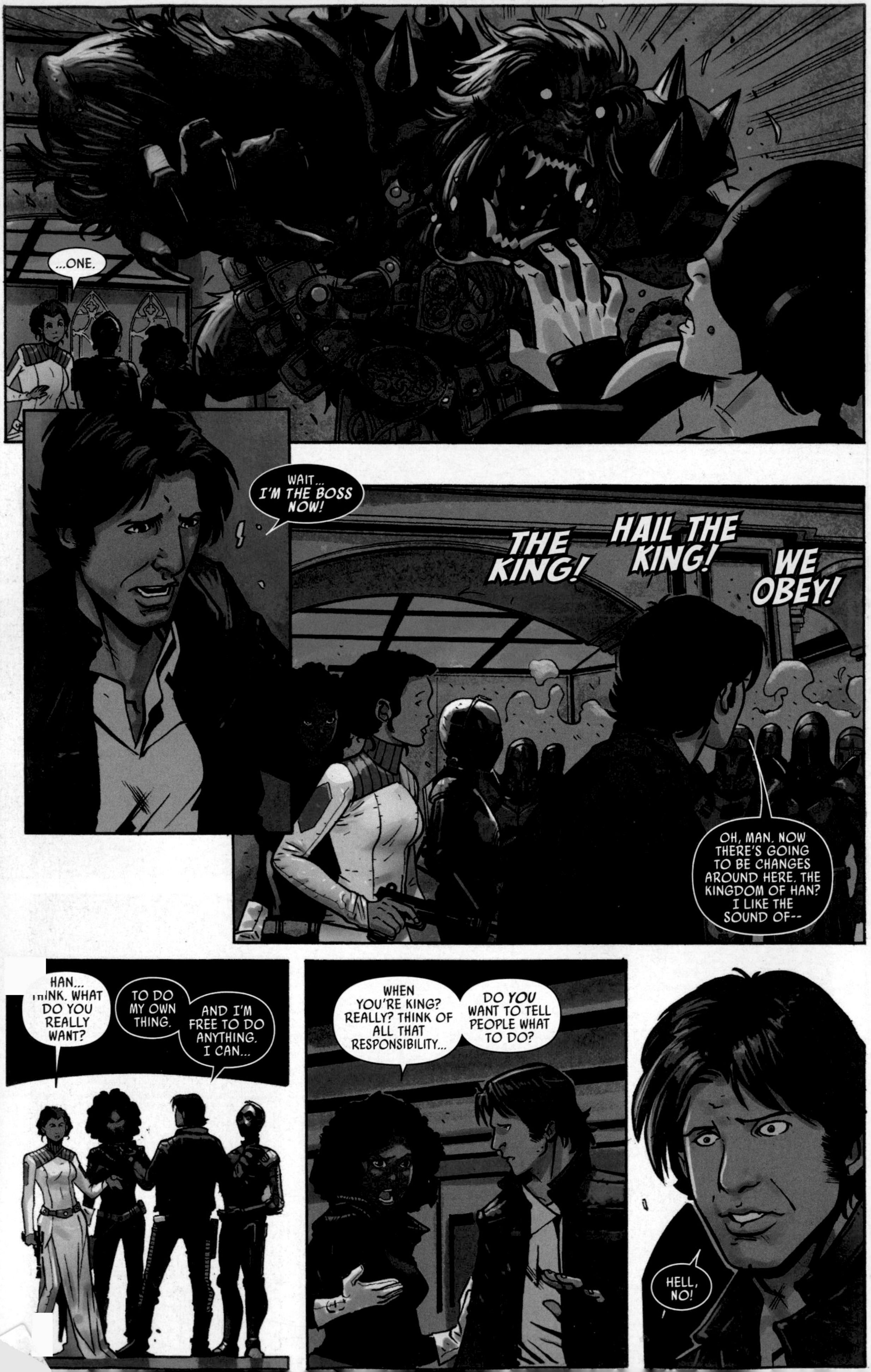

...ONE.
WAIT... I'M THE BOSS NOW!
THE KING!
HAIL THE KING!
WE OBEY!
OH, MAN. NOW THERE'S GOING TO BE CHANGES AROUND HERE. THE KINGDOM OF HAN? I LIKE THE SOUND OF--
HAN... THINK. WHAT DO YOU REALLY WANT?
TO DO MY OWN THING.
AND I'M FREE TO DO ANYTHING. I CAN...
WHEN YOU'RE KING? REALLY? THINK OF ALL THAT RESPONSIBILITY...
DO YOU WANT TO TELL PEOPLE WHAT TO DO?
HELL, NO!

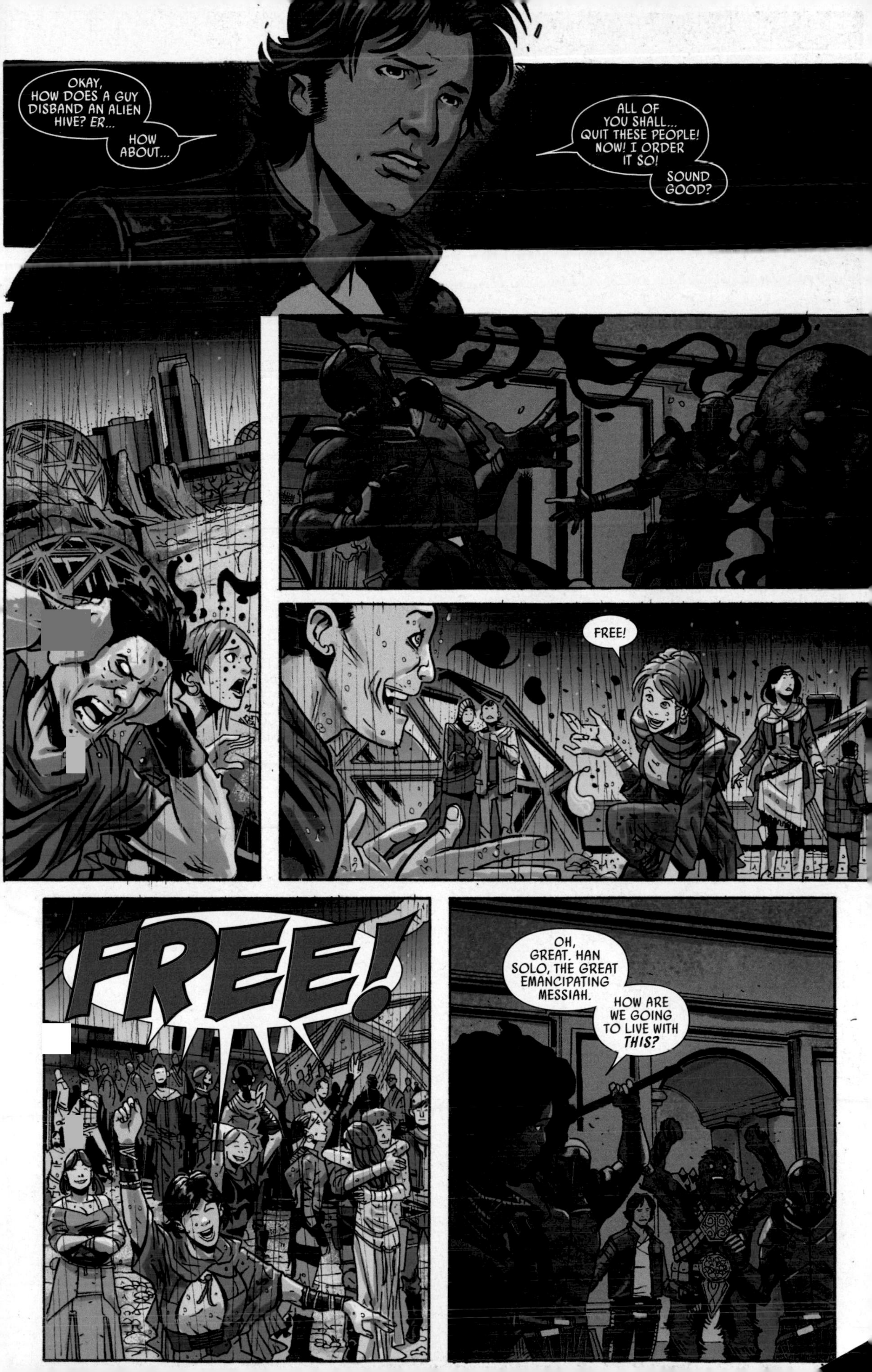
OKAY, HOW DOES A GUY DISBAND AN ALIEN HIVE? ER...
HOW ABOUT...
ALL OF YOU SHALL... QUIT THESE PEOPLE! NOW! I ORDER IT SO!
SOUND GOOD?
FREE!
FREE!
OH, GREAT. HAN SOLO, THE GREAT EMANCIPATING MESSIAH.
HOW ARE WE GOING TO LIVE WITH THIS?

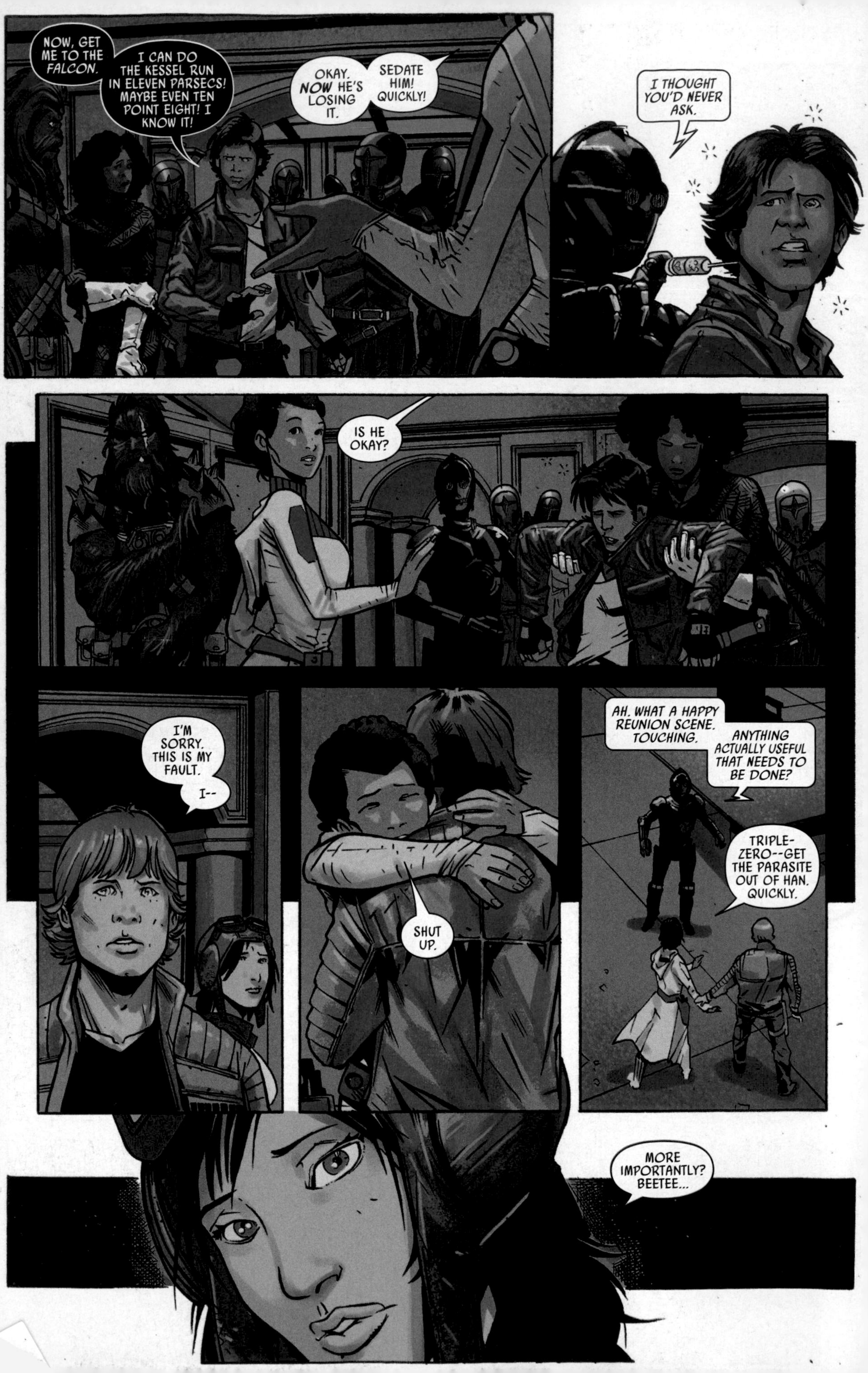
NOW, GET ME TO THE FALCON.
I CAN DO THE KESSEL RUN IN ELEVEN PARSECS! MAYBE EVEN TEN POINT EIGHT! I KNOW IT!
OKAY. NOW HE'S LOSING IT.
SEDATE HIM! QUICKLY!
I THOUGHT YOU'D NEVER ASK.
IS HE OKAY?
I'M SORRY. THIS IS MY FAULT.
I--
SHUT UP.
AH. WHAT A HAPPY REUNION SCENE. TOUCHING.
ANYTHING ACTUALLY USEFUL THAT NEEDS TO BE DONE?
TRIPLE-ZERO--GET THE PARASITE OUT OF HAN. QUICKLY.
MORE IMPORTANTLY? BEETEE...

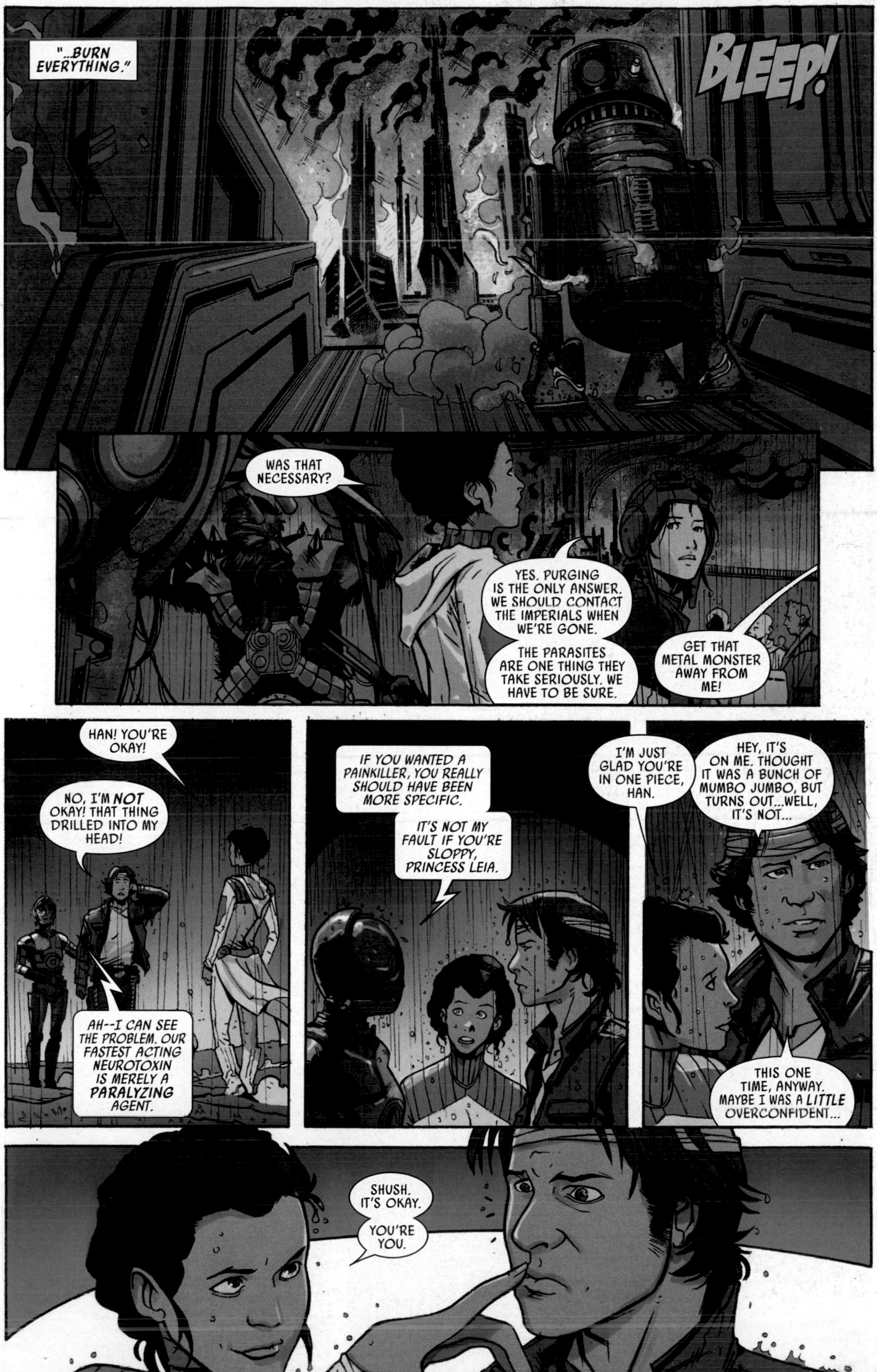
"...BURN EVERYTHING."
BLEEP!
WAS THAT NECESSARY?
YES. PURGING IS THE ONLY ANSWER. WE SHOULD CONTACT THE IMPERIALS WHEN WE'RE GONE.
THE PARASITES ARE ONE THING THEY TAKE SERIOUSLY. WE HAVE TO BE SURE.
GET THAT METAL MONSTER AWAY FROM ME!
HAN! YOU'RE OKAY!
NO, I'M NOT OKAY! THAT THING DRILLED INTO MY HEAD!
AH--I CAN SEE THE PROBLEM. OUR FASTEST ACTING NEUROTOXIN IS MERELY A PARALYZING AGENT.
IF YOU WANTED A PAINKILLER, YOU REALLY SHOULD HAVE BEEN MORE SPECIFIC.
IT'S NOT MY FAULT IF YOU'RE SLOPPY, PRINCESS LEIA.
I'M JUST GLAD YOU'RE IN ONE PIECE, HAN.
HEY, IT'S ON ME. THOUGHT IT WAS A BUNCH OF MUMBO JUMBO, BUT TURNS OUT...WELL, IT'S NOT...
THIS ONE TIME, ANYWAY. MAYBE I WAS A LITTLE OVERCONFIDENT...
SHUSH. IT'S OKAY.
YOU'RE YOU.

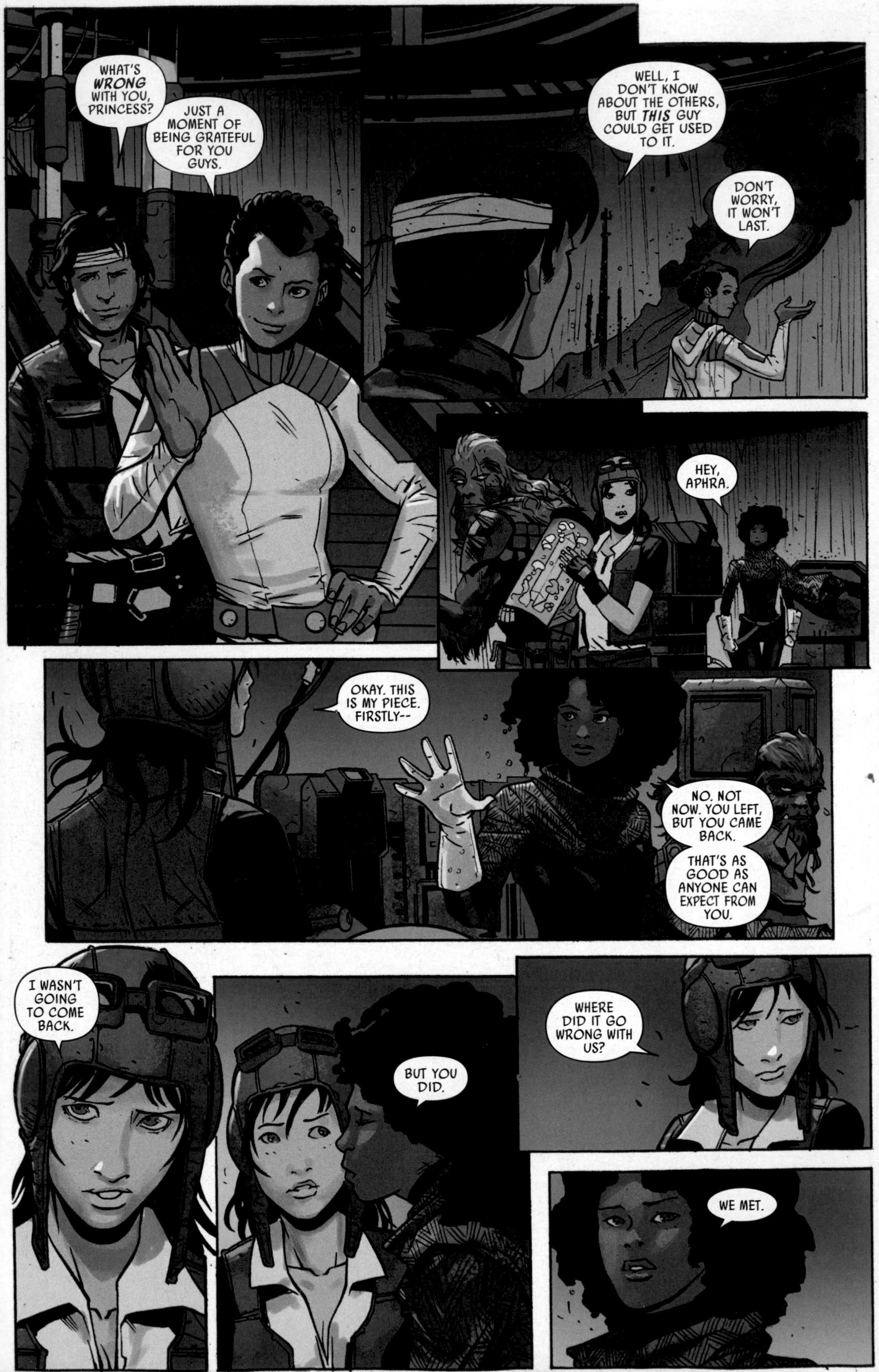
WHAT'S *WRONG* WITH YOU, PRINCESS?
JUST A MOMENT OF BEING GRATEFUL FOR YOU GUYS.
WELL, I DON'T KNOW ABOUT THE OTHERS, BUT *THIS* GUY COULD GET USED TO IT.
DON'T WORRY, IT WON'T LAST.
HEY, APHRA.
OKAY. THIS IS MY PIECE. FIRSTLY--
NO. NOT NOW. YOU LEFT, BUT YOU CAME BACK.
THAT'S AS GOOD AS ANYONE CAN EXPECT FROM YOU.
I WASN'T GOING TO COME BACK.
BUT YOU DID.
WHERE DID IT GO WRONG WITH US?
WE MET.

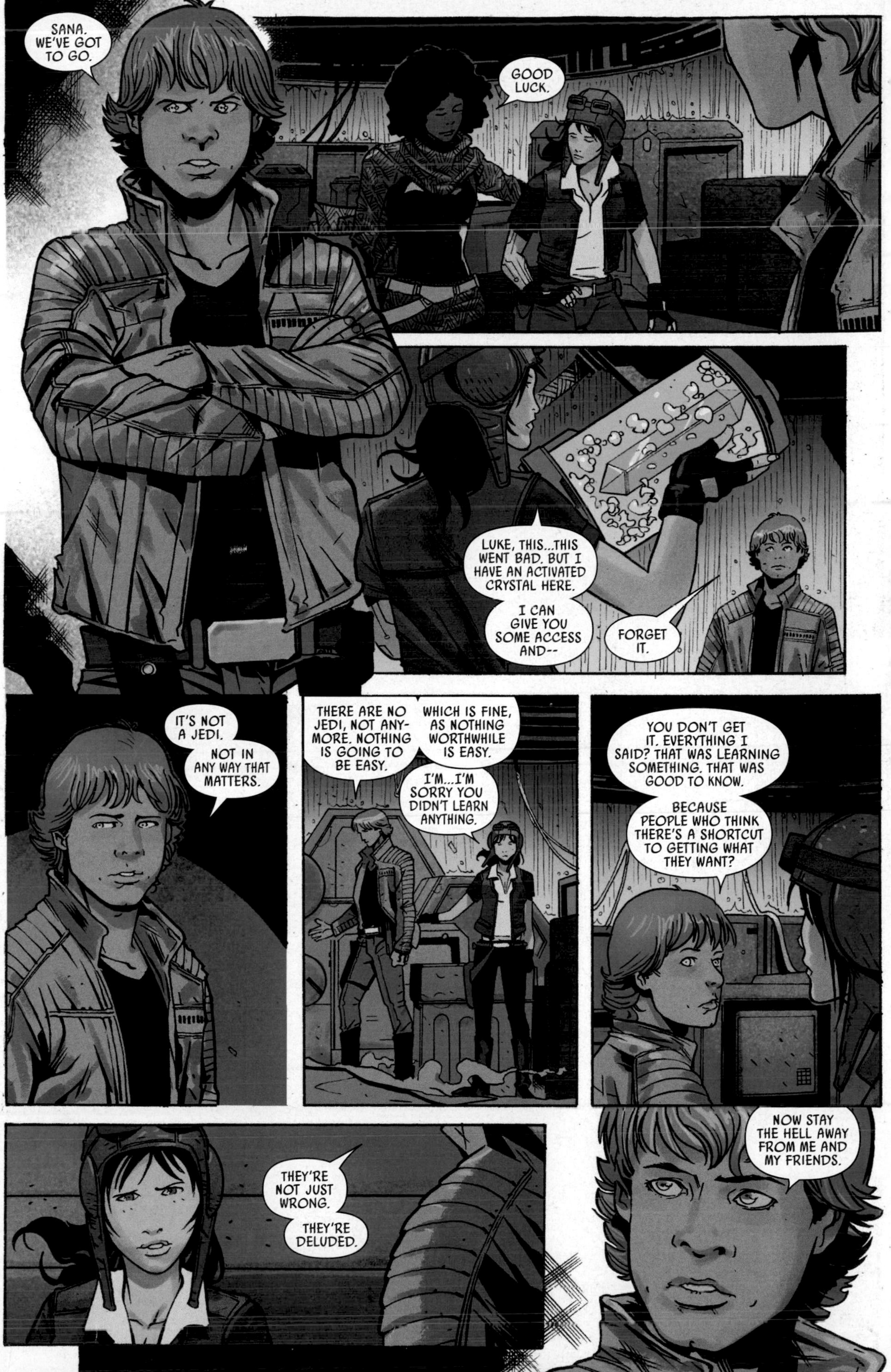
SANA. WE'VE GOT TO GO.
GOOD LUCK.
LUKE, THIS...THIS WENT BAD. BUT I HAVE AN ACTIVATED CRYSTAL HERE.
I CAN GIVE YOU SOME ACCESS AND--
FORGET IT.
IT'S NOT A JEDI.
NOT IN ANY WAY THAT MATTERS.
THERE ARE NO JEDI, NOT ANY-MORE. NOTHING IS GOING TO BE EASY.
WHICH IS FINE, AS NOTHING WORTHWHILE IS EASY.
I'M...I'M SORRY YOU DIDN'T LEARN ANYTHING.
YOU DON'T GET IT. EVERYTHING I SAID? THAT WAS LEARNING SOMETHING. THAT WAS GOOD TO KNOW.
BECAUSE PEOPLE WHO THINK THERE'S A SHORTCUT TO GETTING WHAT THEY WANT?
THEY'RE NOT JUST WRONG.
THEY'RE DELUDED.
NOW STAY THE HELL AWAY FROM ME AND MY FRIENDS.

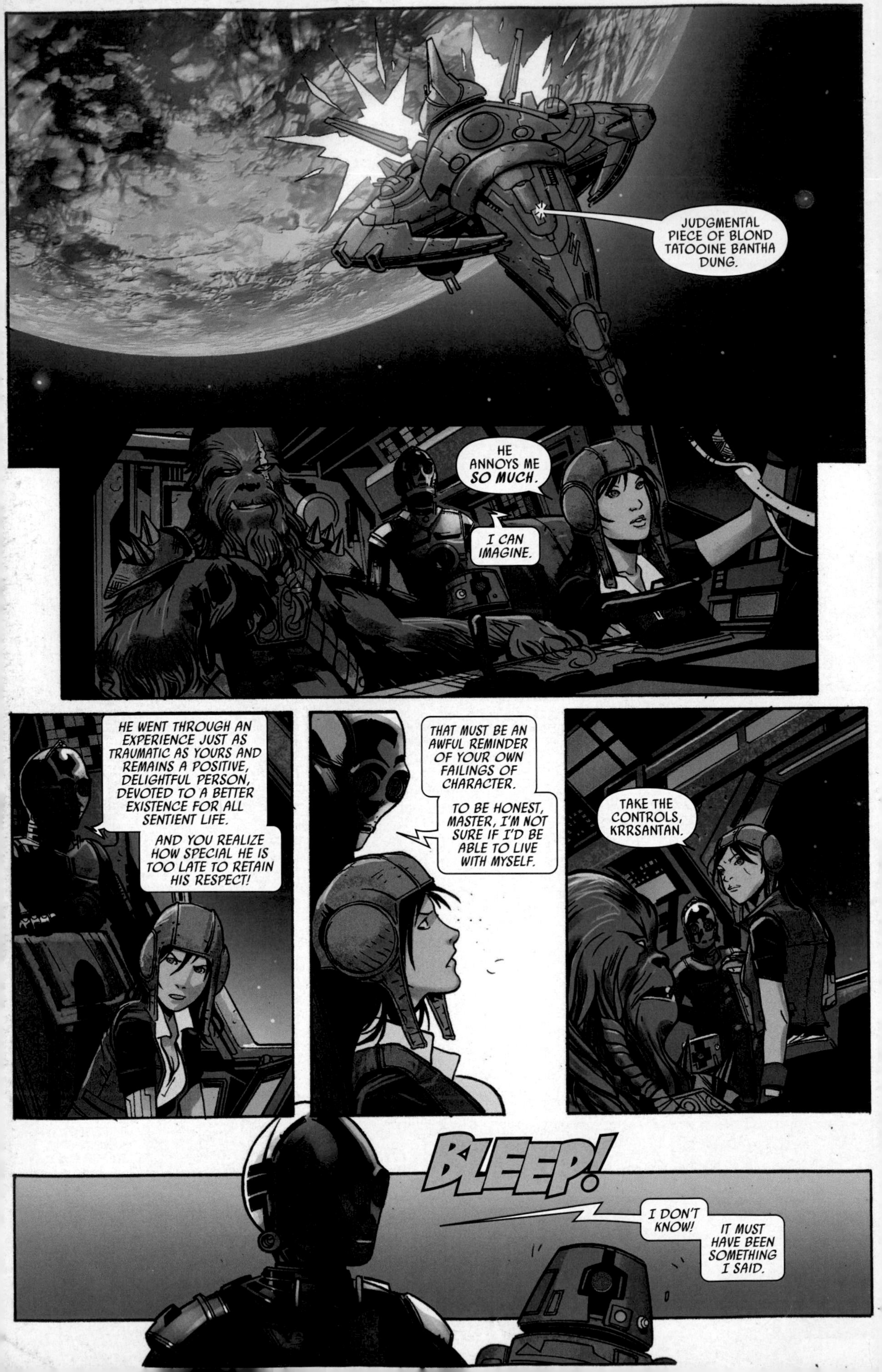
JUDGMENTAL PIECE OF BLOND TATOOINE BANTHA DUNG.
HE ANNOYS ME SO MUCH.
I CAN IMAGINE.
HE WENT THROUGH AN EXPERIENCE JUST AS TRAUMATIC AS YOURS AND REMAINS A POSITIVE, DELIGHTFUL PERSON, DEVOTED TO A BETTER EXISTENCE FOR ALL SENTIENT LIFE.
AND YOU REALIZE HOW SPECIAL HE IS TOO LATE TO RETAIN HIS RESPECT!
THAT MUST BE AN AWFUL REMINDER OF YOUR OWN FAILINGS OF CHARACTER.
TO BE HONEST, MASTER, I'M NOT SURE IF I'D BE ABLE TO LIVE WITH MYSELF.
TAKE THE CONTROLS, KRRSANTAN.
BLEEP!
I DON'T KNOW!
IT MUST HAVE BEEN SOMETHING I SAID.

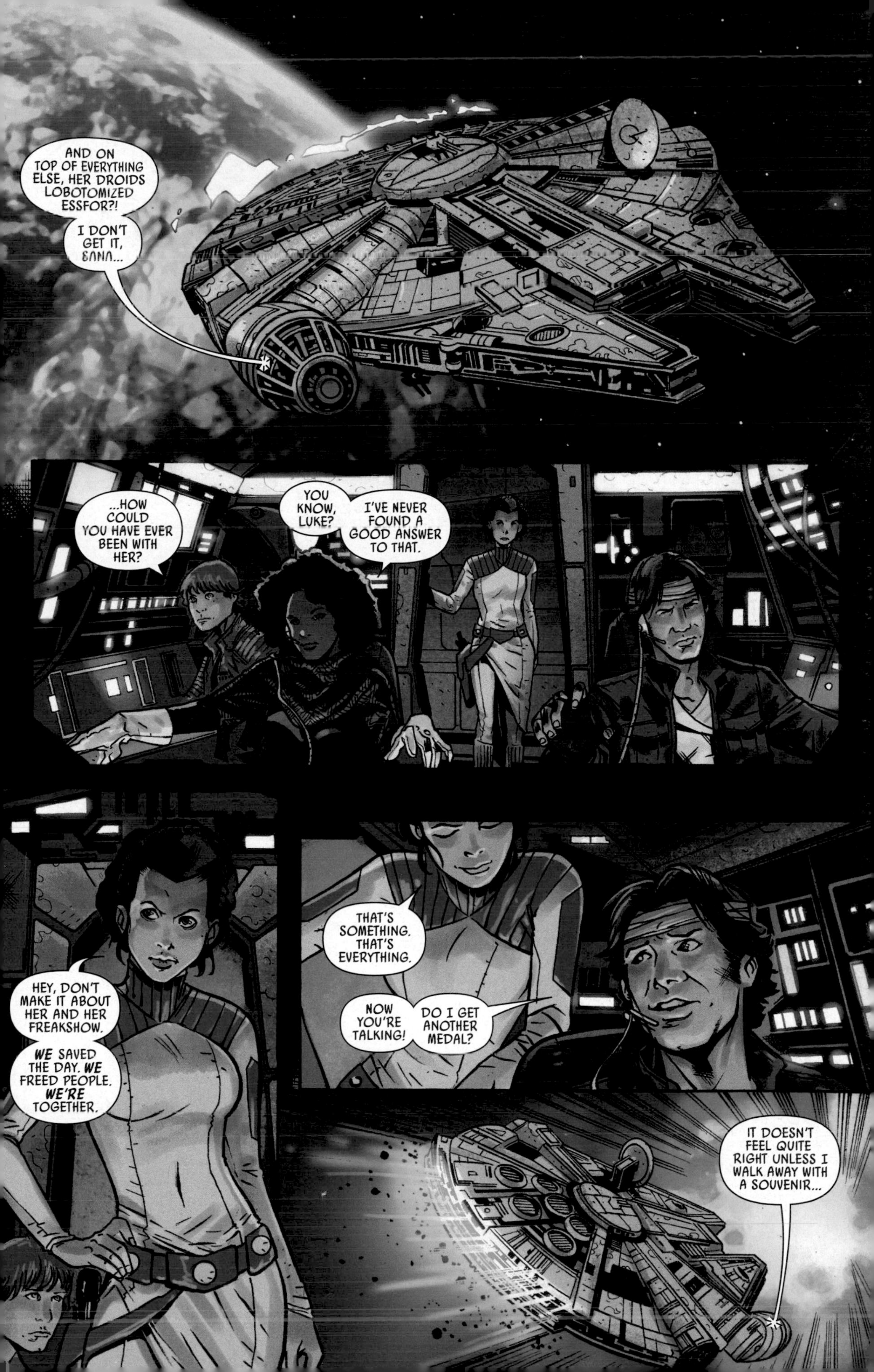
AND ON TOP OF EVERYTHING ELSE, HER DROIDS LOBOTOMIZED ESSFOR?!
I DON'T GET IT, SANA...
...HOW COULD YOU HAVE EVER BEEN WITH HER?
YOU KNOW, LUKE?
I'VE NEVER FOUND A GOOD ANSWER TO THAT.
HEY, DON'T MAKE IT ABOUT HER AND HER FREAKSHOW.
WE SAVED THE DAY. WE FREED PEOPLE. WE'RE TOGETHER.
THAT'S SOMETHING. THAT'S EVERYTHING.
NOW YOU'RE TALKING!
DO I GET ANOTHER MEDAL?
IT DOESN'T FEEL QUITE RIGHT UNLESS I WALK AWAY WITH A SOUVENIR...

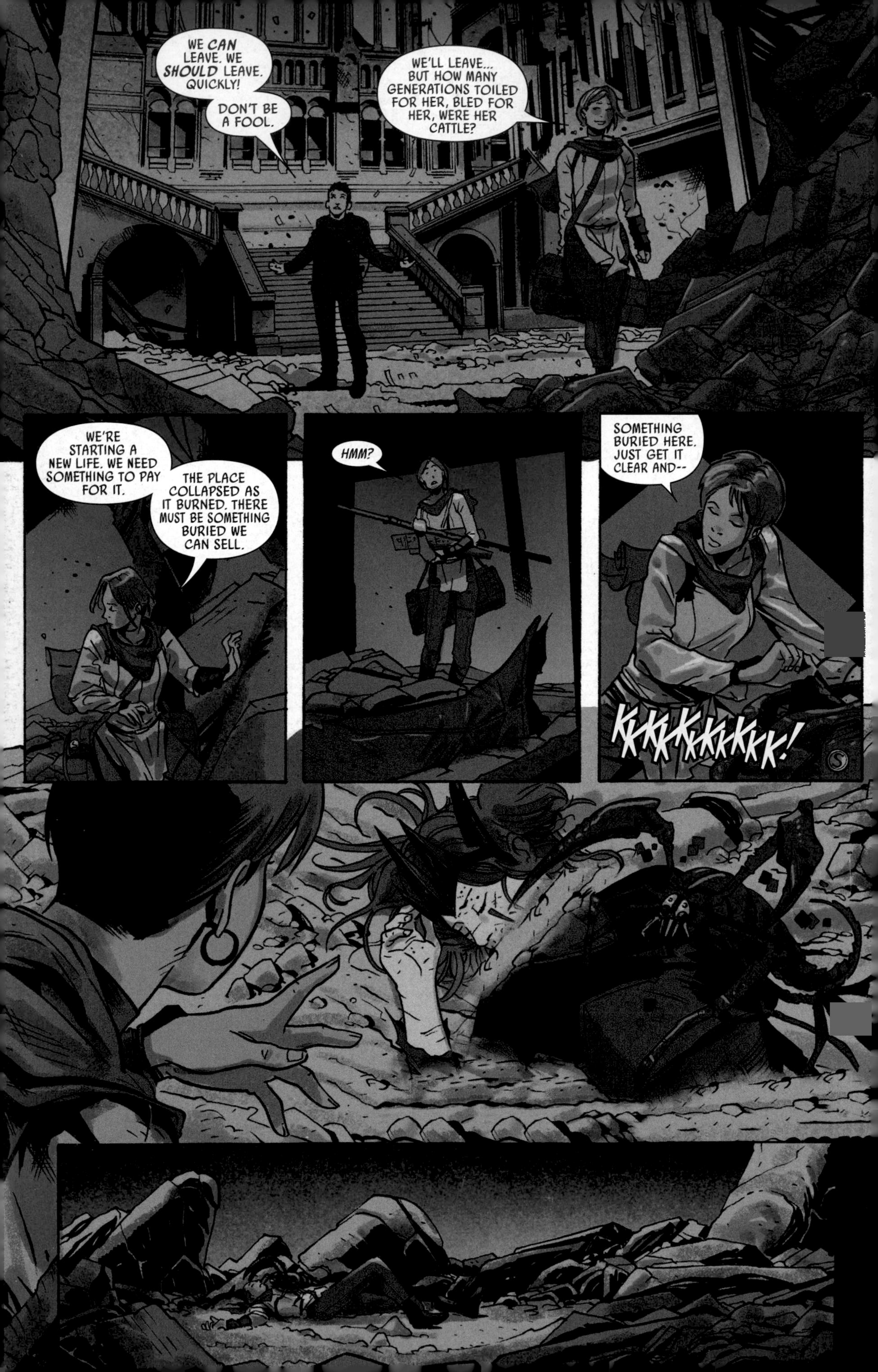

WE CAN LEAVE. WE SHOULD LEAVE. QUICKLY!
DON'T BE A FOOL.
WE'LL LEAVE... BUT HOW MANY GENERATIONS TOILED FOR HER, BLED FOR HER, WERE HER CATTLE?
WE'RE STARTING A NEW LIFE. WE NEED SOMETHING TO PAY FOR IT.
THE PLACE COLLAPSED AS IT BURNED. THERE MUST BE SOMETHING BURIED WE CAN SELL.
HMM?
SOMETHING BURIED HERE. JUST GET IT CLEAR AND--
KKKKKKKKKKK!

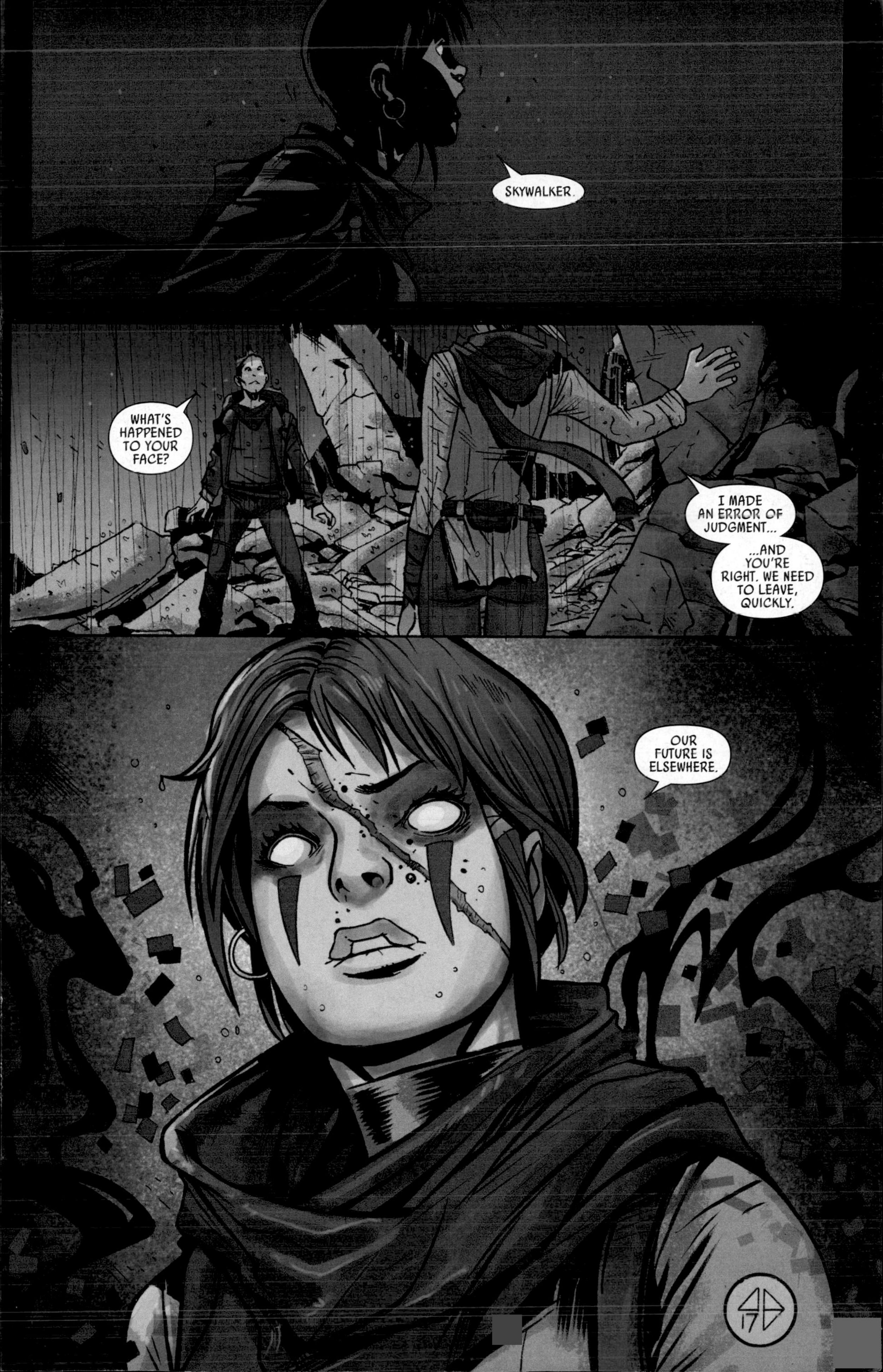
SKYWALKER.
WHAT'S HAPPENED TO YOUR FACE?
I MADE AN ERROR OF JUDGMENT...
...AND YOU'RE RIGHT. WE NEED TO LEAVE, QUICKLY.
OUR FUTURE IS ELSEWHERE.

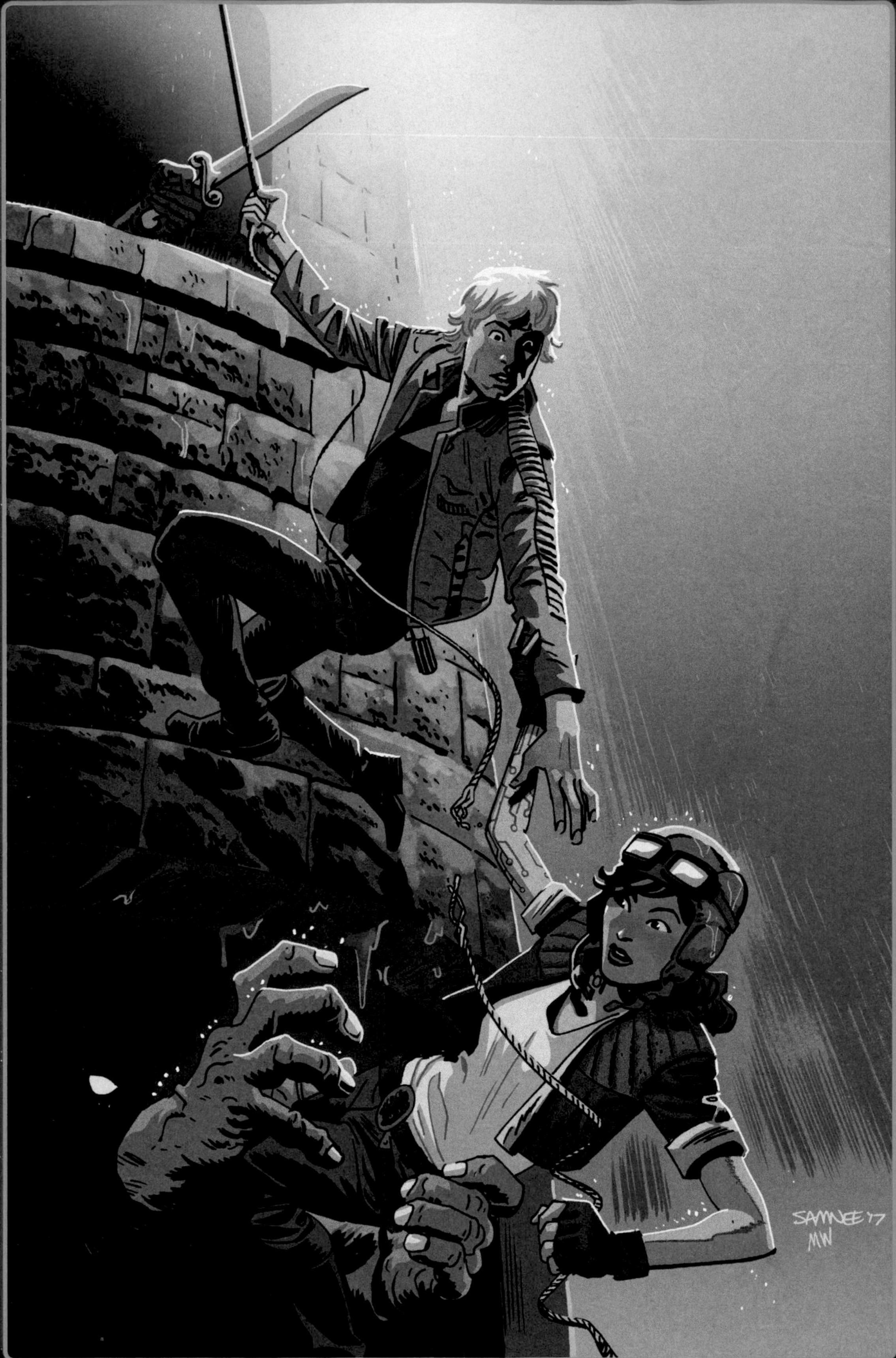
SAMNEE '17
MW

STAR WARS: THE SCREAMING CITADEL 1
VARIANT BY CHRIS SAMNEE & MATTHEW WILSON

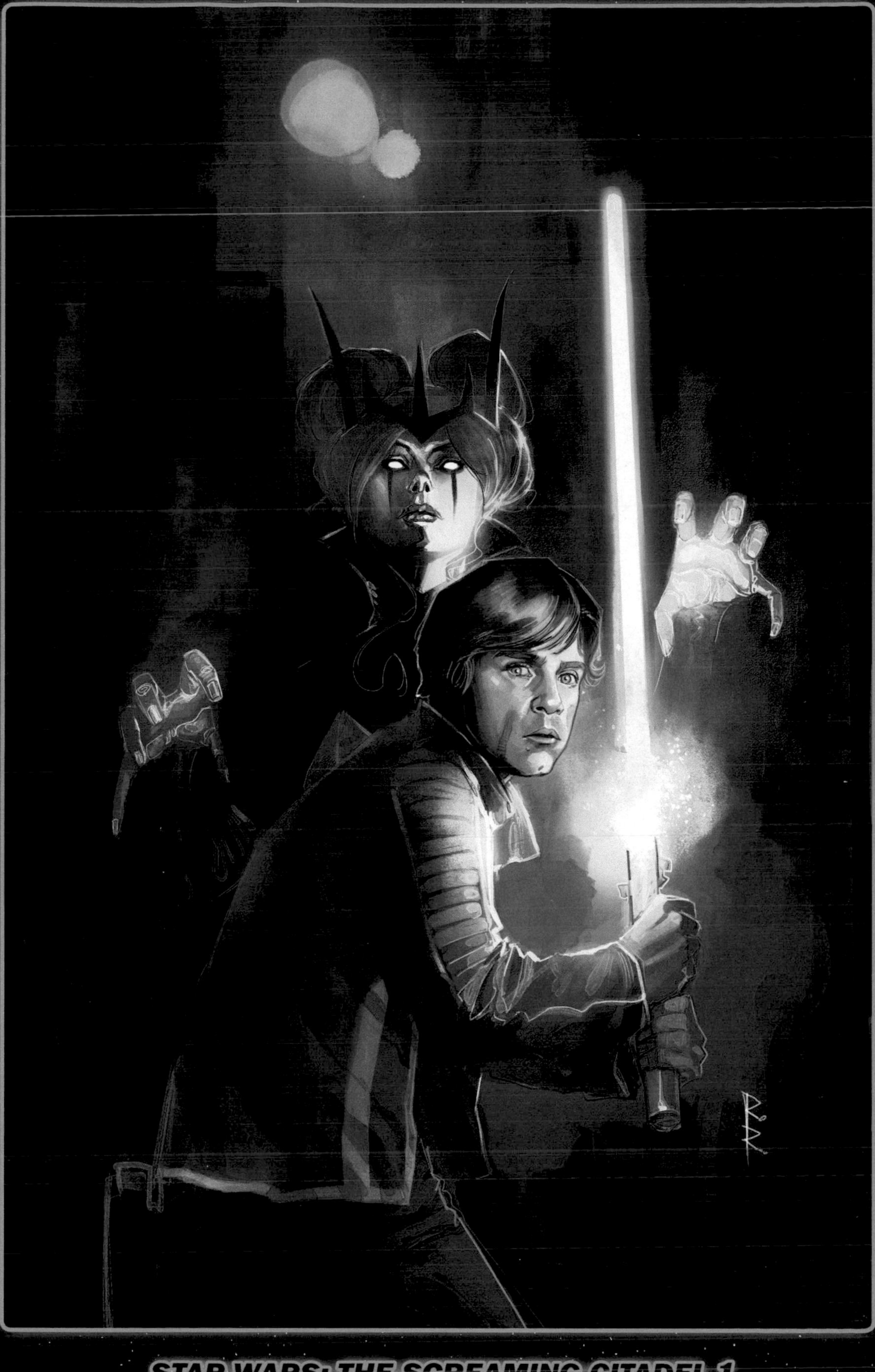

STAR WARS: THE SCREAMING CITADEL 1
VARIANT BY ROD REIS

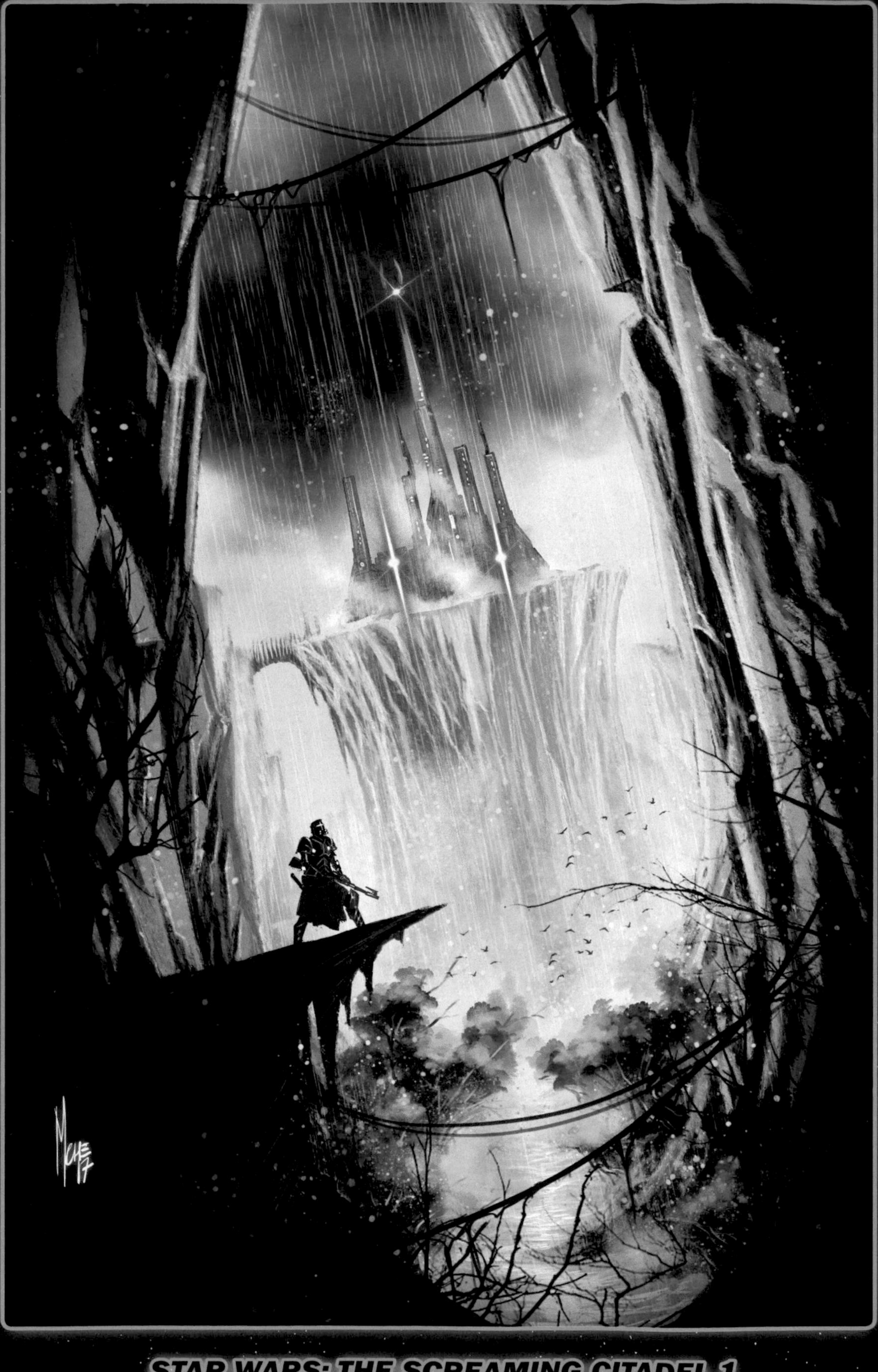
MCHE 17

STAR WARS: THE SCREAMING CITADEL 1
VARIANT BY MARCO CHECCHETTO

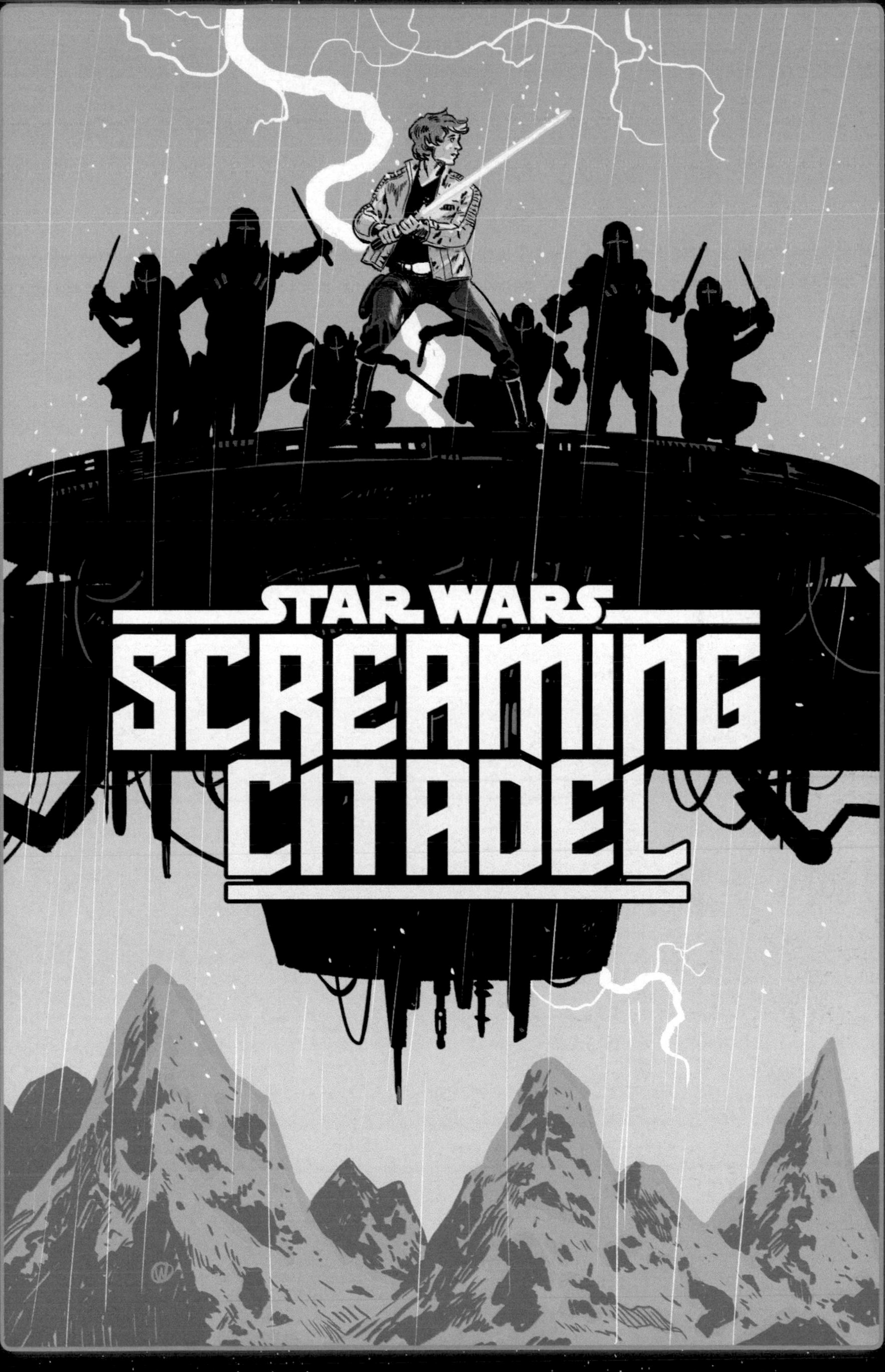
STAR WARS
SCREAMING CITADEL

STAR WARS: THE SCREAMING CITADEL 1
VARIANT BY MATT WALSH

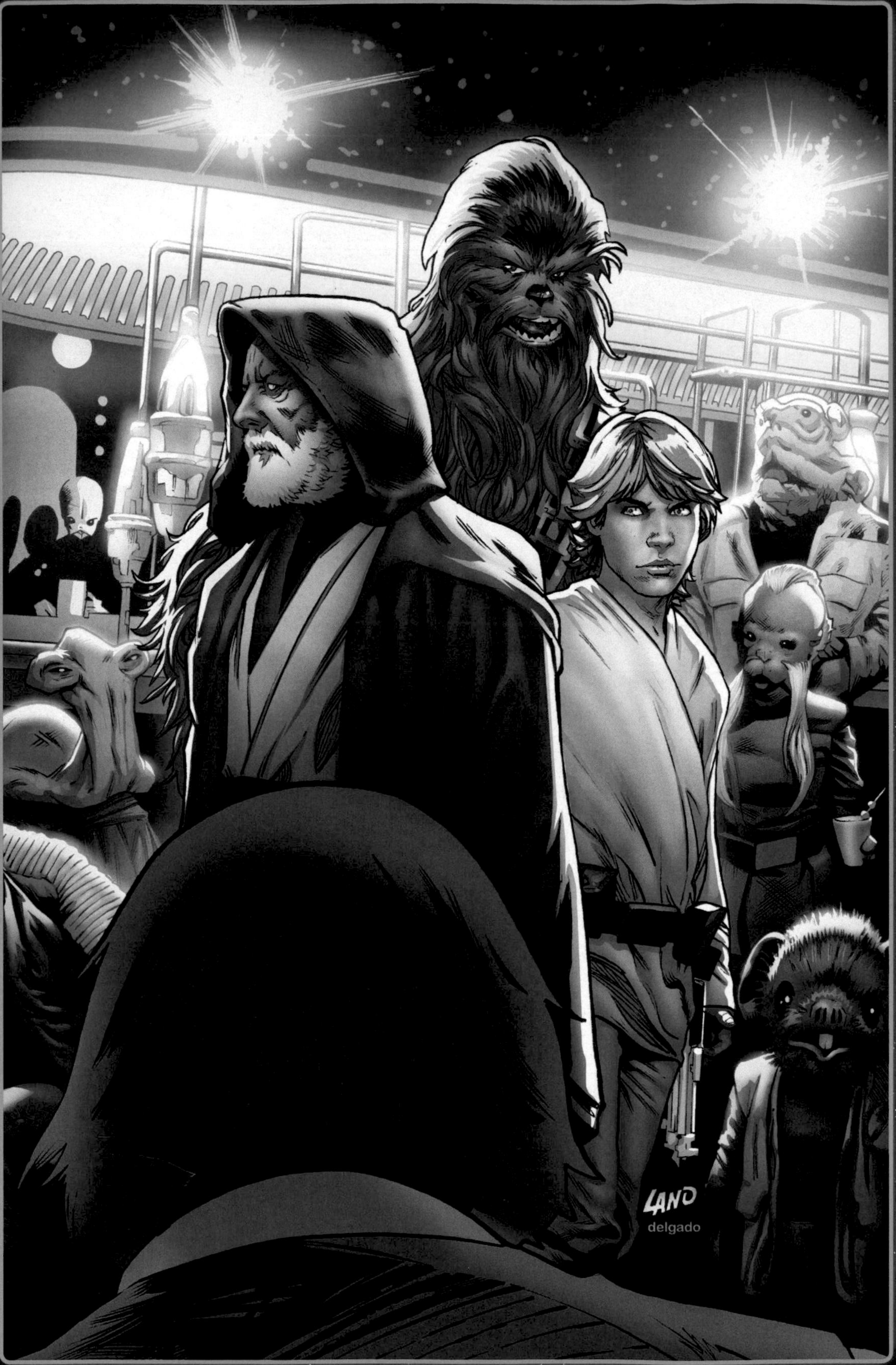
LAND
delgado

STAR WARS: DOCTOR APHRA 7
40TH ANNIVERSARY VARIANT BY GREG LAND & EDGAR DELGADO

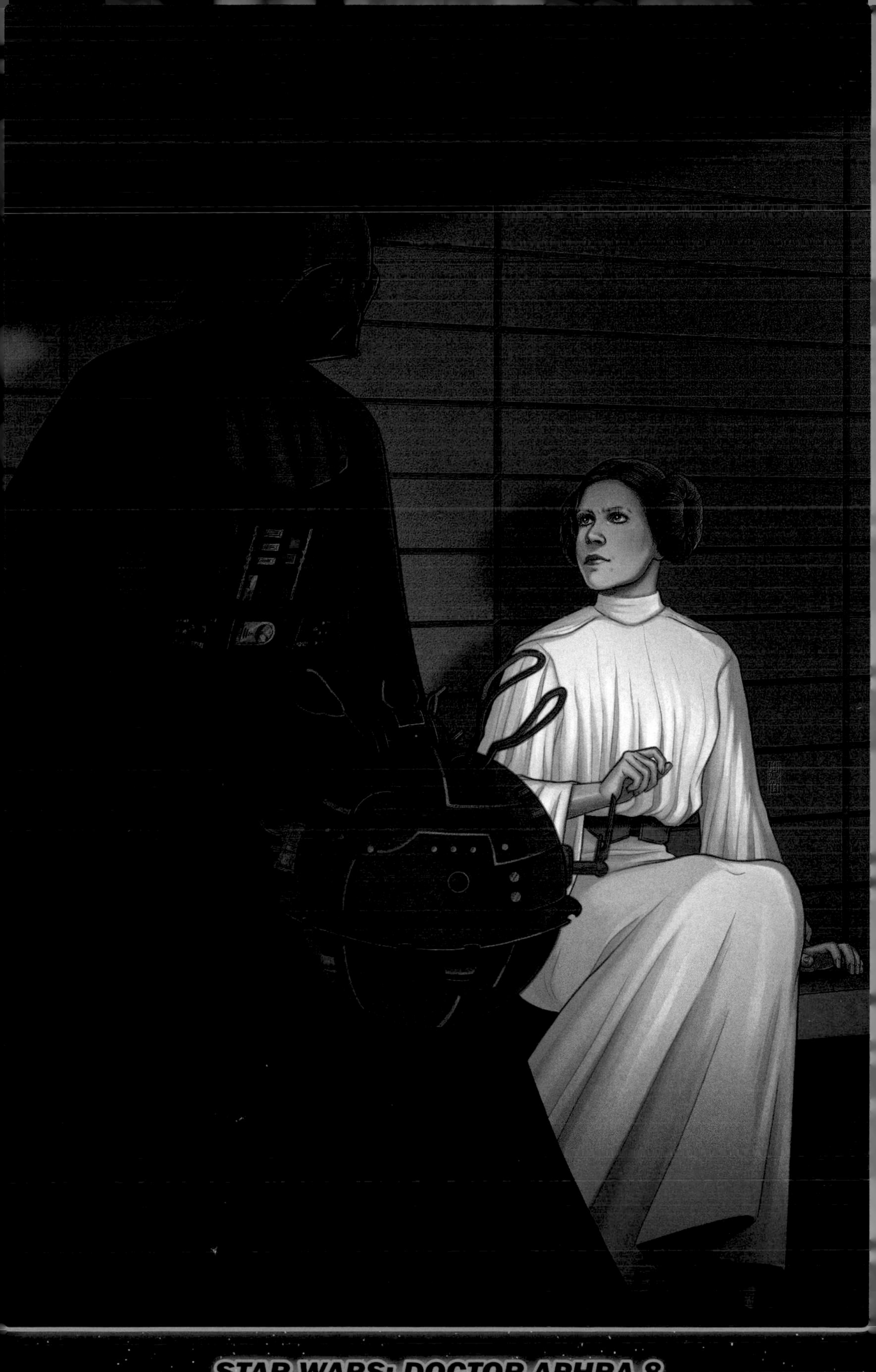

STAR WARS: DOCTOR APHRA 8
40TH ANNIVERSARY VARIANT BY JEN BARTEL

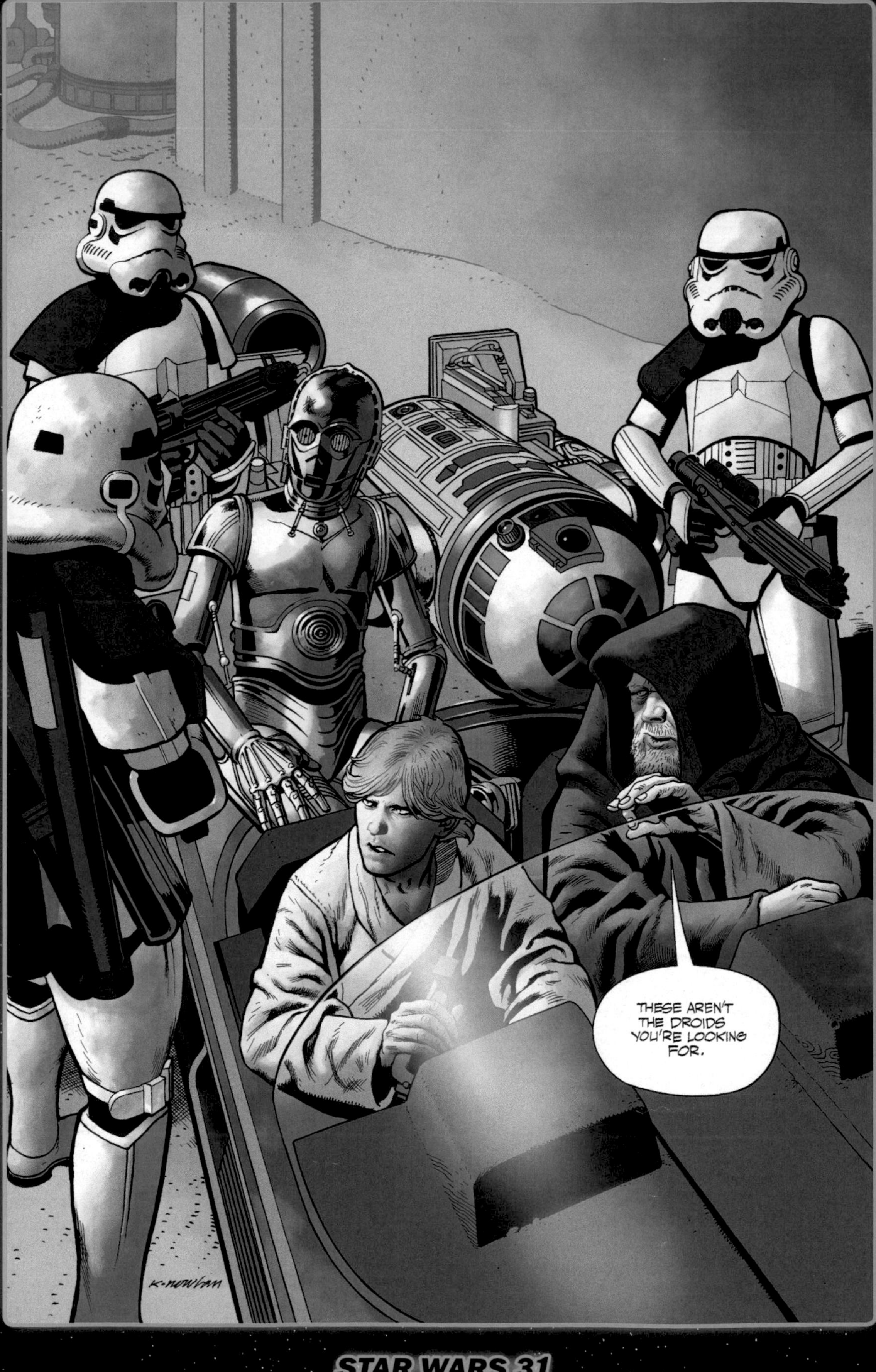
THESE AREN'T THE DROIDS YOU'RE LOOKING FOR.
K-NOWLAN

STAR WARS 31

40TH ANNIVERSARY VARIANT BY KEVIN NOLAN

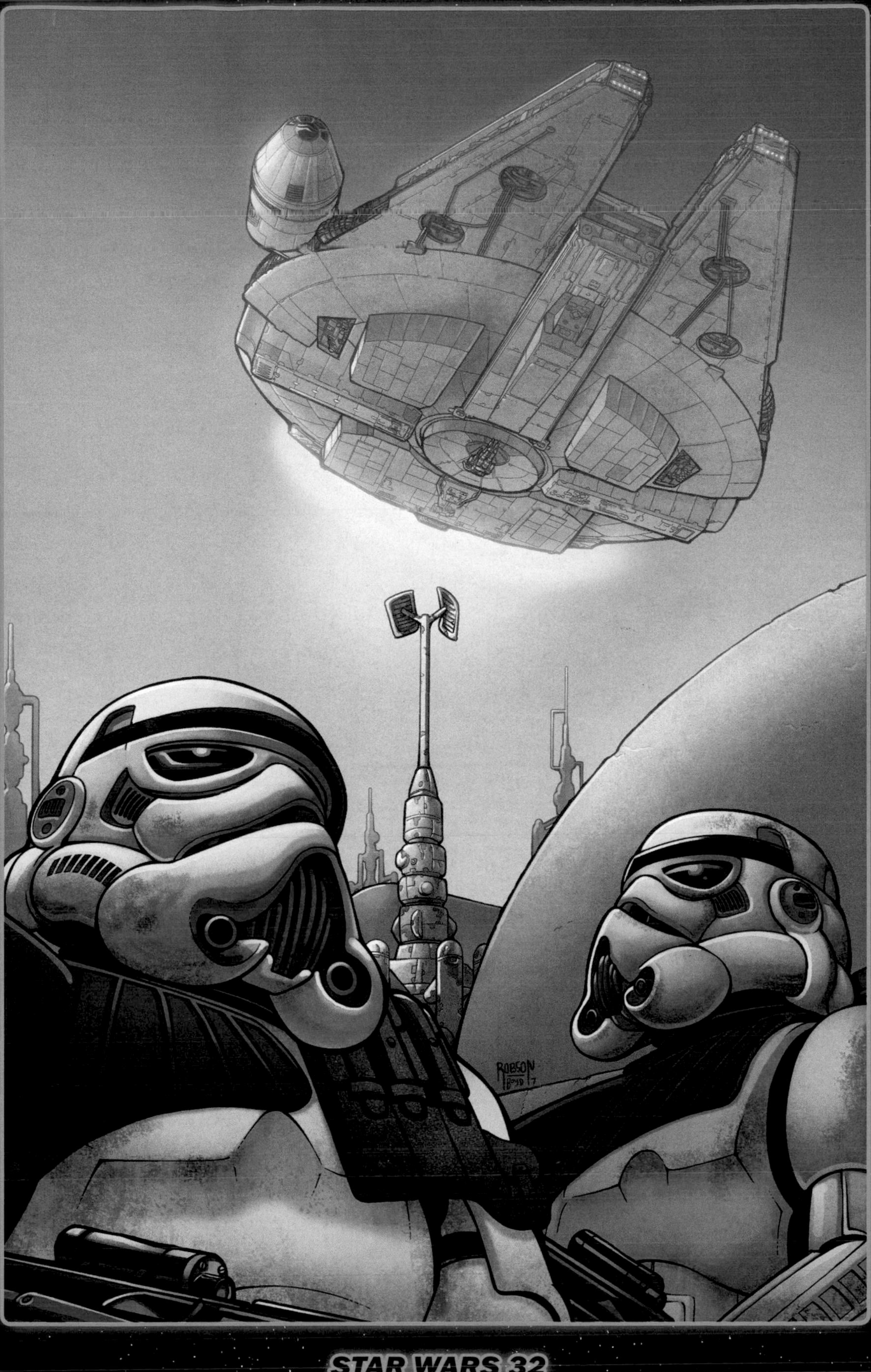

STAR WARS 32

40TH ANNIVERSARY VARIANT BY WILL ROBSON & JORDAN BOYD

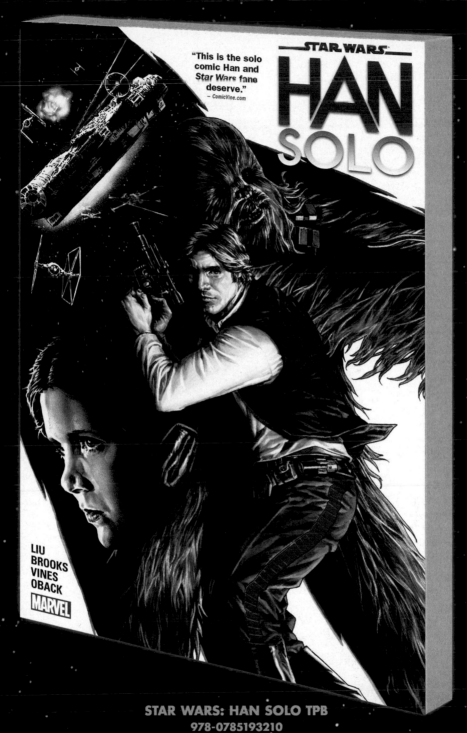

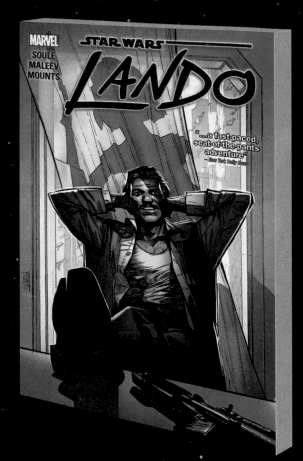
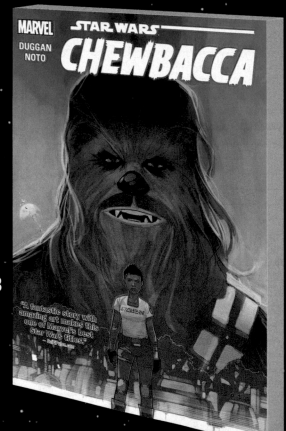

RETURN TO A GALAXY FAR, FAR AWAY!

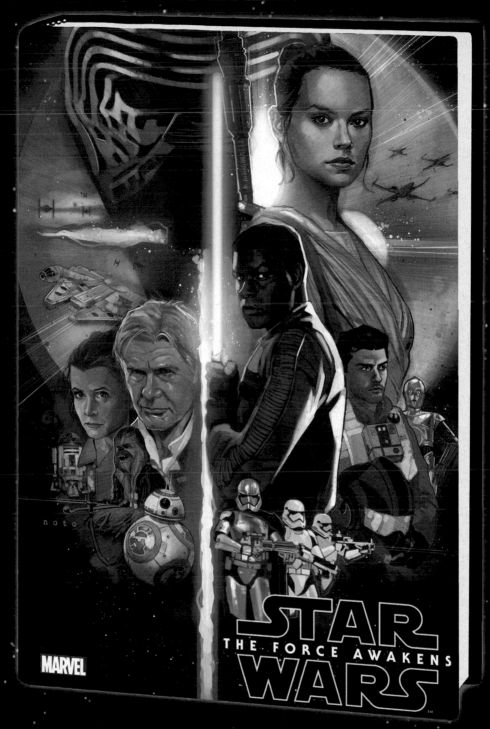

STAR WARS: THE FORCE AWAKENS ADAPTATION HC
978-1302901783

ON SALE NOW

AVAILABLE IN PRINT AND DIGITAL WHEREVER BOOKS ARE SOLD

RETURN TO A GALA

THE CLASSIC MARVEL ADAPTATIONS

NOW WITH REMAS

MARVEL
STAR WARS
A NEW HOPE
EPISODE IV
INTRODUCTION BY PETER MAYHEW

STAR WARS: EPISODE IV – A NEW HOPE HC
978-0-7851-9348-7

STAR
THE
EMP
STRIKES
EPISO
INTRODUCTION BY B

STAR WARS: EPISODE V
978-0-7851-9367-8

AVAILABLE WHEREVER BOOKS ARE SOLD

MARVEL Disney LUCASFILM

XY FAR, FAR AWAY!

OF THE BIGGEST MOVIES IN HISTORY,
TERED INTERIORS!

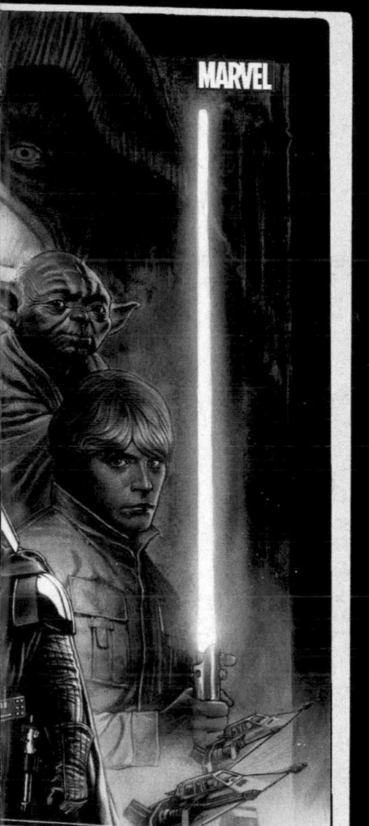
MARVEL
IRE
BACK
WARS
E V
DEE WILLIAMS

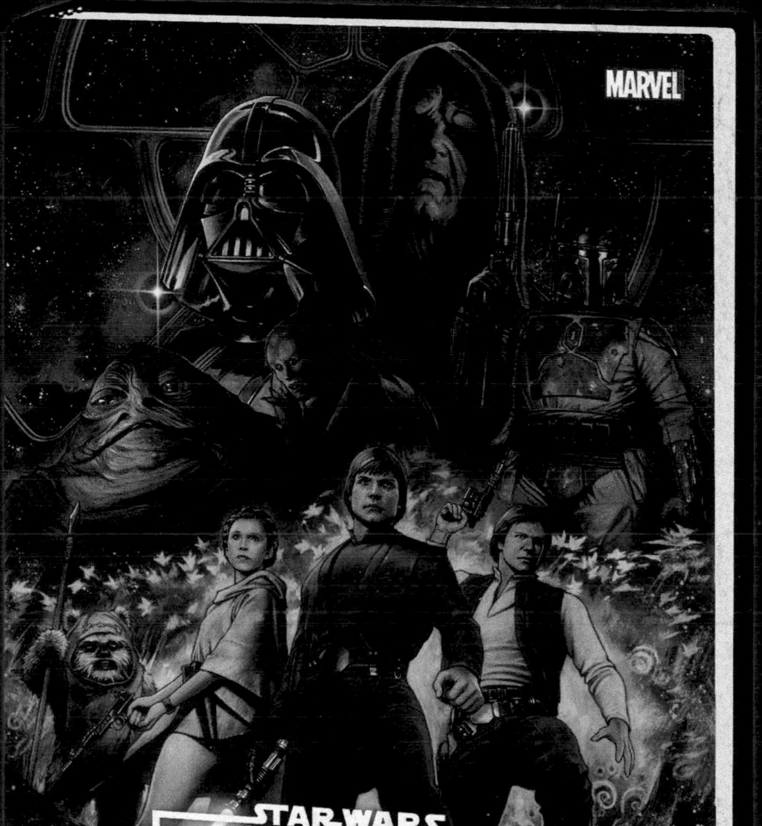
MARVEL
STAR WARS
RETURN OF THE
JEDI
EPISODE VI

EMPIRE STRIKES BACK HC

STAR WARS: EPISODE VI – RETURN OF THE JEDI HC

978-0-7851-9369-2